A History
of the Ninth Regiment
Illinois Volunteer Infantry,
with the
Regimental Roster

Shawnee Classics

A Series of Classic Regional Reprints for the Midwest

Personal Memoirs of John H. Brinton
Civil War Surgeon, 1861–1865
John H. Brinton

Stagecoach and Tavern Tales of the Old Northwest
Harry Ellsworth Cole
Edited by Louise Phelps Kellogg

The Great Cyclone at St. Louis and East St. Louis, May 27, 1896
Compiled and Edited by Julian Curzon

"Black Jack"
John A. Logan and Southern Illinois in the Civil War Era
James Pickett Jones

The Outlaws of Cave-in-Rock
Otto A. Rothert

A Woman's Story of Pioneer Illinois
Christiana Holmes Tillson
Edited by Milo Milton Quaife

Army Life of an Illinois Soldier
Including a Day-by-Day Record of Sherman's March to the Sea
Charles W. Wills

A History of the Ninth Regiment Illinois Volunteer Infantry,

with the Regimental Roster

By the Chaplain,
Marion Morrison

Foreword by John Y. Simon

Southern Illinois University Press
Carbondale and Edwardsville

Foreword by John Y. Simon copyright © 1997 by the Board of Trustees, Southern Illinois University. First published 1864 by John S. Clark, Printer. All rights reserved. Printed in the United States of America.

00   99   98   97   4   3   2   1

Library of Congress Cataloging-in-Publication Data
Morrison, Marion, b. 1821.
A history of the Ninth Regiment Illinois Volunteer Infantry, with the regimental roster / by the chaplain, Marion Morrison ; foreword by John Y. Simon.
    p.   cm. — (Shawnee classics)
Originally published: Monmouth, Ill. : J.S. Clark, 1864. With new foreword.
    1. United States. Army. Illinois Infantry Regiment, 9th (1861–1865) 2. United States—History—Civil War, 1861–1865—Regimental histories. 3. Illinois—History—Civil War, 1861–1865—Regimental histories. 4. United States. Army. Illinois Infantry Regiment, 9th (1861–1865)—Registers. I. Title. II. Series: Shawnee classics.
E505.5 9th.M67 1997
973.7'473—dc21   96-46355   CIP
    ISBN 0-8093-2043-6 (alk. paper). —ISBN 0-8093-2042-8 (pbk. : alk. paper)

The paper used in this publication meets the minimum requirements of American National Standard for Information Sciences—Permanence of Paper for Printed Library Materials, ANSI Z39.48-1984. ♾

CONTENTS

ILLUSTRATIONS vii

FOREWORD BY JOHN Y. SIMON ix

ACKNOWLEDGMENTS xiii

PREFACE 3

I. [ORIGIN OF THE REBELLION AND MEASURES TAKEN] 5

II. FROM THE RE-ORGANIZATION TO TIME OF
   LEAVING PADUCAH 13

III. FROM PADUCAH TO PITTSBURG LANDING 20

IV. FROM BATTLE OF SHILOH TO BATTLE AT CORINTH 28

V. FROM THE ATTACK ON CORINTH, OCT. 3RD, 1862,
   UNTIL REGIMENT WAS MOUNTED 38

VI. FROM THE MOUNTING OF THE REGIMENT
   TO LEAVING POCAHONTAS 49

VII. FROM THE TIME OF LEAVING POCAHONTAS TO
   THE PRESENT 71

BIOGRAPHICAL SKETCHES OF THE FIELD AND STAFF OFFICERS
   BIOGRAPHICAL SKETCHES 89

EXCERPTS FROM THE ADJUTANT GENERAL'S REPORT
   REGIMENTAL ROSTER 98

   HISTORY OF NINTH INFANTRY 125

   NINTH INFANTRY (CONSOLIDATED) REGIMENT 129

ILLUSTRATIONS

FOLLOWING PAGE 48

COL. AUGUSTUS MERSY
LT. COL. JESSE J. PHILLIPS
LT. COL. SAMUEL T. HUGHES
CAPT. WILLIAM F. ARMSTRONG
CAPT. ISAAC CLEMENTS
CAPT. ALEXANDER G. HAWES
1ST LT. CYRUS H. GILMORE
1ST LT. GEORGE W. WILLIFORD
2D LT. ALFRED COWGILL
2D LT. WILLIAM C. HAWLEY
SGT. JACOB MILLER
SGT. ALONZO F. MCEWEN
SGT. JAMES M. ARTHURS
CPL. CHARLES N. BROWN
PVT. LEVI GIBBS

FOREWORD

Many Germans fled political repression in their homeland in the 1830s and 1840s to settle along the upper Mississippi Valley. Although the burgeoning commercial center of St. Louis attracted some, idealists abhorred the existence of slavery in Missouri. Opposite St. Louis these refugees found both free soil and economic opportunity in St. Clair County, Illinois. When the Civil War erupted in April 1861, German immigrants on both sides of the Mississippi River responded by enlisting for military service to preserve the Union. Speeches in both German and English declaimed in Belleville's public square prompted enthusiastic volunteers to march to Springfield under the command of August Mersy, an employee of a Belleville bank, but also a veteran of the failed 1848 revolt in Baden, where he had held high rank.[1]

In Springfield, concern about Mersy's limited command of English induced Gustave Koerner, the prominent German political leader in St. Clair County, to reject Mersy.[2] Koerner had served as lieutenant governor of Illinois from 1853 to 1857, entering office as a Democrat and leaving as an ardent Republican, having switched to the newly organized antislavery party. No voice commanded more respect in Belleville. The Ninth Illinois Infantry Volunteers went off to war under Colonel Eleazer A. Paine, an Ohioan and West Point graduate, with Mersy as lieutenant colonel. Mersy complained privately that Paine was "an old fogy, a martinet," and was constantly electioneering.[3] Within a few months, however, Paine's promotion left Mersy in command of the Ninth. In the interim, the three-months enlistment of the regiment had expired and the troops faced the choice of reenlistment for three years or going

1. Earl J. Hess, "The Obscurity of August Mersy: A German-American in the Civil War," *Illinois Historical Journal*, 79 (1986): 127–28.
2. *Memoirs of Gustave Koerner,* Thomas J. McCormack, ed. (Cedar Rapids: Torch Press, 1909), 2: 122–23.
3. Hess, "Mersy," 129.

home. Most reenlisted, but at least a few of the Belleville Germans withdrew and joined the Twelfth Missouri under Colonel Peter Joseph Osterhaus, a former resident of Belleville, who organized a more preponderantly German regiment. More than 78 percent of those who enlisted in the Twelfth (and for whom information is available) were born in German states.[4]

Enough German immigrants remained in the Ninth Illinois to produce a multicultural regiment, one of many in the federal army. Friedrich Hecker, a prominent political refugee living in St. Clair County, raised two more German regiments in Illinois, Koerner another, while prominent German leaders organized their countrymen elsewhere in the North. New York State alone produced ten German regiments. Although officers maneuvered and wrangled, Mersy proudly reported that in the ranks "Germans & Americans live so happily together."[5]

Confederate leaders expected their armies to triumph over Yankees and foreigners. Proud and hard-fighting regiments like the Ninth soon proved them wrong. Once Ulysses S. Grant began his Tennessee River campaign, the Ninth found itself in the thick of battle. At Fort Donelson, on 15 February 1862, the Ninth bore the brunt of an unexpected Confederate attempt to break Grant's siege lines. No regiment resisted more stubbornly nor suffered so grievously. Of 600 men engaged in the two-and-one-half-hour battle, 36 were killed, 165 wounded, and 9 missing, for a casualty rate of 35 percent.[6]

Less than two months later, the Ninth was encamped at Pittsburg Landing in Tennessee expecting to advance on the enemy at Corinth, Mississippi, when Confederates suddenly disrupted a Sunday morning with a surprise attack at Shiloh Church, driving back Grant's panic-stricken forces. The Ninth did not take the first shock of attack but advanced about midmorning through throngs of fleeing soldiers to secure the Union line between a peach orchard and a pond that achieved lasting fame as "bloody pond." Outnumbered and flanked, the Ninth held their line for three and one-half hours, withdrawing, as they had at Donelson, only after exhausting their ammunition. Casualties at Shiloh eclipsed

4. Earl J. Hess, "The 12th Missouri Infantry: A Socio-Military Profile of a Union Regiment," *Missouri Historical Review,* 76 (1981–82): 60.
5. Hess, "Mersy," 131.
6. Peter E. Cozzens, "'My poor little Ninth': The Ninth Illinois at Shiloh," *Illinois Historical Journal,* 83 (1990), 34.

those of any other Union regiment: 61 killed, 300 wounded, and 5 missing, for a total of 366 men lost, 63 percent of its strength of 578.[7] "My poor little Ninth," murmured Colonel Mersy.[8]

The depleted ranks of the Ninth needed strengthening, but new regiments offered opportunities for new commissions; ambitious potential officers frequently snared recruits, while old regiments of tested warriors declined in effectiveness. Less promising material replenished the ranks of the Ninth. In April 1863 the 128th Illinois, primarily recruited in Williamson County and filled with opponents of emancipation, had dwindled from 860 to 161 men, principally because of desertions. Adjutant General Lorenzo Thomas discharged most of the officers and ordered an inspection of the remaining officers and men to weed out those too old or unfit for service.[9] In August, the 103 survivors joined the Ninth. Also in August, 105 imprisoned deserters (including some from the 128th) were sent to the Ninth from Fort Pickering at Memphis. Only two ever deserted again. Contact with the seasoned fighters of the Ninth transformed undesirables into acceptable soldiers. Now mounted on mules (horses were scarce), the Ninth guarded supply lines, leaving the heavy fighting of the first eighteen months of war behind them. When the original three-year enlistment of the Ninth expired in July 1864, only 40 veterans of the original regiment reenlisted, but enough men from among the deserters and the survivors of the 128th joined them to form a body of 150. A reorganized Ninth served for another year, completing the war.

The Ninth was one of the first regiments to become the subject of a unit history. All drew upon the recollections of veterans, and Chaplain Marion Morrison had the advantage of capturing fresh memories. A former professor at Monmouth College and editor of a Presbyterian newspaper, Morrison joined the regiment in September 1863 and began to chronicle its history, which he carried to the eve of the Atlanta campaign in March 1864. A biographical sketch of Morrison appeared at the conclusion of the 95-page history that he published in 1864.

7. William F. Fox, *Regimental Losses in the American Civil War 1861–1865* (Albany: Albany Publishing Co., 1889), 354.

8. James Oates, *A Gallant Regiment and the Place it Holds in National History* (Belleville: Post and Zeitung Publishing, n.d.), 4.

9. J. N. Reece, ed., *Report of the Adjutant General of the State of Illinois* (Springfield: Journal Co., 1900), 8: 532.

Southern Illinois University Press has supplemented this reprinting of Morrison's book with the regimental roster published in 1900 by the Illinois Adjutant General's office.

The chaplain's nephew, also named Marion Morrison, who served with the Eighty-third and Sixty-first Illinois Volunteers, died in Los Angeles in 1915. When his grandson, yet another Marion Morrison, began a movie career, that name "didn't sound American enough," so studio officials credited him as John Wayne.[10]

In 1886 the veterans of the Ninth held their first reunion, then met annually at various Illinois sites. Each year they published an ever shorter roster of living veterans. But enthusiasm did not wane proportionately. In 1889, daughters of the veterans prepared a regimental flag for use at reunions. The original flag, made by the women of St. Clair County in 1861, rested in the State Capitol, inscribed with the names of 110 engagements credited to the regiment. In accepting the new banner, one veteran recalled how "young men largely of foreign birth . . . had sought new and better homes for themselves here; they had taken the oath of allegiance to this government, and when native-born sons, forgetful of the duty they owed to their native land, disregarding their duty to the government that had protected them and theirs, sought the destruction of this government, these young men came forward and offered to make good their oaths with their lives if need be." The old flag, tattered and riddled with bullet holes, had circled the Confederate States, then returned with its folds "washed clean of human slavery—their only stain—in the blood of its bravest followers."[11] Such idealism continues to deserve respect.

John Y. Simon

---

10. Ralph Eckley, "John Wayne's Uncle Once Taught Math at Monmouth College" and "More on Marion Morrison," undated clippings from the *Monmouth Review Atlas,* Monmouth College Archives, Monmouth, Ill.; Judith M. Riggin, *John Wayne: A Bio-Bibliography* (New York and Westport, Conn.: Greenwood Press, 1992), 39: Pilar Wayne, *John Wayne: My Life with the Duke* (New York: McGraw-Hill, 1987), 8.

11. *Ninth Illinois Infantry Association: Proceedings of the Fourth Annual Reunion . . .* (n.p., n.d.), 4.

ACKNOWLEDGMENTS

The publisher thanks Mark Westhoff, commander of the reactivated Ninth Illinois, and Kathryn M. Harris, Illinois State Historical Library, for their invaluable assistance with this publication. The author of the foreword thanks Wayne C. Temple, Illinois State Archives, and Beth Cox, Monmouth College Archives.

A HISTORY

OF THE

NINTH REGIMENT

ILLINOIS VOLUNTEER INFANTRY.

BY THE CHAPLAIN,

MARION MORRISON.

MONMOUTH, ILLS.:

JOHN S. CLARK, PRINTER.

1864.

PREFACE.

In this sketch of the military career of the 9th Ill. Vol. Inft., my object has been, to present the facts connected with its organization, and its connection with the various battle-scenes through which it has passed. I have entered upon the compilation of these facts with some degree of hesitation. I have thrown it into the present shape, only on the earnest solicitation of a number of the officers and men of the Regiment. Originally nothing more was contemplated than a newspaper sketch. It was thought that even the prominent facts in the Regiment's history, could not be given in such an article, without making it so long that publishers would not wish to insert it in their papers, or the readers of such papers be willing to read it.

It has been the writer's aim, not only to give the facts connected with the various battles in which the Regiment has been engaged, but to narrate many incidents on marches and scouts, both of a general and individual character. Often these incidents will throw more light upon the real workings of soldier life, than accounts of great battles.

I am indebted for most of the facts connected with the marches and battles of the Regiment, to the kindness of Adjutant Klock. Most of the incidents I have gathered from the officers and men in the Regiment. Much dependence had to be put in these, since the writer has only been with the Regiment from the first of September, 1863.

It was felt to be due the Regiment, that a sketch of this kind be prepared. It has never had a correspondent to herald its deeds of daring in the news of the day, as many other regiments have. Hence, although it has performed a great amount of hard and very valuable service, still it has but seldom been noticed in the papers. Let justice be done. Nothing more.

If I can but succeed in putting together the substantial facts in the History of this Regiment, so that they can be preserved by the boys, in a convenient form for reference, and afford material to aid the future historian in making up the history of this war, I will have accomplished the object I have in view.

CHAPTER I.

Cause of the Rebellion—Measures taken by the leaders to deceive the masses—James Buchanan—Lincoln's journey to Washington, and entering upon his duties—Call for 75,000 Volunteers—Organization of 9th Ill.—Roster of officers—Six Regiments organized in Illinois—Nature of "Three months' service"—Kentucky neutrality—Scouting—Incidents—When mustered out—Reorganization.

Every lover of his country will remember, with peculiar emotions, the events of the Winter and Spring of 1861. On the election of Abraham Lincoln to the position of President of the United States, in the autumn of 1860, the Southern portion of our once peaceful and happy country were indignant at the result. They had so long been accustomed to have everything their own way, so far as President-making was concerned, that they could not endure the thought of being superceded in their favorite work. For years they had elected Presidents who were either Southern men, or Northern men whose views agreed with their own on the great question at issue with them—Slavery. Now that a Northern man was elected to the Presidency, who, it was known, would use his constitutional powers to check the spread of that ruinous system, they were determined not to suffer it. Loud talkings of secession from the Union, spread rapidly throughout the South.

The leaders in this wicked rebellion did not allow the mass of the people to know the exact position which the newly elected President had taken, and the policy he would pursue with reference to the slavery question. If they had, we would never have heard of the rebellion now raging in our land. Their watchword was, that whenever he would enter upon the duties of his office, he would at once take measures to have the slaves set free throughout the entire South; that slaves would everywhere be stirred up to insurrection. Thus the leaders aroused the minds of the masses, and prepared them for the terrible ruin into which they were about to plunge them.

During the Fall after the election of the present President, it was my privilege to meet with a citizen of Mississippi, who was visiting Illinois on matters of business. He had spent two or three weeks in

5

Springfield and vicinity, attending to that business. Speaking of the state of feeling existing in his State, and contrasting that with the feelings manifested in Illinois, he said, "I would give half I am worth, if the people of the South could only see and know what I have seen and learned since I have been in Illinois." He had had an interview with the President elect; had made the acquaintance of many of his prominent friends; and had become fully satisfied that he, together with the mass of the people South, was entirely mistaken as to the position which the incoming administration would occupy on the question of slavery. "Why, sir, if my fellow citizens could only see things as I now see them, there would be no difficulty. If they could only be convinced that the incoming Administration would not interfere with the system of slavery as it exists in the slave States, but were only opposed to its further extension, there would be no further difficulty. But," says he, "I cannot hope to see that state of feeling now produced. If I should go home and tell them what I have seen and what I have heard, my life would be in danger. I would be denounced as an abolitionist. My friends dissuaded me from making the journey to this State. 'If you go to Illinois you will be mobbed.' I feared the result myself, but my business was urgent. I am agreeably surprised to find that here a man can express his opinions on this vexed question, with perfect safety." This Southern man expressed himself thus, on the eve of this rebellion, with tears in his eyes.

But time passed. The leaders in this rebellion were making Herculean efforts to be prepared for the crisis. James Buchanan occupied the Presidential chair. He was just the instrument they needed in that position. His heart was with them. Most of the Cabinet he had gathered around him, were notorious traitors, and ready to resort to any means to carry out their wicked ends. Hence they robbed the government of its treasures, its arms, and its fortifications. During the Winter, one State after another passed acts of secession, and he looked quietly on, but made no demonstration towards stopping it. Armed forces were gathering in the various seceding States. Fort Sumter was still in possession of the government. Fortifications were erected in Charleston harbor to reduce it. Its few inmates were in a starving condition. No supplies were sent them.

The term of office of James Buchanan expires. The President elect enters upon his journey from Springfield, Illinois, to Washington, D. C. He leaves his home, feeling fully aware of the great work before him. He is satisfied that without Divine aid he will be unable to meet the crisis. Hence, on taking his departure, while standing upon the steps of the cars, he asks the friends he was leaving behind, to seek that aid on his behalf. A plot is laid for his assassination, in the City of Baltimore. But that Providence, whose aid he desired, revealed the plot, and he is enabled to reach Washington, on an extra train and at an hour unexpected. At the proper time he is duly initiated into his office. He looks around and sees the sad condition of the affairs of State. He firmly grasps the helm, however. Although the ship of state is in a leaky condition; although many a plank was torn off; although many were still in it ready to strike other leaks; although but little money with which to repair it; still he takes firm hold. He gathers around him, as counselors, and co-workers, those in whom he could place confidence. Every exertion which could possibly be made, is made, to set things "to rights" again.

It is not long until Fort Sumter is fired upon by the enemies of their country. The roar of the cannon, whose balls shattered the walls of that Fort, echoed throughout the land and aroused an indignant people to arms. In the meantime the President calls for 75,000 volunteers to enter the service for three months. He has been blamed for calling for so few, and for so short a time. That call, however, doubtless saved the capital of our nation, which was then sorely beleagured.

In compliance with this call, the State of Illinois furnished six regiments for the "three months' service." That call was made on the 15th day of April, 1861. The county of St. Clair promptly sent six companies; the county of Madison three companies, and the county of Montgomery one company. They rendezvoused at Springfield, Illinois, on the 23d day of April, 1861, and were organized and mustered into the service on the 25th of the same month. It was the third regiment organized in Illinois, and was numbered as the 9th Regt. Ill. Vol. Inft.

The roster of officers of companies, as reported, is as follows:

Company A.—Aug. Mersy,   Captain.
    "   " —Jacob Kercher,   1st Lieutenant.
    "   " —Birt Affleck,   2d Lieutenant.
Company B.—Rodolphus Beckier,   Captain.
    "   " — ——— Ledergarber,   1st Lieutenant.
    "   " —H. Clay Hay,   2d Lieutenant.
Company C.—I. F. Tiedeman,   Captain.
    "   " — ——— Conner,   1st Lieutenant.
    "   " —Hamilton Lieber,   2d Lieutenant.
Company D.—Alexander G. Hawes,   Captain.
    "   " — ——— Cox,   1st Lieutenant.
    "   " — ——— Roman,   2d Lieutenant.

Company E.——————— Catine,	Captain.
" " ——————— Scheitlier,	1st Lieutenant.
" " ——————— Scheminger,	2d Lieutenant.
Company F.—Van Cleve,	Captain.
" " —Loren Webb,	1st Lieutenant.
" " —Geo. Adams,	2d Lieutenant.
Company G.—————— Tucker,	Captain.
" " ——————— Davis,	1st Lieutenant.
" " ——————— Ash,	2d Lieutenant.
Company H.—Jesse J. Phillips,	Captain.
" " —John W. Kitchell,	1st Lieutenant,
" " —Wm. F. Armstrong,	2d Lieutenant.
Company I.—Jos. G. Robinson,	Captain.
" " —Thos. J. Newsham,	1st Lieutenant.
" " ——————— Gerly,	2d Lieutenant.
Company K.—John H. Kuhn,	Captain.
" " ——————— Shutterer,	1st Lieutenant.
" " —Emil Adam,	2d Lieutenant.

An election for field officers was held on the organization of the Regiment, which resulted in the choice of—

ELEAZER A. PAINE,	Colonel.
AUGUST MERSY,	Lt. Colonel.
JESSE J. PHILLIPS,	Major.

The following were appointed staff officers :

Dr. Bell, of Springfield,	Surgeon.
Dr. S. M. Hamilton, of Monmouth,	Assistant Surgeon.
John W. Kitchell,	Adjutant.
——— Davis,	Quarter Master.
J. J. Ferree,	Chaplain.

No sooner was the Regiment fully organized, than it was called to duty. The Rebels were evidently making their arrangements to take possession of, and occupy Cairo, Ill. They saw at once, if they could do this, they would be able to cut off all communication between the Ohio and Mississippi rivers. They would thus occupy a position from which they would be able, not only to command these rivers, but to make inroads into the State of Illinois. They contemplated making their battle-grounds on Northern soil. It did not at all enter into their original plans, to wage this war upon the sacred soil of the South. Their soldiers were promised the privilege of sacking Northern cities, and overrunning Northern States. But promptly the government took possession of Cairo, and thus saved Illinois from the invasion of the enemy. While the Border Free States of Pennsylvania, Ohio, Indiana and Iowa have suffered from Rebel raids, more or less, Illinois has thus far escaped.

To carry out this design of occupying Cairo, ere the enemy got possession of it, orders were issued on the 30th of April, 1861, to the 9th Regt. Ill. Inft., to report at Cairo, Ill. It arrived at that point May 1st, 1861, at 9 A. M. It was the third Regiment on the ground at Cairo.

The first six regiments from Illinois, that were organized under that call of the President, were:

7th Regiment,	Colonel	Cooke	Commanding.	
8th	"	"	Oglesby	"
9th	"	"	Paine	"
10th	"	"	Prentiss	"
11th	"	"	Wallace	"
12th	"	"	McArthur	"

These regiments were distributed as follows: The 7th Regiment was ordered to Alton, Ill.; the 8th, 9th and 10th to Cairo, Ill.; the 11th to Villa Ridge, Ill.; the 12th to Casey's Station, on the O. & M. R. R.

At an election which was held for a Brig. General to take the command of the above regiments, B. M. Prentiss was elected. His "Head Quarters" were at Cairo, Ill.

After the Regiment arrived at Cairo, Ill., Lieut. Conner, of Co. C, resigned. Sergt. W. C. Kneffner, of Co. D, was elected as 1st Lieut. of Co. C, and commissioned by the Governor. Jacob Kircher was commissioned as Captain of Co. A, and J. W. Kitchell as Captain of Co. H.

After the election of J. W. Kitchell as Captain of Co. H, 1st Lieut. Thos. J. Newsham was appointed Adjutant of the Regiment.

The Regiment remained on duty at Cairo during the term of service for which they were called out.

Many of the soldiers, supposing that they would be furnished with clothing by the government, took very little clothing with them, and that of the most ordinary kind, thinking that when they should draw clothing they could not take care of what they took with them. The result was, that many of them had no change of clothing for the three months they were in the service. They had no regular uniform. Some of the companies were clothed with such a uniform as they had selected and supplied for themselves. When the Regiment arrived in Cairo, no provision was made for them in the way of tents. War was a new thing then, and the Quartermaster and Commissary stores were not always ready to be drawn upon at a moment's warning. The supply of rations was, at times, very irregular. The men had not been accustomed to making themselves comfortable in camp; consequently they sometimes found it pretty hard living. After they had been there a few days, it was determined to go into camp on the edge of the Mississippi river, between the town and the river. The camping ground was covered with very large trees of drift-wood. These must be cleared off. No details for fatigue duty were made; but Col. Paine, taking hold along with the rest, said "Come, boys, we must red these logs off, and clear up this ground." And at it they went, and after a time they had the logs all cleared away, the stumps burnt out, and a pretty respectable camping ground prepared. Much hard service was endured during these three months. Although no fighting was necessary, yet some of the soldiers who were with the Regiment then, and are with it still, speak of those three months as the hardest part of their military life. The duty consisted principally in working on the fortifications, and guard duty. This was very onerous.

To make it harder on the boys, they were poorly provided with food and clothing. Little or no provision was made for blankets. Many of them, if they got their shirts washed, had to take them off and go without while it was being done. If they did this, they were immediately attacked by a powerful and numerous enemy, in the shape of mosquitoes. While the rebels like to attack and surprise our boys, when clothed with new uniforms, this numerous army prefer to make the attack when our soldiers are entirely stripped of their coats and their shirts.

During the time the Regiment was in camp at Cairo, Kentucky was pursuing that policy which proved so ruinous to her. She was attempting to enforce a strict *neutrality* with reference to the war. Parties were organized. No efforts were made to prevent disloyal men from organizing companies, and committing hostilities. The State was soon filled with rebels against the government. Several scouting parties were sent from Cairo into Kentucky for the purpose of scattering those parties and watching their movements. In most of these, the 9th Ill. Inft., was represented by detachments.

In July, an expedition which was under command of Col. J. J. Morgan of the 10th Ill., and which consisted of twelve companies, and one section of artillery, was sent to Indian Creek, Mo., to break up an organization of Rebels encamped at that place. The expedition was made up of detachments from each of the regiments in camp at Cairo at that time. The 9th Ill. was represented by Companies C and H.

The Rebels prowled about in Missouri and Kentucky, and there were frequent rumors of attacks to be made upon Cairo. But the three months rolled past without any attack.

There are some incidents that occurred during this period, worthy of notice here. One of them occurred with our present highly esteemed Surgeon, Dr. Guilick. He was then a private in the Regiment. One day he was stationed to guard a powder magazine. It was an important post. The Dr. had served in the army in Germany. He knew a picket should never leave his post until relieved from duty. The rule for picket, is two hours on duty and four off, during the twenty-four. The first two hours passed away, no relief came. Two hours more passed. He supposed that surely at that change he would be relieved. Still no relief came. Another two hours passed. Still no relief. Relief-hour after relief-hour passed. But no relief for the Dr. He began to feel the need of his dinner, but no relief came, and he stuck to his powder. That article was an important item in warfare, and he was determined to guard it. Night was drawing near; still no relief. Its quiet hours passed by, and still no relief came. The morning dawned, and there it beheld the Dr. tramping faithfully his beat, wondering, I suppose, if there was *no relief.* The twenty-four hours rolled round, and the Dr. was there still, having had nothing to eat and nothing to drink. Another thing which caused the time to pass heavily with him, like almost all Germans, in fact almost all soldiers, he was very fond of his pipe. But there was the powder he was guarding, and it was not safe to have fire near it. At the end of the twenty-four hours he was relieved. Our worthy Dr. has been with the Regiment ever since. He is still faithful to his post. He still carries out his tenacity in sticking to his post until relieved. There is only one thing, so far as I know, that will cause the Dr. to abandon his proper post. When the Regiment is engaged in battle, unless there is immediate need for him in the rear to care for the wounded, he will leave his post, as a non-combatant, and seeking some position in the advance, he is seen deliberately firing away at the enemy with his revolver. If there is a man wounded he hastens to the rear to attend to him. That done, and he is off again to his firing-post.

Another incident. I think it occurred during the three months' service. At any rate it was during some scout. The camp was in an old cornfield, on a hill-side. The only place the boys could well lay was in the hollows between the corn rows. Col. Phillips (then Major) made his bed between two corn rows. He laid one gum blanket underneath him, and another over him. As it was beginning to rain, he

covered his face with his gum blanket, gathering it carefully under his
head. During the night it rained heavily; but the Major slept on.
When he awoke in the morning and attempted to uncover his head,
the first attempt to remove the blanket failed. By a more determined
effort he succeeded. But oh, horrible! The water had run down the
furrow, sweeping the mud before it. It had been piled up against his
head, the blanket keeping him dry. But instantly on raising the
blanket, rush came mud and water over his face and head! If he had
only had sense enough to commence uncovering at the other end, he
might have crept out snug and dry, although the water had been
pouring down on both sides of him. The Col. has since manifested
much skill in fighting a retreat with his regiment. But it seems he
had not yet learned the art of retreating, for he seemed determined in
spite of all opposition, to go it, head foremost. But he conquered, and
had the consolation of knowing that his severest wounds were in the
face; and although naturally very careful of his good-looking face, I
doubt not he would rather be wounded there than in the back. Save
a brave man always from being wounded in the back.

Still another incident. Rats had become very abundant in town
and around the camps. In fact, rats, fleas and mosquitoes were the
principal enemies with which our boys had then to contend. The side
walks in town were made of plank. Under these was a beautiful place
for the rats to run and play. Sergeant Williford (now Captain) was
Sergeant of the guard in the town one night. That he might have
something to do, by which he could while away the dull hours of the
night, he armed himself with an old cavalry sabre and took his position
at a point where there was a break in the side-walk, there to watch the
movements of the enemy. They had to pass through this opening, and
as one after another made his appearance, each met a death blow from
the Sergeant's sabre. He has now no knowledge of the multitude of
the slain, as he ceased to count the dead. I know not but that the
grand strategy by which he here deceived the enemy and the multi-
tudes slain on that night, were the beginning of his rise which has
resulted in his present commanding position.

The Regiment was mustered out of the service on the 25th day of
July, 1861. Because of the aspect of affairs in Missouri, but a small
number of troops could be sent to Cairo, Ill., to take the place of the
six regiments from Illinois, whose term of service was about to expire.
Consequently an application was made by Gen. Prentiss to the Commander-in-chief, for permission to re-organize those six regiments in the
field. This permission was granted; the re-organization of the several

regiments was perfected, and the regiments recruited. The application made to the authorities for this permission was telegraphed, and granted in a dispatch from General Scott.

CHAPTER II.

FROM THE RE-ORGANIZATION TO TIME OF LEAVING PADUCAH.

Re-organization—Roster of officers—Drill at Cairo—Change to Paducah—Promotions and assignments to duty—Attack on Saratoga—Reconnoisance towards Columbus by 1st Brigade—Commissions—Reconnoisance towards Fort Henry—Regiment paid—Incidents.

As will be seen from the preceding chapter, the 9th Ill. Inft. was mustered out of the service on the 25th of July, 1861, and an order dispatched from Gen. Scott granting permission to re-organize it. It was consequently organized for the three years' service, at Cairo, Ill., and mustered into the service for three years, unless sooner discharged, on the 28th day of July, 1861. The Regiment reported for duty on the same day to Brig. General B. M. Prentiss, commanding the forces at Cairo, Ill.

The field, staff, and line officers were "mustered in" as follows:

Colonel—E. A. Paine,   July 26th, 1861.
Lieut. Col.—Aug. Mersy,   "   "   "
Major.—Jesse J. Phillips,   "   "   "
Surgeon.—S. M. Hamilton,   "   "   "
Assistant Surgeon.—Emil Guelick,   "   "   "
Adjutant.—Thos. J. Newsham,   "   "   "
Regt. Quartermaster.—Wm. G. Pinckard, Aug. 26th, 1861.
Chaplain.—James J. Ferree,   July 26th,   "
Co. A.—Captain, John H. Kuhn,   "   "   "
    " —1st Lieutenant, Emil Adam,   "   "   "
    " —2d Lieutenant, E. J. Weyrich,   "   "   "
Co. B.—Captain, Wm. C. Kneffner,   "   "   "
    " —1st Lieutenant, Hamilton Lieber,   "   "   "
    " —2d Lieutenant, Fred. Vogler,   "   "   "
Co. C.—Captain, D. F. Tiedeman,   "   "   "
    " —1st Lieutenant, Oscar Rollmann,   "   "   "
    " —2d Lieutenant, Chas. Schevir,   "   "   "
Co. D.—Captain, Rodolph Beckier,   "   "   "
    " —1st Lieutenant, Edward Krebbs, Aug. 10th, "
    " —2d Lieutenant, Wm. Bohlen,   "   "   "

Co. E.—Captain, Alex. G. Hawes, July 26th, 1861.
 " —1st Lieutenant, Wm. D. Craig, Aug. 6th, "
 " —2d Lieutenant, R. B. Patterson, July 26th, "
Co. F.—Captain, Loren Webb,   " " "
 " —1st Lieutenant, Wm. Britt,   " " "
 " —2d Lieutenant, Geo. W. Williford, " " "
Co. G.—Captain, Edgar M. Lowe, " " "
 " —1st Lieutenant, John S. Sutten, " " "
 " —2d Lieutenant, Isaac Clements, " " "
Co. H.—Captain, Wm. F. Armstrong, " " "
 " —1st Lieutenant, Cy. H. Gillmore, " " "
 " —2d Lieutenant, Alfred Cowgill, " " "
Co. I.—Captain, Jas. G. Robinson, " " "
 " —1st Lieutenant, Wm. Purviance, July 31st, "
 " —2d Lieutenant, S. T. Hughes, " " "
Co. K.—Captain, Geo. B. Poor, July 26th, "
 " —1st Lieutenant, John L. A. Reeves, " " "
 " —2d Lieutenant, Jas. C. McClery, " " "

After the re-organization of the Regiment, it remained at Cairo, Ill., until September 5th, 1861. During this time they were principally engaged in doing guard duty and drilling. The great matter was to have men well drilled. War was a new occupation to most of them. They were men who had been spending their lives quietly at home on their farms, behind their counters, in their offices, and among their tools in the work-shop. The peaceful walks of life were those they were accustomed to tread. When their country was threatened by those who would destroy it, at the call of that country, they left those peaceful walks and rushed to its defence. It was new work, and they must be trained for it. Much patient drill must be passed through. The officers themselves, many of them, must learn what a military life is, and how to do its work. The men must, day after day, endure the patient drill. They must learn the picket's duty, and how to perform it. They must learn that while on picket each picket is, for the time being, commander-in-chief of his post. When he cries "Halt," his order is law. No Captain; no Colonel; no General, dare disobey it, unless he has his pass or can give the "countersign." A Corporal in Co. E, once narrated to me his first experience in picket duty. He was handling his gun rather awkwardly. The officer of the guard came along and reproved him for his awkwardness. "Let me have your gun, sir, until I show you how to hold it." Anxious to learn every part of a soldier's duty, in all the simplicity of his heart, he handed his gun over to the officer. "Now, sir, what are you going to do for your gun ? Suppose I was the enemy, what kind of a fix would you be in?" He at once saw the embarrassment of his position. "Did you ever stand picket before?" "No, sir." "On that account you are excusable; but on no other. Never give up your gun again; no officer, no General has any right to it." It was a wholesome lesson. He profited by it. From that time forward, no man ever got his gun when on picket.

On the 5th day of September, 1861, the Regiment left Cairo, Ill., embarked on a steamer and moved up the Ohio River to Paducah, Ky. Here it occupied the advance position on the Columbus road.

Col. E. A. Paine was promoted to be Brigadier General, September 3d, and Lieut. Col. August Mersy being absent, Major Jesse J. Phillips assumed command of the Regiment.

On the 8th day of September, 1861, Brig. Gen. C. F. Smith relieved Brig. Gen. Paine of the command at Paducah, and Lieut. Col. Mersy returned and relieved Major Phillips of the command of the Regiment.

Adjutant Newsham was detached as Acting Assistant Adjutant General, and Quartermaster Pinckard as Acting Assistant Quartermaster.

About the 20th of September, Brig. Gen. Paine was assigned to the command of the 1st Brigade. This Brigade consisted of the following regiments: 9th Ill. Inft., 12th Ill. Inft., 40th Ill. Inft., 41st Ill. Inft., Buel's Battery, and Thielmann's Independent Cavalry Battalion. Lieut. Adam, of Co. A, 9th Regt., was detached as Act. Assist. Adj. Gen. of the 1st Brigade.

On the 3d day of October, 1861, Adjutant Nusham was promoted to be Captain and Assistant Adjutant General, and assigned to duty on Gen. Smith's staff.

By this time the boys were getting anxious for a fight. To use a common expression, they were "spoiling for a fight." They felt that now they were ready to fight with and conquer the whole South. On October 15th, 1861, a portion of the Regiment had an opportunity to try their pluck. Major Phillips, with Companies B, H, and I, filled to their maximum by details from other companies, with Lieut. Patterson as aid to commanding officer, moved up the Cumberland River above Eddyville, where they disembarked. It was ascertained that a detachment of 300 rebel cavalry were in camp at Saratoga. Major Phillips moved upon them, surprised and completely routed them; killing from 10 to 15, wounding from 25 to 30, and capturing 20. Major Phillips' detachment had Capt. Kneffner slightly wounded, and Corporal Greblig of Co. B, and private Gatewood of Co. K, severely wounded. It returned to camp on the 16th of October, bringing in the prisoners and a large amount of captured property.

First Lieutenant John L. A. Reeves, of Co. K, resigned, and his resignation was accepted October 2d, 1861.

On the 6th day of November, 1861, the 1st Brigade, Brig. General Paine commanding, moved on the Columbus road to Mayfield Creek, and bivouacked for the night. The next day they moved forward to Milburn, Ky., 31 miles from Paducah, and 11 miles from Columbus, bivouacked there for the night, and commenced the return march by daylight on the 8th. Reached camp at Paducah by 2 P. M., of the 9th. This was about the first heavy marching the boys had undergone. It was very fatiguing. There was a disposition to straggle. To prevent it, in the 9th, a rear guard was appointed, which compelled all to keep their places. This, some of the boys who were very tired, no doubt thought to be cruel. But the result was, the 9th Regiment came into camp in Paducah in splendid order, while the 40th and 41st Ill. Regiments seemed to have lost their organization altogether on the return march, and came straggling into camp in small squads, during the entire days of the 9th and 10th. Gen. Smith issued an order highly commending the 9th for their orderly conduct, and condemning those Regiments which returned in such disorder. This pleased our boys so much, that they almost forgot their heavy marching, and there was no more complaining about rigid discipline.

On the 9th of September, 1861, Capt. John H. Kuhn was appointed Provost Marshal of Paducah, and his Co. (A) was detached to act as Provost Guard.

December 2nd, 1861, commissions arrived as follows: For Lieut. Col. Aug. Mersy to be Colone ; Major Jesse J. Phillips to be Lieutenant Colonel; Capt. John H. Kuhn to be Major; 1st Lieut. Emil Adam to be Captain, and 2d Lieut. E. J. Weyrich to be 1st Lieutenant of Co. A. On the 5th of December, Sergeant Scheel, of Co. F, received a commission as 2d Lieutenant of Co. A, but was assigned to duty in Co. D, 2d Lieut. Bohlen of that Co. having been transferred to Co. A.

Capt. Geo. B. Poor, of Co. K, resigned, and his resignation was accepted on the 10th of December. First Lieutenant E. J. Weyrich, of Co. A, resigned on the 25th of December.

Capt. Armstrong, of Co. H, was appointed Provost Marshal, to relieve Major Kuhn, and his Co. (H) relieved Co. A, as Provost Guard, on the 6th of December, 1861.

On the 15th of January, 1862, the entire force at Paducah, except the 40th Ill., moved towards Viola, 13 miles, and bivouacked for the night at Hickory Creek. Brig. Gen. C. F. Smith commanded the Division in person. Col. McArthur, of the 12th Ill. Inft., was in command of the 1st Brigade, and Brig. Gen. Lew. Wallace, of the 2d Brigade. The Division was about 5,000 strong. On the 15th, moved to Mayfield Creek, 28 miles from Paducah. On the 17th, the command marched 23 miles to Clark's River, and bivouacked for the night on its banks. On the 18th and 19th, owing to rain and mud, the command moved a very short distance. It reached Calloway Landing, on the Tennessee River, 20 miles below Fort Henry, on the 22d of January. Finding no enemy in that vicinity, and none nearer than Fort Henry, the command returned to camp at Paducah, Ky., arriving there January 25th, 1862. It had marched altogether, during the reconnoisance, 125 miles. The most that was accomplished, was accustoming the men to hard marches.

Second Lieutenant Wm. Bohlen, resigned, and his resignation was accepted on the 31st day of January, 1862. On the same day a commission arrived for private Henry H. Klock, of Co. F, to be 1st Lieutenant and Adjutant, to rank from October 3d, 1861, the date of Adjutant Newsham's promotion.

Major I. N. Cook paid the Regiment up to January 1st, 1862. It had been previously paid by Major C. P. E. Johnston, to September 1st, 1861.

During the time the Regiment was in camp at Paducah, some incidents of interest occurred. All were longing for an adventure of some kind. The routine of camp life was becoming wearisome. One day Major Phillips, of the 9th Ill. Inft., and Major McDonald, of the 8th Mo. Inft., rode outside the pickets. After they had rode out two or three miles, Major McDonald remembered that he had an old acquaintance living ten or twelve miles out that road. It was proposed and agreed upon, that they would ride out and see him. Before reaching there, they passed where the enemy had their picket fires the night before. Things looked suspicious. A rebel soldier was seen riding up to a neighboring house. They proposed to go and take him. But their friend with whom they stopped, insisted on their not doing it, saying that if any fuss occurred there, they would burn his house at once, as they were threatening him anyhow, because of his Union sentiments. Dinner was ready in a short time, and they must stay for dinner. Major Phillips, always disposed to watch rebs. closely, proposed to stand picket while the rest were eating. He then hurriedly drank a cup of coffee, and they mounted their horses and started for camp. In a short time they saw two cavalry men riding before them. Taking

[2]

them to be rebels, they gave them chase. Major Phillips, mounted on a splendid horse, soon came close on them. Suddenly they checked up, wheeled around, and drew their sabres. Before our Major could check his horse, he was close upon them. With pistol drawn, he inquired what command they belonged to. The reply was, "Thielman's Cavalry." The Major mistook it for Tilman's (Rebel) Cavalry. He inquired the second time. The same reply came, and he labored under the same mistake. By this time Major McDonald came fairly up, and they demanded the surrender of the two men, and they surrendered. At this point, they saw a short distance from them, about 25 men coming towards them. They felt that they were in a close place. Says Major McDonald to Phillips, "What shall we do with these two men? shoot them?" "No; we will take them with us, and if they don't keep up, then we will shoot them," was the reply. Says Major Phillips, "I would give a horse to be in Paducah." "Paducah!" says one of the prisoners; "we belong there, too. We are Willson's Dragoons." The mistake arose from the fact that the Rebels had a band of cavalry, known as Tilman's Cavalry, while the Federals had a battalion of cavalry, known as Thielman's Cavalry. The prisoners being Germans, the one was mistaken for the other. This matter explained, their prisoners were released, and they returned to camp. Having reached camp, Major Phillips reported to Gen. Smith, when the following interview took place. I give the substance:

"General." "Well, Major." "General, having permission to go outside of the pickets to-day, I gained some valuable information, which I thought the good of the service required that I should report to you." "How many men had you, Major?" "General," (afraid to confess there were but two,) "Major McDonald was in command of the expedition." "How many men had Major McDonald?" "I was with him." "But, sir, how many men did you have?" Finding the truth must come, he replied, "The Major commanded me, and I commanded him." "Well, sir, you both deserve to be punished, and if you had shot those two men, I should have had you both cashiered. But as it is, I will let it pass. What is the valuable information you have gained?" "I learn, at a certain point, a Rebel company is to be organized on to-morrow." "Well, sir, as you are fond of adventure, you will take a detachment of forty men, and proceed to that point and disperse or capture them." But as the next day was very rainy, the expedition was abandoned.

Another incident. Major Phillips and Captain Kuhn rode outside the pickets late in the evening. After getting outside the pickets, they saw some fresh wagon-tracks. Captain Kuhn, who was then acting

Provost Marshal, said that there were two wagons, loaded, that went out, of which he was suspicious, but that with his instructions he could not examine them. They concluded to follow them. They had gone but a short distance until the road forked, and there were fresh tracks on each road. The Major took one road, and the Captain took the other. The Major soon came in sight of them, and pushing on, came up with them. On inquiring what they were loaded with, he was told that they were some groceries for a store in the country. Things looking suspicious, he procured an ax and broke open some of the boxes, and found that it was a regular lot of military stores. By this time Captain Kuhn came up, and after a little consultation, they concluded to let them go on, and told them that all was right, they could go on. They returned immediately to town. They had gone out about five miles. On their return, the Major again presented himself to General Smith. "General." "Well, Major." "General, Captain Kuhn and myself rode outside of the pickets, this evening. After getting out a short distance, we saw wagon-tracks, which were suspicious. We followed them a few miles and came up with them, and I am satisfied they are loaded with goods to supply a rebel camp. We did not bring them in, from the fact that the Captain's instructions, as Provost Marshal, would not justify him in doing it." "Another of your fool-hardy dashes, Major." "Yes, General; but I thought the good of the service demanded it." "Well, sir, how many men will you have to bring those wagons in to-night?" "Five men, General." "Adjutant, make a detail for five men, to report here immediately for duty." The men came, and the Major started on his expedition. He overtook the wagons, which had been driving on all night, and brought them back to Paducah, and turned them over to the Quartermaster.

Still another incident. Citizens were frequently coming into town. There was not much difficulty in getting in, but they could not go out again without a pass. One young fellow from Kentucky, having, as he supposed, some of the *noble blood* in him, said he would not apply for a pass. He said the "niggers" had to have passes, and he was not going to put himself on an equality with "niggers." So he refused to apply for a pass. After staying in town a few days, he made an attempt or two to run the pickets, and as a consequence, was put in the guard-house. After staying in town a month or two, the young nobleman was compelled to put himself on an equality with the "niggers," and apply for a pass.

Still another. When out on a scout, at a time when every house would be guarded as the troops were passing, and not a chicken or goose must be touched, the Quartermaster went into a house to purchase some chickens for his mess. The woman refused to sell any. "Well," says he, "we must have something to eat. If you wont sell your chickens, we will steal your geese." "If I sell you some chickens, sir, will you *swear* that you won't steal my geese?" He promised he would. Two or three chickens were caught for him, and then the old lady got upon a chair and reached down an old Bible for him to swear on, that he would not steal her geese. I guess he swore for her, but not very reverendly.

One more incident. Perhaps on the same scout as the above, it was suspected that Company K had stolen a goose. Col. Mersy got wind of it. He addresses Lieut. Col. Phillips as follows: "Col. Phillips, I tink Co. K steal one coose. You take de charge de right wing, while I goes to see." The Col. rode off to Co. K, but could find no goose. He returned to the command, thinking, I suppose, that Co. K was "all right on the goose."

That day is now passed in the army. As our army now marches along, the boys weary and suffering for water, there is not a guard stationed at every well to prevent their quenching their thirst. When they are hungry, if chickens and geese are convenient, they are not interfered with if they try to catch them. Often have I seen our boys coming in from a scout, many of them having a chicken or a goose swinging at each side of their saddle.

CHAPTER III.

FROM PADUCAH TO PITTSBURG LANDING.

Preparations for opening the Cumberland, Tennessee and Mississippi Rivers—Fort Henry taken—Fort Donelson taken—Part taken by 9th Ills., number killed and wounded—List of killed and wounded— Trip to Nashville and back—Incidents.

At the opening of the year 1862, it was becoming evident that to crush the "hideous monster" rebellion, would require a great effort on the part of the government. While our armies were being raised and disciplined, the rebels were planting themselves firmly at many points in the South-west, as well as the East. Columbus, Island No. 10, Memphis, Vicksburg, Port Hudson, and other points on the Mississippi River, were being strongly fortified. Fort Henry and Fort Donelson were fortified, and commanded the entrance of the Cumberland and Tennessee Rivers. General Fremont had urged the early occupation of these points, before the enemy should fortify them. But for some reason, (I suppose a good one on the part of the government,) the enemy were allowed to make these points strong-holds. Magnificent preparations were making, however, to take possession of these rivers, by the government, as great national thoroughfares. Gunboats, floating batteries &c., were being built with that view. These were brought to bear, early in 1862, on the work of opening the Cumberland and Tennessee Rivers, and dislodging the enemy of their strong-holds on these rivers. A heavy land force must of course co-operate with the fleet. In this work, the 9th Ill. Inft. was destined to act a conspicuous part. The material for the greater portion of its history is found in the part it has taken in subduing the rebellion in Tennessee, Mississippi and Alabama. At Cairo and at Paducah its work of discipline had been carried on until it was well prepared for meeting the enemy on the field. It left Paducah, a large and well-drilled Regiment.

On the evening of February 4th, 1862, Companies A, B, C, D and E, under command of Col. Mersy, struck tents at Paducah, and embarked on board the steamer "Wilson," with camp and garrison equipage. This wing of the Regiment moved up the Tennessee River the same night, and reported to Brig. Gen. John A. McClernand at Brown's Landing. The remainder of the Regiment, (except Co. H, Provost Guard,) under command of Lieut. Col. Phillips, came up on the steamer "B," on the evening of the 5th February. The two wings of the Regiment formed a junction on the left bank of the Tennessee River, five miles below Fort Henry, on the night of the 5th. They moved up the river towards Fort Heiman, on the 6th, reaching and occupying the Fort the same night. Brig. Gen. Smith's Division had left Paducah, and passed up the river to this point. They did not reach here in time to participate in the engagement. Fort Henry was reduced by the gunboats alone, none of the infantry taking part in the engagement.

When Fort Henry surrendered, the enemy quartered at Fort Heiman evacuated the place, leaving behind them all their camp and garrison equipage.

Brig. Gen. Smith's Division was ordered to move across the river and garrison Fort Henry, on the 7th. But the heavy rains had swollen the Tennessee River to such an extent that it was impossible to reach the boats, in order to cross. Hence, a Division already on that side of the river was assigned to that duty.

It was the high stage of water, and the consequent difficulty of landing, that prevented the land forces from co-operating with the gunboats in the attack against Fort Henry. Had they been permitted to co-operate as designed, they would have been able to cut off the retreat of the enemy, and capture the whole force. This would have prevented the reinforcement at Fort Donelson, and made the engagement there less sanguinary. But perhaps the victory would not have been any more complete than it was.

The enemy that had evacuated Forts Henry and Heiman fell back and strengthened Fort Donelson. The next thing in the programme, was to reduce Fort Donelson. The gunboats consequently were to descend the Tennessee River and ascend the Cumberland, while the land forces would march across the country, only twelve miles, and attack in the rear. In accordance with this plan, Gen. Smith's Division, still camped on the opposite side of the river, on the 12th of February, 1862, crossed the river with two days' rations, and no transportation, and moved towards Fort Donelson and bivouacked for the night about four miles from that place. At 11 o'clock at night, moved forward again, two and a half miles further, and bivouacked. At 11, A. M., of the 13th, moved forward to support McAllister's Battery, remaining here until 2, P. M. At this hour, McArthur's entire Brigade, (the one to which the 9th Ill. belonged,) were ordered to the left of McClernand's Division, to prevent a flank movement of the enemy on his left. The Brigade remained here until night, when it moved one-half mile further to the right. Company A, Capt. Adam commanding, was detached at this place, to support a battery, and Lieut. R. B. Patterson, of Co. E, was ordered with Co. A.

On the evening of the 13th, from having been warm and pleasant when they left camp, the weather changed and became extremely cold. Rain, sleet and snow fell alternately during the night. No fires were allowed. Hence, they suffered much from cold.

At midnight, a heavy volley of musketry was fired in front of Col. McArthur's Brigade. We were immediately ordered into line, and moved three-quarters of a mile further to the right, occupying a position in Gen. McClernand's Division and reporting to him.

The Brigade was moved again on the 14th, to the extreme right of our line, reaching that point after dark. The 41st Ill. occupied the extreme right, and the 9th Ill. next. At daylight of the 15th, the enemy made a furious attack on this part of Gen. McClernand's line. The 9th and 41st Ill. Regiments moved forward one hundred yards, to a high ridge, from which they held the rebel columns in check. The 9th moved forward to the ridge in echelon, the 41st in line of battle. At the second onslaught of the enemy, the 41st broke and fell back, and the 12th Ill. promptly occupied their place. The 9th Regiment held its position for two and a half hours, when all its supports on the right and left giving way, and its ammunition being exhausted, it fell back, slowly and in good order. The enemy did not press our front, but moved rapidly on our right flank. So rapid was their movement in this direction, that twice we were compelled to halt and make demonstrations to prevent their charging us. About 11 o'clock, A. M., the Regiment passed through the second line of battle, received a new supply of ammunition, and moved to the left and rejoined Gen. Smith's Division, to which they properly belonged.

On the morning of the 16th, the 9th Regiment was ordered forward to complete the work so gallantly begun by the 2d Iowa Inft. on the previous day. That Regiment had charged the rebel breastworks, and in part taken possession of them. To make another charge, and completely drive them out, was the work assigned to the 9th for this day. But before the final order to charge was given, the enemy surrendered *unconditionally.* The 9th Ill. Inft. and the 2d Iowa Inft. were granted the honor of first marching into the outer works of the enemy. On entering the works, the 9th Ill. took charge of the following rebel regiments: The 14th Mississippi, 32d, 14th and 18th Tennessee, and 2d Kentucky, in all about 2,000 men.

The 9th Ill. went into the fight, on the 15th, with about 600 men reported for duty. Its loss during the action was, 35 killed on the field, 160 wounded, and 6 taken prisoners. Most of those taken prisoners were wounded and unable to fall back with the Regiment. Companies A and H were not engaged in the fight. Company H had been left as Provost Guard at Paducah, and Company A, as mentioned above, had been detached on the night of the 13th to support a battery, and had not rejoined the Regiment at the time it was engaged.

Among the wounded, were the following officers: Capt. Robinson of Co. I, and Capt. Beckier of Co. D, both slightly; 1st Lieuts. Lieber of Co. B, Britt of Co. F, and Sutton of Co. G. These were all severely wounded. Lieut. Lieber lost his left arm, and Lieut. Sutton was disabled for life.

The following is a list of the killed and wounded in the various companies:

COMPANY A.—Supporting a battery, lost none.

COMPANY B.—*Killed,* Corp. Lugenbuehler, Corp. Dettweiler, Benkers, Jacob Eierkuss, Henry Gonnermann, Henry Hurick, Christian Koch, Albert Newmann, Leech. In all 9 killed. *Wounded.*—First Lieut. Hamilton Lieber, Privates Adolph Aldo, Peter Bauer, John Berger, Charles Daehner, Albert Donner, Michael Fath, Joseph Gantner,

Paul Geist, Sergt. Louis Grieser, Privates Jul. Hoffmann, John Krieger, Charles Lobe, Frederick Menne, Louis Messerschmitt, Hermann Moser, Josep Oberfell, Simon Pohn, Corp. John Sehab, William Schlott, Sergt. John Schmidt, Henry Schneider, Anton Schwarzkopf, Frederick Lensel, Henry Weber, Daniel Werner, Christian Wickermann, Joseph Cropp. In all 28 wounded.

COMPANY C.—*Killed*, Lorence Bersig and Heinrich Hillmann.—2. *Wounded*, Henry Arndt, George Fichter, John Graus, Christopher Klein, John Pietz, Adam Reesh, John Riedel, Adam Lammons, Henry Schmidt, William Vogt, Peter Weis, William Miller, and Corp. Charles King. In all 13 wounded.

COMPANY D.—Company D had 20 men wounded, including the Captain. The most of them were slight wounds, which did not disable the men. Three only were dangerously wounded.

COMPANY E.—*Killed*, Privates Cassius C. Atchinson and Jas. Dyer.–2. *Wounded*, Corps. John A. Gilmore and Frank M. Tillotson, Privates John Beatty, John A. J. Bragg, Russell W. Cool, Wm. Evans, Michael Farley, John Fletcher, Dennis C. Frothingham, Jas. B. Gilmore, Simon Hagar, Joseph B. Jones, Wm. T. Kelley, John Kemberlin, F. M. Moore, Francis J. Murphy, Geo. Snyder, John Till, Wm. G. Triplett, David M. Durham, Geo. M. Gilmore. In all 21 wounded.

COMPANY F.—*Killed*, Privates David N. Ashton and Constant Roland.—2 killed. *Wounded*, 1st Lieut. Wm. Britt, Sergts. Thos. C. Kidd and Andrew J. Webster, Corp. Andrew J. White, Privates Geo. M. Campbell, E. Carrey, John W. Dye, Wm. M. Ellis, James Getty, James Hicks, Nathan Lynch, Geo. McIrish, Eli J. Singleton, Richa Lumpkins, Thos. J. Wallace, Frank Wagner, John Rank, Joseph L. Garrett, Harlow Bassett. In all 19 wounded. This is not a complete list. There were 23 wounded. The records of the company have been destroyed.

COMPANY G.—*Killed*, Benjamin Jacob, Emsley Walker, James Willhelm. In all 3 killed. *Wounded*, 1st Lieut. John S. Sutton, N. G. Brown, Wm. B. Dubois, Thos. J. Pleasant, Jas. Canton, Jas. E. Mason, Jacob Willhelm, John J. White, John A. Stotlan, William J. Higlai, C. C. Akin, Jos. H. Watley, John Collin, Jas. M. Brown, and Wm. R. Gore. In all 15 wounded.

COMPANY H.—Absent at Paducah as Provost Guard.

COMPANY I.—*Killed*, James N. Johnson, Augustus Cluge, G. W. Kinder, Charles Loymer, David Lain, Alonzo Livingston, Hugh McMahen, John McKinney, Charles McDermot, Geo. M. More, Joseph P.

Stevenson, David Williams. In all 12 killed. *Wounded*, Capt. Joseph G. Robinson, 2d Lieut. S. T. Hughs, Sergts. Geo. Woodbury and W. Jarvis, Corps. R. R. Swain, John G. Irwin and F. A. Courmon, Privates Wm. Baird, John Baird, D. G. Breyfogle, Jas. G. Ballard, Zachariah Burgess, Aaron C. Bordon, Jos. Crews, G. W. Clark, Charles Dayton, Emanuel Davis, John Ellett, Henry Fitzsimmons, Theodore Fisher, H. Fuller, John Graham, James Hawratty, William Helms, David Johnson, David Kyle, Geo. Lent, Geo. Lawson, Sam'l Morehead, James Mitchel, Chas. S. Patton, Samuel Read, John R. Vanhooser, William Willson. In all 34 wounded.

COMPANY K.—*Killed*, Corp. Walter Walsh, Privates Reuben M. Anderson, And. J. Burton, Charles Casebeer, John Emery, Johna. Hazlewood, David Newcomb, Jas. Patterson. In all 8 killed. *Wounded*, Sergts. A. J. Snider and John Barbour, Corps. Chas. N. Brown, Geo. Lincoln and Samuel W. Sloan, Privates Jas. Broadie, Jos. N. Condon, Simon P. Casey, Wm. A. Daily, Frank F. Cogles, John Gibson, Albert W. Kimball, Aaron Lipe, John Mallory, Albert Mitchell, John Seivers, Wm. Thompson and H. C. Ulen. In all 18 wounded.

The desperate struggle in which our Regiment was engaged, and the persistence with which the boys fought, may be seen from the list of killed and wounded as presented above. Only about 600 went into the fight. Of these, 195 were killed and wounded; just about every third man.

The boys had, it will be remembered, when they left Fort Heiman on the morning of the 12th of February, only two days' rations. They received nothing more until the evening of the 15th, after they had been engaged in the severe battle of that forenoon. Thus their two days' rations had to last them four days. Many of the officers, who had entrusted their haversacks to their servants, became separated from those servants, and were almost without anything to eat for the last forty-eight hours. There was no chance for foraging there. Often now, our Regiment will go out on a scout with three days' rations, and live very well on it for six or eight days. Such was the battle of Fort Donelson, and the part the 9th took in it.

The Regiment remained at Fort Donelson until the 22d of February, when the Brigade proceeded up the Cumberland River to Fort Sevier near Clarksville, where they disembarked and went into camp on the 25th.

Major Kuhn, formerly Provost Marshal of Paducah, and Co. H of the 9th Regiment, his Provost Guard, reported to the Regiment for duty on the 23d. The Regiment remained in camp here until the 27th, when it embarked on board the steamer "Woodford," and proceeded up the river to Nashville, Tenn., arriving there on the morning of the 28th. Here it remained until March 1st, when it returned to camp at Fort Sevier.

When our forces advanced up the Cumberland River to Clarksville and Nashville, they found no enemy to oppose them. After the rebels surrendered Fort Donelson, they seemed to be seized with terror. The rebel Governor and Legislature fled from Nashville in terror, taking with them whatever they could of State property. The writer, being then in Illinois, well remembers the public rejoicing there was over the result of this victory. There seemed to be a feeling prevailing in the North that the "backbone" of the Rebellion was broken, and that we would soon have peace. But two years have passed away, (I write this sketch on the 16th of February, the anniversary of Fort Donelson's surrender,) and, although we have several times since that been cheered with the promise that the "backbone" of the Rebellion was broken, still it lives. It is said a snake's tail does not die until sunset, even though its back may be broken and its head mashed. Perhaps, as the rebs. had, at first, a snake for their emblem, this may be the reason it is so long dying. Maybe it is only the tail of it that now remains alive. When, however, sunset will come, and its tail cease to live, is difficult to determine. May it be soon.

Some incidents occurred during this period, worthy of note. During the time the Regiment was engaged in battle at Fort Donelson, James Getty, of Co. F, aged about 60 years, was observed by Lieut. Williford of his Co., to decline laying down to load. He stood, loaded his gun, and fired as deliberately as if he had been shooting at a target for a wager. The Lieut. told him he had better lay down to load, or he would get shot. His reply was, "I reckon I know my business," and again raised his gun and deliberately lowered it upon his selected rebel. Soon the Lieut. saw him tumble over, and supposing he was killed, went to him. But he jumped up, and said he guessed he was not much hurt. He was shot in the shoulder, but he gathered up his musket and went to firing again. It was not long until another ball struck his pocket-book. He had some silver in it. The ball struck a silver half dollar, and mashed it up, driving it against his thigh, bruising it very much. Two or three buckshot were lodged in him. Still he stood firing away at the enemy. I might also say in this connection, that this same man, at the battle of Shiloh, when the Regiment ran out of ammunition and had to fall back for a new supply, fell in with some other Regiment; procured a supply of ammunition from some one, and went to fighting again. When that Regiment in turn fell back, he happened in with some other one, and there fought. In this way he spent the whole of that terrible Sabbath day. When he ceased fighting with any company, he was careful to go to the commander of it, and get a certificate, stating that he had been fighting with it. When he returned to his company in the evening, he had certificates from several Captains and one Colonel. He preserved these certificates, so that he might show, when he returned to his Regiment, that he had not been *straggling*, but *fighting*. He went into the fight on the next day, and was shot in the head. From this wound he recovered, but was afterwards discharged on account of it.

Another incident. Surgeon Gulick (then Assistant Surgeon) was taken prisoner by the "Texan Rangers," while attending to his duties in the hospital. He insisted, that being Surgeon, he should not be retained as a prisoner; that there were a large number of wounded men under his charge, and no one to care for them but himself. The rebels persisted, however, in taking him. They told him that they had some wounded men, and he must come and attend to them. One of them was leading his horse along, taking him back to where their wounded were. He was in the rear of a rebel Regiment. The man who led his horse was shot. The Doctor does not say *by whom* he was shot. He put spurs to his horse to make his escape. He had to ride through a rebel Regiment. A perfect shower of musket balls followed him. To increase his danger, our own soldiers supposing him to belong to a party of rebels making a charge, fired upon him from the front. He was riding Surgeon Hamilton's horse. Strapped to his saddle was a buffalo robe. He had often joked with Dr. Hamilton about having that tied on there as a protection when he would be making his escape from the enemy. Five balls passed into this robe, and were lodged among its folds. The Doctor made his escape; but thinks he would never attempt to make another such.

Still another incident, with which the Doctor was connected. After the battle at Fort Donelson, he was placed on board a steamer with 275 wounded men, and shoved out into the river, without any medicine, without anything for the men to eat, with no instruments but carpenter tools, and in that condition remained for three days. If he attempted to take off a limb, he had to use a common cook's knife for a dissecting knife, and a carpenter's saw to sever the bone. He had no bandages with which to wrap up the wounds, except he take the only shirt they had. This truly was a trying position in which to place a good surgeon.

Still another. The present color-bearer received a shot in the arm. The ball was lodged there. The Doctor cut the ball out, but he would

not wait to have a bandage put on it, but snatched his musket and
rushed to the fight again.

One more incident. At the battle of Fort Donelson a soldier of Co.
K found in the knapsack of a Southern soldier, who had been killed in
battle, the picture of a beautiful young lady. He carefully preserved
it. At the battle of Shiloh, this soldier was killed. On examining his
knapsack, to make the proper inventory of his goods, the Orderly of
his company found this picture. He remembered the circumstance of
its being found. He carefully preserved it. It was a great favorite
with the boys in the company, and received the name of "The Daughter
of Co. K." When the Regiment was on the march from Corinth to
Athens, in November, 1863, it passed through the town of Pulaski,
Tenn. As Lieut. Oats, of Co. K, was riding along the streets of Pulaski,
he saw a young lady standing at the door of one of the residences of the
town, whom he at once recognized as the original of the picture in possession of Co. K. Speaking of the matter to others in the company,
they all agreed that this was the original. The Lieutenant learned
afterwards, to a certainty, that it was the same. The picture still
remained in his possession, until near the last of January, 1864. At
the time Gen. Roddy's forces made a dash upon our camp, when the
Regiment was nearly all out, the officers, as well as men, lost everything
that was in their tents. Among other things, the picture of "The
Daughter of Co. K," was taken. Its loss is much regretted by the boys.

CHAPTER IV.

FROM BATTLE OF SHILOH TO BATTLE AT CORINTH.

*Trip up the Tennessee River—Remain on boat—Battle of Shiloh—
Losses in this battle—Losses in 9th Regt. Ill. Inft.—List of killed
and wounded—Advance upon Corinth—Pursuit—Officers commissioned—Garrison Rienzi.*

Having ascended the Cumberland River, and ascertained that the
enemy had evacuated all the prominent points on it, Gen. Grant now
marshals his forces for a trip up the Tennessee River, hoping from it
to reach Corinth, where the enemy were strongly fortifying themselves
and collecting in great number.

The 9th Ill. Inft. was destined to take part in this expedition.
Hence, it struck tents at Fort Sevier on the 6th March, 1862, and
embarked, with camp and garrison equipage, on board the steamers
"Lady Pike" and "Commercial." It moved down the Cumberland

River on the morning of the 7th, and passed Fort Donelson on the 8th, reaching Paducah the same evening. It moved up the Tennessee on 10th March, and joined Gen. Grant's flotilla six miles above Fort Henry.

The trip up the Tennessee River, with this great army, is described by the boys, as grand beyond all description. There were, I believe, ninety-five steamboats loaded with soldiers. The weather was beautiful and pleasant. Bands of music were playing. Everything that was calculated to charm was there. Doubtless very many of this great multitude did not realize that in a short time so many of them must fall in the deadly conflict. The terrors to come were forgotten in the joys and grandeur of the hour.

This fleet, containing a grand army, reached Savannah, Tenn., on the 12th of March, 1862. Here the boats remained tied up until the 18th of March, when we moved up to Pittsburg Landing, disembarked and went into camp, one-quarter of a mile from the river, on the 19th. On the 23d, our camp was moved one-half mile further back from the river. At this point the 81st Ohio, and the 13th and 14th Missouri Infantry, were attached to the Brigade. The two latter were afterwards exchanged for the 22d Ohio and 66th Illinois Infantry.

On the 1st of April Col. Mersy was ordered to the command of the Brigade, in the place of Col. McArthur, who had been placed under arrest.

On the morning of the 6th, at daylight, the enemy made a furious attack on Gen. Prentiss' Division. The enemy moved forward in echelon by Divisions, point foremost, the evident intention being to break, by a furious attack, the centre of our line. But in this they did not succeed. Gen. Prentiss was compelled, however, to fall back a short distance to his supports. Here he gallantly maintained his position for a long time.

But my object in this sketch, is not to give an account of this terrible battle, but of the part the 9th Illinois took in it.

Our Division was held in reserve, and consequently did not reach the field of action until after noon. Col. McArthur had been released from arrest, and resumed command of his Brigade. Brig. Gen. W. H. L. Wallace relieved Major General Smith of the command of our Division, the latter being too unwell to do duty on the field. We were moved to the left of Prentiss' Division. On the way the Regiment met with hundreds of stragglers hastening in confusion to the sheltering cover of the river bank for protection. About fifty of these were pressed into our Regiment. Nearly all of them were killed or wounded during the day.

The Regiment held its place in the line for two hours, against a vastly superior force of the enemy. The 41st Ill. Inft. was on our right, and the 12th Ill. Inft. on our left. The latter Regiment fell back three hundred yards, after being exposed to the fire of the enemy for over an hour. Thus our left flank was exposed to a flank movement of the enemy. Of this they soon took advantage, and poured a murderous fire down the ravine which we occupied. After holding this position until a new line was formed, three hundred yards in the rear, the Regiment fell back hastily behind it. It was not long, however, until this line was broken by the terrible assault of the overwhelming forces of the enemy. A new line, of immense strength, was finally formed one-half mile from the landing. All the available artillery was gathered to this point; the victorious advance of the enemy was checked, and their masses for the first time during the day recoiled before the murderous discharges of grape and canister from one hundred iron throats.

Gen. Prentiss' Division not falling back soon enough to this new line, were completely surrounded, and compelled to surrender to the enemy. The Division numbered about 3,000 men.

After the repulse of the enemy at this point, no further attack was made, and night soon closed the conflict of the day. During the night the gunboats kept up a constant firing of 64-pound shells among the enemy, and finally compelled them to fall back six hundred yards. This gave our forces a fine chance to operate in the morning. During the night also, some 20,000 fresh troops from Buell's army were ferried across the river. Maj. Gen. Wallace's Division, from Crumpt's Landing, came up on the left flank of the enemy. So that on the morning of the 7th we had 20,000 fresh troops on the front of the enemy, our gunboats on their right, and Gen. Wallace's Division of 6,000 fresh troops on their left flank. The contest was not long. The enemy soon gave way. Then began a retreat which finally, at 3, P. M., became a perfect rout, as they fled in wild dismay toward their works at Corinth. The miserable condition of the roads prevented pursuit for more than half of the distance. Hence, we succeeded in capturing only 1,000 prisoners.

The entire Union loss in this engagement was, 1,700 killed, 9,000 wounded, and 3,800 taken prisoners. The rebel loss was about 2,300 killed, 12,000 wounded, and 1,000 taken prisoners. Total Union loss, 14,500. Total rebel loss, 15,800.

Here, in this one battle, were 4,000 American citizens left dead upon the battle-field, and 21,000 more wounded. · By whom was this terrible destruction of life? Had some savage foe invaded our once happy and peaceful land? Ah, no! It was the hand of brother against brother; fellow-citizen against fellow-citizen! It arose on the one hand, from a determination to rivet tighter and tighter the chains of human bondage, even at the cost of the overthrow of that government under which our country has been so highly prospered; and on the other hand, from a determination that so good a government should not be overthrown to support any such unhallowed cause Oh, the sadness of human strife, and especially when it arises from a *family quarrel!*

The loss of the 9th Ill. Inft. in this battle, was 61 killed on the field, and 287 wounded. Among the killed, was Lieut F. Vogler, of Co. B· Among the wounded, were Col. Mersy, Lieut. Col. Phillips, Adjutant Klock, Assistant Surgeon Gulick, Captains Adam, Kneffner, Beckier, Hawes, Webb, Armstrong and Robinson, and Lieutenants Rollmann, Scheel, Williford, Clements, Purviance, McCleery, (mortally,) Lowe and Krebs. Lieut. Krebs was severely wounded and taken prisoner.

The following is a list of the killed and wounded in the various companies, during this battle:

COMPANY A.—*Killed*, Sergt. Peter Schoppert, Corp. Joseph Brown, Privates George Andrea, Henry Glink, Ambrose Lamber and William Herrman. In all, 6 killed. *Wounded*, Capt. Emil Adam, Lieut. Oscar Rolmann, Sergt. Andrew Bastian, Corps. Anton Hund, Anton Schwertner and Henry Burmeister, Privates Friedrich Bremenkamp, Henry Brenner, John Baner, Erasmus Fries, Nickolaus Frank, Anton Gaulocher, (afterward died,) Ferdinand Hoas, Wm. Holl, Michael Hortweck, James Loehr, Charles Miller, Henry Mueller, August Meyer, Jacob Nickolaus, George Schaefer, Jacob Wehrli, Martin Weis, Jacob Duttenhoefer, Adam Schalter, Benidiekt Stranbinger, William Stahl, George Winter, Christian Rose, Nickolaus Vonburg, Friedrich Koch, Theodore Bachlg, Henry Tahncke, Chas. Ribke, Michael Braun and Andreas Sehuehman. In all, 36 wounded.

COMPANY B.—*Killed*, Lieut. F. E. Vogler, Sergt. John Schmidt, Privates Edward Dettmar, Albert Kineoke, Conrad Maul, John Mesh, Frank Scheffer and Henry Weber. In all, 8 killed. *Wounded*, Sergt. John Mallmann, Privates Lorenz Ackermann, Joseph Ammon, Mathias Arnold, Jacob Bauer, Morand Barrmann, George Betz, Gustar Blank, Joss. Cropp, Albert Donner, Frederick Entz, Amald Gerig, Charles Grin, Conrad Hellmuth, Gerhard Janssen, Valentin Kadel, August Lopold, Louis Linne, Paul Martin, Ignaz Menne, Sabastian Pfister, John Raffel, Peter Reppel, George Salz, Henry Schmidt, Jacob Spiess, Philipp Spiess, Corp. Hermann Suemnicht, Jacob Sulzer, Daniel Werner, Christ. Wickermann, Ferdinand Wisshack, Corp. Augustus Wurmb. In all, 33 wounded.

COMPANY C.—*Killed*, Wm. Klingenberg, John Lamprecht, George

Lehr, Michael Lehr, Friedrich Lippert, Geo. Luther, Henry Riditer, Sergt. Chas. Hahle, Christiân Schenk, Wm. Slorch and August Wichard. In all, 11 killed. *Wounded*, First Lieut. Oscar Rollmann, A. Arramus, Anton Becker, Henry Behm, Andrew Benci, Philipp Erbe, Chas. Friedrich, Wm. Gaebe, Jacob Haberkorn, John A. Helferich, Frank Helferich, Jacob Herpin, Christian Keith, Christian Macdel, Frank Moser, Andrew Nadber, Jacob Randall, Antoo Saebert, Charles Schenk, Fred. Scheve, Henry Schemph, Peter Schneider, Nicklaus Schouelber, John Spaule, John Salzmann, Freiderich Slaab, Henry Vishsel. In all, 27 wounded.

COMPANY D.—*Killed*, Jacob Becker, Charles Geesel, Henry Geesel, Adam Loebig, Christian Kahn, Adam Keitz, Jacob Kieps, Philip Laner, Albert Scheleberg, Schelz Tert, Wm. Vogelpohl and Henry Vohs. In all, 12 killed. *Wounded*, Capt. Beckier, Lieuts. Krebs and Scheal, John Baehr, Herman Bange, Isiter Bayett, Joseph Beck, Rudolph Bekier, Wm. Beeverson, Jos. Ersenhauer, Anlon Garllhoeffner, Fred. Havermann, Conrath Heidmann, Chas. Huber, Edward Krebs, William Lieser, Chas. Miller, George Metzker, C. Moeninger, C. Roth Roffy Fried. Scheel, Os. Stocker, Bernhard Vogel, and Tweibert Henry. In all, 34 wounded.

COMPANY E.—*Killed*, Sergt. Silas Bunker, Privates John Anson, Frank M. Moore, Wm. D. Nevius, James McKenzie, John C. Cadie. In all, 6 killed. *Wounded*, Corps. Jas. G. Carnahan, Joseph R. Cox, and Philip Anderson, Privates Jas. M. Blake, Matthew Bromley, Geo. H. Campbell, Chas. Dryden, Michael Furlong, Daniel Hubbard, John W. Hay, Jos. B. Jones, Jas. Mahone, Geo. Meyer, Francis J. Murphy, Jesse Mack, John N. Shoemaker, Thos. Stalkal, Neal Vestal, Sergt. Lewis C. Bornman, Musician Samuel Williams, Wagoner Wm. Minor, Wm. Mock. In all, 22 wounded.

COMPANY F.—*Killed*, Sergt. And. J. Webster, Corps. Joshua Gear and Frank Pothast, Privates Demean McCulloch, John Chantick, Toliver Foster, Thos. Cox, Joseph Koontz, Geo. McLeish, Charles Hills, John W. Snofpr, Private of the 71st Ohio, name not known. In all, 13 killed. *Wounded*, Capt. Webb, Lieut. Geo. Williford, Sergts. Jos. C. Gales and R. N. Heinberger, Corp. And. J. White, Privates John B. Choenewith, Jas. Rodgers, James Duncan, N. B. Winters, John McCarter, John Stutfouth, John H. Lauchly, James Getty, Jos. L. Miller, James Hobbs, Wm. T. Miller, John H. Collins, M. N. Fisher, Harlow Bassett, Jas. M. Hickman, And. Grudin, Henry Grundin, R. Pimpkins, Geo. W. Warren, John M. Ticknor, Marcus Burns. In all, 26 wounded.

COMPANY G.—*Killed*, David Jones, Alpheus Bascum, Jas. Walker, Thos. J. Ouly and Wm. H. Bascom. In all, 5 killed. *Wounded*, Lieut. Clemens, N. G. Poraine, John B. Russell, E. B. Rhoads, Wm. Hampton, John J. White, (afterwards died,) John W. Brown, Wm. L. Brown, N. G. Brown, Henry Brown, John J. Zippy, John J. Stripling, Wm. R. Bradley, Wm. Addison, Lewis R. Applegate Robert Marshall, Daniel Ryan, Thos. Stotlar, A. B. Suttin, W. S. White, John McCord, Lewis Wise, Jun., Allen Edwards, S. P. Hartsell, Charles W. Miller, Bennet Strotlar. In all, 26 wounded.

COMPANY H.—*Killed*, Sergt. Francis D. Hubbel, Will. R. Haller, Daniel C. White, Thos. Wright. In all, 4 killed. *Wounded*, Captain W. F. Armstrong, Sergts. Daniel Pentzer and Jacob Miller, Privates Nickolaus Keller, Alonzo F. McEwen, Paul Roberts, Jas. W. Osborn, Sidney B. Phillips, John Arny, Wm. Boldeman, Dennis Bahon, Chas. Biernbrier, Wm. S. Cheeney, Wm. A. Cottingham, Ira G. Dart, John Droesch, Thos. Fry, Will. H. Ilsley, Wm. Keep, John B. Livingood, John F. Moore, Patrick Mogneham, Layfayette Mason, Jas. S. McGuillion, Edward Nail, George Ralph, Francis M. Stickel, Almon D. Simmons, Jos. E. Taulber, Moses H. Turner, Patrick Whalen, Erasmus Gaw, Jas. A. Clotpelter, George H. Dry, John Salzmann, and Daniel C. Carriker. In all, 36 wounded.

COMPANY I.—*Killed*, Nathan Abbot, John Bass, Reegon Edward, John N. Larance and Frederick Swartz. In all, 5 killed. *Wounded*, Captain Jos. G. Robinson, 1st Lieutenant Wm. H. Purviance, Sergt. W. W. Jarvis, Corp. G. W. Stice, Privates John Baird, Norman Barber, Isaiah Bery, G. W. Clark, Thomas C. Gillham, Wm. Helms, Thomas Hauskins, John Jaka, S. B. Jarvis, Chas. C. Lewis, Albert Mills, Geo. McKinley, Chas. A. Redman, John Wilson and Henry Wormyer. In all, 19 wounded.

COMPANY K.—*Killed*, George Sloan, Wm. Foster, Jas. L. Kriddler, Thos. Walton. In all, 4 killed. *Wounded*, John Richmond, Samuel W. Sloan, Geo. W. Burton, Sen., Geo. W. Burton, Jun., John Burke, Chas. W. Boles, Henderson Cogdall, John L. Creed, John Clifford, Wm. A. Carding, Frank F. Cogles, John Horn, Thos. J. Hagler, Laro May, Sam'l L. Miller, Robert E. Ramsey, Jonathan Stone, and Chas. L. Tomlinson. In all, 18 wounded.

The terrible conflict which was endured by the 9th Ill. Inft., in this battle, will be seen from the number of killed and wounded. There was present for duty when the Regiment went into the engagement, 570 men. Of these 348 were killed and wounded, and ten were captured. One commissioned officer was killed, and 19 wounded. Only four

[3]

commissioned officers were left unhurt. I heard one of the soldiers who was present at the time, say, that when they ceased fighting on Sabbath evening, there were 70 men in line for duty, out of the whole Regiment. It is said that Col. Mersy, when the Regiment was first drawn up in line after the battle was over, shed tears, saying, "Vel, vel; dis is all dat is left of my little Nint!" It must have been a sad sight to see a Regiment, which numbered over 1,000 men when at Paducah a few months previous, cut down to this small number. But such is war.

Such was the battle of Shiloh, and such the part taken in it by the 9th Ill. Inft. The writer well remembers the feeling which prevailed in the North with reference to it. There was rejoicing over it as a victory. Still it was regarded as a dearly bought victory. There was a very decided feeling that somebody was at fault. That the rebels had completely surprised our army. That our pickets were out but a very short distance. Hence, the surprise. Gen. Grant, as chief in command, was faulted. It was charged that he was drunk at the time. That he had disobeyed orders, and landed his men on the wrong side of the river, etc. I heard a citizen of Chicago, not a month ago, say that if Gen. Grant had made his appearance in Chicago immediately after the battle of Shiloh, he would have been mobbed, such was the feeling of indignation.

It is not my province here to write a defense of Gen. Grant. Nor is it needed. His own brilliant career since that, has set him right in the minds of the people. A man who has captured more prisoners and more guns than the world-renowned warrior, Napoleon Bonaparte, certainly does not need, at this day, a written defense of his military career. Suffice it to say, the officers and men who fought under him, even at Shiloh, become restless if a word is said against him.

Immediately after this battle, Gen. Halleck, who had charge of the South-Western Department of the army, with his "Head Quarters" at St. Louis, left that place for the field of strife and took command of the army in person. Expectation was high in the North. It was thought that now surely the rebels will be "pushed to the wall." Never since the war broke out, has there been such intense anxiety in the North-west, as that which filled the public mind during the time which intervened between the battle of Shiloh and the evacuation of Corinth. Many hearts were sad over friends who fell at Shiloh. Every days' news was anxiously awaited, expecting it to bring an account of another terrible conflict. The suspense was long and painful. When the news finally came that Corinth was ours, but that the enemy had evacuated it, there was a feeling of sadness ran through the public mind. They were not prepared for that. They were prepared to hear of many slain in the effort to take Corinth, but not to hear that the enemy had fled and was out of reach.

The 9th Ill. Inft. remained in camp on the battle-ground of Shiloh, exposed to all the sickening influences of the nearness of so many dead animals, as well as offensive odor arising from the shallow and imperfect burial, which necessarily had to be given to so great a multitude of dead. In conversation with a citizen from Illinois, who visited the battle-ground a week or ten days after the battle, I learned from him that the offensive smell of the dead was almost insufferable. That, together with the diet upon which the soldiers had to live, produced disease to an alarming extent. Here the Regiment remained in camp until the 29th of April, over three weeks. On that day it removed, with camp and garrison equipage, towards Corinth ten miles, and bivouacked. It moved forward again on the 30th, five miles further, and went into camp. Here the Regiment had muster and inspection by Col. Mersy commanding.

Here Brig. Gen. R. J. Oglesby took command of our Brigade, in place of Col. McArthur who was severely wounded in the late battle, Brig. Gen. T. A. Davies took command of our Division, in place of Gen. W. H. L. Wallace who was mortally wounded.

On the first of May, moved camp five miles further towards Corinth, and remained there until the 4th of May. On that day removed to Monterey, Miss., and went into camp a little West of that town, and remained there until the 8th of May, when another forward movement was made, to within seven miles of Corinth, finding no enemy.

The country here is very poor and broken, and water very scarce and unfit for use. A great many of the men were sick with the Diarrhea and Typhoid Fever. The Regiment remained here until the 14th of May, when it moved two miles further in the direction of Corinth.

The Division moved forward again on the 16th, about one mile, and formed a line, with Brig. Gen. Hurlbut's Division on our right. On the 17th, moved forward again one mile, and one-half mile on the 19th. This brought our line within two and a-half miles of Corinth, and within range of 32-pounder rifled guns. None were fired, however, and the plain inference was, that the enemy had none. On the 21st of May, our line advanced 400 yards, and again on the 29th 400 yards more. The pressure now became so heavy, that the enemy evacuated Corinth, and moved Southward toward Okolona.

Thus it will be seen, our army was just one month moving from

Pittsburg Landing to Corinth, a distance of about thirty miles. Just one mile per day. And this after having remained 22 days in camp, before leaving the battle-ground. This, too, in pursuit of a fleeing enemy. It will be difficult ever to convince the country that this great delay was necessary. And yet many military men, who were present, regard it as a master-piece of Generalship. The country through which this vast army must pass, was entirely uncultivated. No army could have subsisted in it, even for a few days. Had our army advanced rapidly, they were exposed to a flank movement which would have thrown the enemy between them and the river, and cut off, as a natural consequence, our supplies. That done, and our whole army would have been at the mercy of the enemy. There was certainly great caution. But it was thought it was all needed.

When an advance was made, after halting, in an incredibly short time, breast-works were thrown up to prepare for an attack. It is amusing, even now, to hear the boys laughing at their expertness with the spade. They all turned out to be pretty good Irishmen, so far as the use of the spade is concerned.

Immediately upon the evacuation of Corinth, Gen. Davies' Division, to which the 9th Ill. Inft. belonged, was ordered, with Gen. Pope's army, in pursuit of the fleeing enemy. The rapidity with which that pursuit was prosecuted, will be seen from the following record of our daily marches. Is it to be wondered at that they were not overtaken? On the first day we moved out five miles, and bivouacked for the night near Farmington. Moved forward again on the 31st, three miles, and went into camp on the Mobile and Ohio Railroad. Here we remained in camp until the 5th of June.

The following events occurred while in camp here: On the 1st of June the Regiment was paid for the months of January, February, March and April, 1862.

On the 2d of June commissions arrived as follows: First Lieut. James C. McClery, to be Captain Co. K; 2d Lieut. G. G. Low, to be 1st Lieut. Co. K; and Sergt. James Oats, to be 2d Lieut. Co. K. Sergeant Mallmann, to be 2d Lieut. Co. B; and Sergt. Gottlab, to be 2d Lieut. Co. A.

On the 5th of June we again moved forward, eight miles, and went into camp. On the 6th, moved forward and went into camp near Boonville, Miss. Here we remained until the 12th of June. General Davies, commander of the Division, being absent on sick-leave, General Oglesby was in command of the Division; Col. Mersy of the Brigade, and Major Kuhn of the Regiment.

On the 12th of June, the Regiment moved on its return towards Corinth, fifteen miles, and went into camp. On the 13th, moved again and occupied its old camping ground two and a-half miles south of Corinth.

On the 17th of June, Col. Wright, of the 22d Ohio, being senior Colonel, relieved Col. Mersy of the command of the Brigade, and Col. Mersy went home on sick-leave.

The Regiment remained in camp here until August 16th, 1862. During this time the following changes occurred: Captain Webb resigned, and his resignation was accepted July 15th, 1862. Lieutenant Purviance, of Co. I, was discharged August 16th, for inability from wounds received in action at Shiloh.

On the 16th of August, in compliance with orders from Gen. Davies, Division commander, the Regiment moved, with camp and garrison equipage, to Rienzi, and reported for duty to Brig. Gen. Granger, commanding at that place, by whom it was assigned to Col. Schaeffer, commanding 2d Brigade.

Regimental Quartermaster, W. G. Pinckard, was promoted to be Captain and Assistant Quartermaster, to rank from April 30th, 1862.

There are some incidents during the period covered by this chapter worthy of note. During the battle of Shiloh, Lieut. Col. Phillips was wounded. It occurred late on Sabbath evening. He says the only time he had ever been scared since he has been in the army, was when they were carrying him off the battle-field wounded. The thought occurred to him, that now there was almost six feet exposed to the fire of the enemy instead of one foot, forgetting for the time, that while his body occupied an additional space horizontally, it did not occupy so much perpendicularly, as when he was on his horse.

CHAPTER V.

FROM THE ATTACK ON CORINTH, OCT. 3D, 1862, UNTIL REGIMENT
WAS MOUNTED.

*Rebels prepare to attack Corinth—Order of battle—Result of the
attack on the 3d of October—New line of battle at "White House"—
Line at "Battery Robinett"—Slaughter on the 4th of October—Extracts from a Rebel prisoner's journal—List of killed and wounded
—Outpost duty.*

The Rebel leaders were not satisfied that our forces should occupy
Corinth, uninterruptedly. Hence, in the Fall of 1862 active preparations were made by them to attack that place. A heavy force, under
Generals Price and VanDorn, was fitted up for this purpose. The time
was drawing near when our boys must endure another of those terrible
struggles, two of which they had already passed through.

As I have said, the Regiment had been doing outpost duty at Rienzi,
from the 16th of August until the last of September. On the 20th of
September, Col. Schaeffer's Brigade, with which our Regiment had
been temporarily united, moved Northward, leaving the 9th Ill. and the
59th Indiana, to hold the place. On the 1st of October the 9th Ill.
moved toward Corinth, and bivouacked for the night seven miles South
of our old camp near Corinth. Moved again, on the 2d of October, and
came to the old familiar camp, at noon. Here we occupied our old
position again, reporting to General Oglesby, who commanded the
Brigade.

On the morning of October 3d, 1862, the Regiment was marched
out in its proper position for the terrible conflict. The following order
will show the position it occupied during the fight. It was moved out
two miles Northwest of Corinth, to the old rifle-pits of the rebels. Our
Brigade was on the left of the 2d Division. The 6th Division was on
our left. On the right of the 6th Division, was the 3d Brigade of the
2d Division, (Col. Baldwin commanding,) which had been temporarily
attached to that Division. Gen. McArthur commanded the 6th Division; Gen. Davies the 2d Division, and Gen. Hamilton the Ohio
Division. This latter Division was held in reserve. Immediately on
our right was the 1st Brigade of the 2d Division. Such was the position our Brigade occupied at the opening of this terrible conflict.

The enemy made their first attack upon Gen. McArthur's Division,
which was placed immediately upon our left. After a short resistance,

Col. Baldwin's Brigade, placed on the right of that Division, gave way and fell back in confusion. This uncovered and exposed to the enemy our left flank. Soon the enemy came through the large gap thus made, and attacked us simultaneously in the front and rear. The 81st Ohio, placed upon the left of our Brigade, gave way and moved in confusion and disorder to the right and rear, followed very soon by the 12th Ill., and then the 9th moved in the same manner.

In attempting to check the too hasty advance of the Rebels, the 9th Ill. lost Capt. Britt, killed, and the two Captains Lowe, and Lieutenants Hughes and Ulen, together with 53 enlisted men, captured.

Gen. Hackleman's Brigade covered our retreat, and we fell back and formed a new line at the "White House." The Brigades occupied the same order in this line as in the former one. Here the advance of the enemy was checked, until darkness put a stop to the conflict for this day.

During the night our line was drawn back to Battery "Robinett." Just before daylight, on the morning of the 4th of October, the enemy cheered by their success of yesterday, opened from a four-gun battery, on the town, compelling our wounded to leave for safer quarters. A General Hospital was established one mile out on the M. & C. R. R., where all the wounded were removed. Before they could all be removed, one or two of them had been killed by the rebel shells in the Tishomingo House. At daylight, the action became general all along our lines. The Rebel columns made desperate charges, and were as often repulsed.

General Oglesby, commanding our Brigade, was wounded the day previous, and Col. Mersy assumed command of the Brigade. Major Kuhn, of our Regiment, was also disabled, and Captain Hawes assumed command of the Regiment during the fight on the 4th of October.

The slaughter of the enemy, in the efforts to capture "Battery Robinett," was terrific. A true picture of the ground, taken ere the dead were removed, shows the ground to be literally covered with the dead, often lying one upon another.

The struggle lasted until about 10 A. M., when the Rebel line was broken, and their whole army retreated in confusion and disorder. Thus ended another of those terrible conflicts which have marked the history of this war. The conflict was fierce and determined on both sides. Our forces were under the command of Gen. Rosecrans. Those of the enemy were under Generals Price and VanDorn. It was regarded a matter of vital importance, at that time, for our forces to hold that place. The importance which the Rebels attached to the work of re-taking it, and the desperate struggle they made in order to do it, will be seen

from some extracts which I will here make from the journal of a Rebel
prisoner, Lieut. Labruzan, of the 42d Regt. Ala. A copy of his notes,
taken as the battle progressed, and after he was captured, was obtained
by some of the boys in our Regiment, and I have thus secured access
to it. The following extract will show the position the enemy occupied
on the day before the battle commenced:

"*Thursday, Oct. 2d.*—The bridge finished about 10 o'clock, when
we took up the line of march. We marched right in front, which
brought our Regt. near the head of the column. Generals VanDorn
and Villipigue were ahead about two or three miles. The army here is
fully 25,000 men under command of Gen. VanDorn, who outranks
Gen. Price. Brig. Gen. Moore commanded our Brigade of five Regiments. Our Division is commanded by Brig. Gen. Manny."

I omit here a portion of his notes as to the march during the day,
and the manner in which he spent the night of the 2d October. It
would be interesting to give the whole of this extract from his journal,
but it would occupy too much space. It would enable us to view that
great battle from a rebel stand-point. Of the first day of the fight, he
writes thus:

"*Friday, Oct. 3d.*—Reveille by the bugle at 4 A. M. Were marching by 4½. Crossed into Mississippi at 7 A. M. Marched just on the
border for some miles. At 6½ heard some artillery firing. Three miles
ahead, skirmishing, which was kept up until after we crossed the M.
& C. R. R., which was at 9½ A. M. Saw a Regiment skirmishing in a
field just below us. The artillery kept up a constant fire about three
times a minute. Our Brigade, under Gen. Moore, marching into the
woods, formed a line of battle, our right resting on the Railroad. We
had not waited more than fifteen minutes, when heavy skirmishing was
heard about a half mile in front, with steady and increasing cannonading.
Two men from each company were detailed to attend to the wounded,
&c. We left blankets and knapsacks here. About 10 o'clock our
Brigade marched forward through a corn-field, and formed into a line
within a half mile of the enemy. Heavy firing just in front. Saw a
Major who was wounded."

He proceeds thus to speak of the fight of the 3d; but I will not
follow him further, on that day. Let us hear him describe the scene
of the 4th:

"*Saturday, Oct. 4th.*—An awful day. At 4 o'clock, before day, our
Brigade was ordered to the left about one-fourth of a mile, and halted,
throwing out lines of skirmishers, which kept up a constant fire. A
Battery in front of the right of our Regiment opened briskly, and the
enemy replied the same. The cannonading was heavy for an hour and
a half. Our Regiment lay down close, and stood it nobly. The shell
flew thick and fast, cutting off large limbs and filling the air with frag-
ments. Many burst within 20 feet, and the pieces popped within 2 or
3 feet. It was extremely unpleasant, and I prayed for forgiveness of

my sins, and made up my mind to go through. Col. Sawier called for
volunteers to assist the 2d Texas skirmishers. I volunteered, and took
my company. Captain Perkins and Lieutenant Wumson being taken
sick directly after the severe bombardment, I had the Co. all the time.
I went skirmishing at 7½, and returned at 9½ o'clock. We got behind
trees and logs, and the way the bullets did fly, was unpleasant to see.
I think 20 must have passed within a few feet of me, humming prettily.
Shells tore off large limbs and splinters. Struck my tree several times.
We could only move from tree to tree, and bending low to the ground,
while moving. Oh, how anxiously I watched for the bursting of the
shells when the heavy roar of the cannon proclaimed their coming. At
9½ o'clock I had my skirmishers relieved, by Captain Rouse's Company.
Sent my men to their places, and went behind a log with Major Furges.
At 10 o'clock, suddenly the fight fairly opened, with heavy volleys of
musketry and the double thundering cannon. This was on the right.
In a few minutes the left went into action in splendid style. At 10¼
o'clock, Col. Rogers came up by us, only saying "Alabama forces."
Our Regiment, with the Brigade rose, unmindful of the shell or shot,
and moved forward, marching about 250 yards and rising the crest of
a hill. The whole of Corinth, with its enormous fortifications, burst
upon our view. The U. S. flag was floating over the forts and in town.
We were now met by a perfect storm of grape, cannister, cannon balls
and Minnie balls. Oh, God! I have never seen the like! The men
fell like grass, even here. Giving one tremendous cheer, we dashed to
the bottom of the hill on which the fortifications are situated. Here
we found every foot of ground covered with large trees and brush, cut
down to impede our progress. Looking to the right and left, I saw
several Brigades charging at the same time. What a sight was there.
I saw men running at full speed, stop suddenly and fall upon their
faces, with their brains scattered all around. Others, with legs and
arms cut off, shrieking with agony. They fell behind, beside, and
within a few feet of me. I gave myself to God, and got ahead of my
company. The ground was literally strewed with mangled corpses.
One ball passed through my pants, and they cut twigs right by me. It
seemed, by holding out my hand I could have caught a dozen. They
buzzed and hissed by me in all directions, but I still pushed forward.
I seemed to be moving right in the mouth of cannon, for the air was
filled with hurling grape and cannister. Ahead was one continuous
blaze. I rushed to the ditch of the fort, right between some large
cannon. I grappled into it, and half way up the sloping wall. The
enemy were only three or four feet from me on the other side, but could
not shoot us for fear of having their heads blown off. Our men were
in the same predicament. Only 5 or 6 were on the wall, and 30 or 40
in and around the ditch. Catesby on the wall by my side. A man
within two feet of me, put his head cautiously up, to shoot into the
fort. But he suddenly dropped his musket, and his brains were dashed
in a stream over my fine coat, which I had in my arms, and on my
shirt sleeves. Several were killed here, on top one another, and rolled
down the embankment in ghastly heaps. This was done by a Regi-

ment of Yankees coming about 40 yards on our left, after finding us entirely cut off, and firing into us. Several of our men cried "put down the flag," and it was lowered, or shot into the ditch. Oh, we were butchered like dogs, as we were not supported. Some one placed a white handkerchief on Sergeant Buck's musket, and he took it to a port hole. But the Yankees snatched it off and took him prisoner. The men fell 10 at a time. The ditch being full, and finding we had no chance, the survivors tried to save themselves as best they could. I was so far up, I could not get off quickly. I do not recollect of seeing Catesby after this, but think he got off before. I trust in God he has. I and Capt. Foster started together, and the air was literally filled with hissing balls. I got about 20 steps, as quick as I could, about a dozen being killed in that distance. I fell down and scrambled behind a large stump. Just then, I saw poor Foster throw up his hands, and saying "Oh, my God!" jumped about two feet from the ground, falling on his face. The top of his head seemed to cave in, and the blood spouted straight up several feet. I could see men fall as they attempted to run, some with their heads to pieces, and others with the blood streaming from their backs. It was horrible. One poor fellow being almost on me, told me his name, and asked me to take his pocket-book if I escaped and give it to his mother, and tell her that he died a brave man. I asked him if he was a Christian, and told him to pray, which he did, with the cannon thundering a deadly accompaniment. Poor fellow. I forgot his request in the excitement. His legs were literally cut to pieces. As our men returned, the enemy poured in their fire, and I was hardly 30 feet from the mouth of the cannon. Minnie balls filled the stump I was behind, and the shells bursted within three feet of me. One was so near it stunned me, and burned my face with powder. The grape-shot hewed large pieces off my stump, gradually wearing it away. I endured the horrors of death here for half an hour, and endeavored to resign myself and prayed. Our troops formed in line in the woods, and advanced a second time to the charge with cheers. They began firing when about half way, and I had to endure it all. I was feigning death. I was right between our own and the enemies fire. In the first charge our men did not fire a gun, but charged across the ditch, and to the very mouth of the cannon, with the bayonet. So also the second charge, but they fired. Thank God, I am unhurt, and I think it was a merciful Providence. Our troops charged by, when I seized a rifle and endeavored to fire it several times, but could not, for the cap was bad. Our boys were shot down like hogs, and could not stand it, and fell back each man for himself. Then the same scene was enacted as before. This time the Yankees charged after them, and as I had no chance at all, and all around me were surrendering, I was compelled to do so, as a rascal threatened to shoot me. I had to give up my sword to him. He demanded my watch also. Took it; but I appealed to an officer, and got it back. I had no means of defending myself for the first time in many years. I cried to see our brave men slaughtered so, and thought where Catesby might be. I have never felt so in all my life. It is now said that our Brigade was never ordered to charge such a place, and that it was a mistake. If so, it was a sad one. Being brought behind the works we found three Regiments drawn up in line, and all of them were fighting our 42d Alabama alone. I helped to carry a wounded man to the Depot, with Lieutenants Marshall, Contra and Preston, they being the only unhurt officers who were prisoners from our Regiment. We and the privates were soon marched to a large house, having a partition for the officers. The men, about 400, in next room. I heard firing again, but I fear we can do nothing. We are treated very politely—more so than I had expected."

Perhaps the reader is now ready to ask what this long extract from a secesh officer's journal, has to do with the history of the 9th Ill. Inft. Well, it is not very intimately connected with it. But it has been preserved by the boys in the 'Regiment, and all agree that it gives a very correct account of that terrible battle. It has, however, this connection with our history: It shows the desperate nature of that struggle, in which our boys took so active a part. It shows that they had a foe to contend with, full of courage and who fought with desperation.

It was truly a terrible battle. One officer who was on the ground, told me that he at one time thought the rebels would succeed in driving us out.

The loss sustained by the 9th Regt. Ill. Inft. in this terrible conflict, was 20 killed and 82 wounded. Captain Britt was among the killed. The following officers were among the wounded: Major Kuhn, Adjt. Klock, Captains Kneffner and Robinson, and Lieutenants Rollmann, Williford, Clements and Cowgill. There were 57 captured, including Captains E. M. and G. G. Low, and Lieutenants S. T. Hughs and B. L. Ulen.

The following is a list of the killed and wounded, in the various companies:

Company A.—*Killed*, Charles Gibrich—1. *Wounded*, William Kortkamp—1

Company B.—*Killed*, Joseph Cropp and Jacob Sulzer.—2. *Wounded*, Captain Kneffner, Anton Weenstroth, Sergeant John Eichenberger, Corporal Louis Fisher, Paul Geist, Ed. Hoffmann, George Jenne, Nicholaus Meyer, Jos. Noelsner, George Salz, Daniel Werner, Sergeant Augustus Wurmb. In all, 12 wounded.

Company C.—*Killed*, Corporal John Fangemann, and Frederich Hugenberg.—2. *Wounded*, 1st Lieutenant Oscar Rollman, 2d Lieut. Charles Sheve, Privates John Miller, Peter Schneider, John Frietz, Christian Jackob, Christian Maedel, Henry Behm, and Jacob Herpein. In all, 9 wounded.

COMPANY D.—*Killed*, Jacob Berthold, Hy. Borchording, John Smith, Christ Truting, Louis Truttman. In all, 5 killed. A number were slightly wounded—names not given.

COMPANY E.—*Wounded*, Corporal Francis J. Murphy, Privates William T. Grimley, Jack L. Stevens, James F. Williams, James Malone, John Lill, John Beatty, William P. Kelley, Neal Vestal. In all, 9 wounded.

COMPANY F.—*Killed*, Captain William Britt, Privates John O. Foeshee, and Fred. Weggourd. In all, 3 killled. *Wounded*, Sergt. W. C. Hawly, Corp. James Fiske, Private William Miller. In all, 3 wounded.

COMPANY G.—*Killed*, Alferd Bartley and John McCord. In all, 2 killed. *Wounded*, Lieutenant I. Clements, Henry Brown, James A. Peragin, William J. Heglar, Robert Marshall, N. G. Brown. In all, 6 wounded.

COMPANY H.—*Killed*, Sam'l Giesinger, John B. Livingood, Sebastian Swendeman. In all, 3 killed. *Wounded*, 1st Lieutenant C. H. Gilmore, 2d Lieutenant A. Cowgill, James Brady, William S. Boone, Dennis Bahon, Charles Biernbrier, William A. Cottingham, Robert Finley, Israel Haller, Charles H. Newcomb, George W. Qualls, Wm. Reckord, Francis M. Stickle, O. W. Boutwell, Venice C. Haller, Ambrose J. Shelton, Jos. W. Warren. In all, 17 wounded.

COMPANY I.—*Wounded*, Thomas Pat, William Baird, John Jaka, James Lang, Jos. E. Stringer. In all, 5 wounded.

COMPANY K.—*Killed*, James Ulen.—1. *Wounded*, George Myers, Levi Gibbs, Henry Stanger, John Burke, Charles W. Boles, Jos. N. Coneden, Peter Hall, Sam'l C. Ulen, Frank M. Winsted. In all, 9 wounded.

The enemy driven from Corinth, our Regiment was again thrown out on the front, a position it had been occupying for some time before the battle. On the 8th of October, it moved South to Danville, Miss., and on the next day the left wing, Companies K, I, H, G, and F, moved on to Rienzi. Col. Mersy took command of all the troops at Rienzi, and Lieut. Col. Phillips, who had now rejoined the Regiment, after his severe wound at Shiloh, of the forces at Danville. The Regiment, with other troops of the 2d Brigade, performed outpost duty at the above named places until the 28th of November, 1862, when they returned and went into camp at Corinth, Miss.

On the 12th of December, the Regiment moved Southward again, going within five miles of Tupelo, Miss., and returned to camp at Corinth on the 19th of the same month; Col. Mersy being in command of the 2d Brigade, and Lieut. Col. Phillips in command of the Regiment.

On the 2d day of January, 1863, we moved three and a half miles East of Monterey, and bivouacked for the night, and returned to camp the next day; Gen. Forrest and his command having escaped across the river. The Regiment remained in camp until March, not having much duty, except guard duty.

During the period embraced in this chapter, some interesting incidents occurred. As I mentioned above, the two Captains Low, and Lieutenant Hughs, together with a considerable number of privates, were taken prisoners. I have given extensive extracts from the journal of a Rebel prisoner, showing the horrors of the battle-field. It may not be amiss to refer to some things connected with the prison-life of some of our boys, who were captured in this battle at Corinth.

The scene, as described by Captain G. G. Low, to the writer, beggars description. The horrors of their retreat was terrible. The Captain thinks if Napoleon's retreat from Moscow was much more terrible, he does not know how it was endured at all. But I shall here allow the Captain to speak for himself, by giving extracts from a written statement, which he kindly furnished me, of his prison life:

"On the morning of the 3d of October, 1862, our Regiment received orders to move early in the morning. We had moved up the day before from Rienzi, to within 2½ miles of Corinth. As we approached Corinth, we could occasionally hear the boom of distant cannon. Conjecture was rife as to what it meant, so little did we expect an action. We passed through Corinth, and to the outer works on the West of it. Sometime before we obtained our position behind the rifle-pits, three had been heavy fighting on our left. We took our position here, feeling confident we could hold it against a vastly superior force. The enemy were gradually approaching from the front, and our line was being engaged, when I noticed a panic in my company. I was on the extreme left of our Regiment. Many of my men broke out of the ditch and started back. I ordered every man back to his place. They told me the 12th Ill. and 81st Ohio were running. I told them it mattered not; we would stay there until we were ordered away. I saw a change of front was necessary, and expected to hear the order to change front to rear, on first company. But it did not come· Soon after, I heard the order to move by the right flank; but it was too late. Already the enemy were in our rear. I saw it would be death for my men to attempt to leave their position, and I surrendered with seventeen of my command.

"We were moved back about three-fourths of a mile. I found that Captain C. M. Lowe and Lieutenant L. T. Hughes of our Regiment, were captured. We were placed under guard at or near a house. Here a woman abused us very much. She insisted that Captain Lowe was the mean Yankee that was there the night before and stole her chickens. The Captain assured her that he had never been there before, and that she must be mistaken. She was certain he was the man, and had it not been for the guard, she would have pitched into him rough-shod. I think she was as hard a specimen of the fair-sex as I have ever seen in the Sunny South; and I have seen many that outraged decency and forever disgraced the name of woman.

"After the excitement of the battle was over, or rather of the scenes through which we passed that day, we had time to reflect. Here we were, prisoners of war, held by a motley set of human beings that, as far as outward appearances were concerned, would be a disgrace to barbarians. I wondered, "Is this the boasted chivalry of the South, sent out to fight the hated poor men of the North, the '*mud-sills*' and '*greasy mechanics?*'" When I saw my poor boys, dressed in their blue uniform, contrasted with these rag-a-muffins, I felt proud of them.

"The "Rebs" had great stories to tell us. Bragg had captured Louisville and all Buell's army. Lee had captured Little Mac. and 40,000 prisoners. Governor Gamble, of Missouri, had turned over 40,000 troops, well armed and equipped, to the Southern Confederacy; and they had come with 70,000 men to capture Corinth, and drive Grant out of West Tennessee, and the war would be over in a few days. All were jubilant.

"At night, we moved in the woods about a mile, and were consoled with a lot of wounded of both armies. About 9 o'clock at night, the news came back that they had captured Corinth, and we would be moved up there in the morning. About this time, Col. Prevene, of a South Carolina Regiment, came to see us, (he was a Mason,) and took Capt. Lowe and myself outside the lines and had a long talk with us. He assured us that Corinth was not taken, and that it would not be; and further, that Gen. VanDorn was (to use his own language) a d—d fool for attacking the place. To-night we had nothing to eat, except a cup of coffee that a Rebel Lieutenant made for us. I furnished the coffee. We passed a restless night.

"The morning of the 4th dawned, and was ushered in with the boom of heavy cannon. This assured us that the place was not taken, but that they had approached very near it, as we could hear the guns of the forts. The cannonading and musketry was incessant from daylight until about 1 P. M. At that time, orders came to move us back to the rear. We took up our line of march to Dixie. Although we were prisoners in the hands of the enemy, yet we were jubilant. We knew they had been repulsed; that the stars and stripes had again been triumphant; and though we had a prison-life, and even starvation staring us in the face, yet there was not a man despondent. We were then suffering for something to eat, but we knew the "rebs." were suffering even more than we were; for they had nothing to eat when they attacked Corinth, and their only hope for something, was the capture of the place. In this they had failed. The retreat soon became a rout. Neither tongue nor pen can describe the sufferings during that memorable retreat. Wagons, with six mules attached, were filled with the wounded and dying, and the cowardly drivers whipping their mules at every jump. The groans of the dying and the curses of the wounded were enough to make the knees of terror tremble. One would think, that if human suffering would expiate the crime of treason, all this army should be forgiven; for they suffered from hunger, thirst, fatigue, and all the ills that follow a defeated, routed, broken and disheartened army. I could not help feeling sorry for the panic stricken wretches.

"At night, we camped about twelve miles from Corinth, on a little branch. I had coffee enough to make us a cup apiece. This, and a few crumbs of crackers, was all we had for twelve of us—eight Federal officers and four Rebel officers." (It will be remembered they had had nothing to eat the day before, and very little on the preceding day.) "We camped near a house, and there was a rooster, the only chicken left on the premises. We offered five dollars for it. The woman would not let us have it.

"On the morning of the 5th of October, we again moved, escorted by a company of the Rebel Jackson's cavalry, under command of Capt. Douglass. Let me mention here, that Capt. D. did all in his power to make his prisoners comfortable. While we were being marched back on the afternoon of the 4th, an aid of Gen. VanDorn's rode up and told him to move the prisoners faster. He said, 'If I move them faster they will fall down from exhaustion.' The aid replied, 'Let them fall, and be d—d. Shoot them if you cannot get them along.' But the Captain took his own gait, and treated all kindly. As we marched along this forenoon we saw a great number of their wounded on all sides of the road. About 1 o'clock we came in sight of Hatchie Bridge. We halted for a few moments, and soon we heard fighting in front of us. We were taken back about one mile, and halted in a hollow. We had been there but a few moments, when rifle shells came whistling in such close proximity that we had to retire further back. Soon we saw the Rebel mass come running back in, if possible, greater confusion than the day before. They thought the whole Rebel army would be captured. They took up the Hatchie about ten miles and crossed us, and we halted about 12 o'clock that night, near Ruckersville, Miss. Here they killed a beef weighing about 300 pounds, for the 320 prisoners and their guards, in all over 400. We had had nothing to eat that day but raw corn. We ate the beef without salt.

"On the morning of the 6th, we started towards Ripley, without anything else to eat. Arriving at that place late in the afternoon, they gave us a very little to eat, perhaps rations enough for fifty men. On the following morning we moved in the direction of Holly Springs, Miss. The day was very hot and the roads dusty. Add to this, the suffering from hunger, and it would be hard to describe the amount of suffering the men endured. We camped at night near a Mr. Robinson's. (To-day we had to march about nine miles out of the way, on account of some one destroying a bridge in the rear of the retreating army.) The officers got a very good supper at Mr. R.'s, by paying one dollar each, in Greenbacks. He would not take anything else. The men got but little to eat.

"On the morning of the 7th, the officers hired a team to take them to Holly Springs, for which they paid $20. We arrived there at 11 o'clock at night.   Here we were taken to Col. Roddy's Head Quarters. He said he was surprised that we, being North-western men, were fighting Southern men.   Captain Lowe told him that we were not in a condition to resent an insult, and did not wish to be insulted.   This ended the conversation.

"The next evening we started by Railroad, under guard, for Jackson, Miss., arriving there about 10 A. M., on the 9th of October. Here we were taken before General Thillman, and paroled for that city and Vicksburg.   We had good rooms at the best hotel in Jackson. On the morning of the 10th we took cars for Vicksburg.   On this trip we had no guard, except one Rebel Captain.   We arrived at Vicksburg about 1 o'clock, and were quartered at the 'Washington Hotel.'   We were limited to certain streets.   Otherwise we had our liberty.   Our fare at the hotel was corn bread, corn coffee, fresh beef and molasses. The ladies were allowed wheat bread, and when the darkies could do so without being detected by their master, they would supply *us* with that luxury.   On the whole, we were treated pretty well by the 'Rebs.' We found them generally dispirited; but said they thought they never could be conquered, &c.

On the 18th of October, we were paroled, and started up the river to meet our flag of truce boat.   The sight of the old flag and hard bread created great joy among our men.   Hard treatment, under a flag of treason, had endeared the old flag to them.   A scanty supply of corn bread, and beef without salt, made 'hard tack' look and taste like the best food cooked.   On the morning of the 19th of October, 1862, we took our course up the river for 'God's country.'"

A little incident narrated by Private Neal Vestal, of Co. E, who was taken prisoner at the same time with Captain Lowe, is worth noting. When the Rebs. were attacked by General Hurlbut, at the Hatchie on the 5th of October, and a panic was arising, a Rebel Captain passing by Neal, he inquired, good naturedly, "Well, Captain, what are you going to do with us now?"   His reply was, "If I had my way, I would shoot you."   At which Neal replied, "I bet *six bits* that man was not in the fight."   At this response went up all along the line, "That is true!"

Col. Augustus Mersy, Belleville
Courtesy of the Illinois State Historical Library

Lt. Col. Jesse J. Phillips, Hillsboro
Courtesy of the Illinois State Historical Library

Lt. Col. Samuel T. Hughes, Edwardsville
Courtesy of the Illinois State Historical Library

Capt. William F. Armstrong. Company H, Hillsboro
Courtesy of the Illinois State Historical Library

Capt. Isaac Clements, Company G, Carbondale
Courtesy of the Illinois State Historical Library

Capt. Alexander G. Hawes, Company E, Belleville
Courtesy of the Illinois State Historical Library

1st Lt. Cyrus H. Gilmore, Company H, Hillsboro
Courtesy of the Illinois State Historical Library

1st Lt. George W. Williford, Company F, Hillsboro
Courtesy of the Illinois State Historical Library

2d Lt. Alfred Cowgill, Company H, Hillsboro
Courtesy of the Illinois State Historical Library

2d Lt. William C. Hawley, Company F, Mascoutah
Courtesy of the Illinois State Historical Library

Sgt. Jacob Miller, Company H, Hillsboro
Courtesy of the Illinois State Historical Library

Sgt. Alonzo F. McEwen, Company H, Hillsboro
Courtesy of the Illinois State Historical Library

Sgt. James M. Arthurs, Company H, Hillsboro
Courtesy of the Illinois State Historical Library

Cpl. Charles N. Brown, Company K, Auburn
Courtesy of the Illinois State Historical Library

Pvt. Levi Gibbs, Company K
Courtesy of the Illinois State Historical Library

CHAPTER VI.

FROM THE MOUNTING OF THE REGIMENT TO LEAVING POCAHONTAS.

Regiment mounted—Scout to Tuscumbia, with its five engagements— Scout to Florence, with two engagements—Move camp to Pocahontas—Scout to New Albany, destroying the town—Mud Creek scout and battle—Scout to Jackson, and battle—Scout to Ripley—Scout to Trenton, Tenn.—Scout to Grenada—Raid to Grenada—Commissions and promotions—Battles of Salem, Graham's Mills and Wyatt's—List of killed and wounded—Incidents.

Our Government, by the beginning of 1863, began to see the necessity of having a larger mounted force. It was proposed that many of the Infantry Regiments should be mounted for scouting purposes. Lieut. Col. Phillips made application to have the 9th Ill. Inft. mounted. He was told that it could be mounted on mules, but not on horses. He replied that he would prefer the mules, as they would endure more hard usage and require less care. Hence, on the 15th of March, 1863, Lieut. Col. Phillips, commanding Regiment, received orders to mount his command, on mules, for scouting purposes. The Regiment was all mounted by the 20th of March.

Col. Mersy was in command of the 2d Brigade, and Lieut. Col. Phillips of the Regiment. This arrangement still continues, to the present date.

Sergeant George Rhuland, of Company A, was commissioned as 1st Lieutenant of said company. He ranks from March 20th, 1863, the date of the receipt of his commission.

The Regiment was paid on the 26th of August, by Major Phelps, for the months of May and June.

On the 14th of April, the Regiment received orders to be ready to move by daylight the next morning. The order was afterwards changed to moving in half an hour. We were soon on the way towards Glendale, where the rebels had made a dash on a small body of the 64th Ill. Vols. We reached Glendale a little too late, as Col. Cornyn had driven the enemy and started in pursuit. The Regiment hastened forward and found him at Yellow Stone Creek. We were delayed one and a-half hours in crossing this very muddy stream. Hence, we bivouacked for the night two miles beyond. Moved forward rapidly, on the 15th, and bivouacked within four miles of Big Bear Creek, on the opposite bank of which, we were informed, there was a large body

[4]

of the enemy. We awaited here, on the 16th, the arrival of the Infantry force from Corinth. All having arrived, we moved rapidly, early on the morning of the 17th. After "shelling the woods" for a short time with our rifled pieces, the following mounted forces, viz: 10th Missouri Cavalry, battallion of the 15th Illinois Cavalry, and the 9th Illinois Mounted Infantry, dashed rapidly across the creek. Captain Richardson was throwing shell over our heads at an imaginary force across the creek. As he did not stop soon enough, a number of his shell flew among our men, but fortunately no one was hurt. As soon as all the mounted force was over, and one section of Tamrath's Battery, we moved forward on the Tuscumbia road.

At Dickson's we ran upon the enemy's videttes, driving them back to "Buzzard Roost" or "Cherokee Bluffs," where they made a stand, and the place being naturally strong, our shell could not dislodge them. Consequently, the 9th Ill. Mounted Infantry was dismounted, and deployed as skirmishers. They advanced rapidly to within one hundred yards of the bluff, and then the right wing swung around on the left flank of the enemy, compelling them to leave the bluff very rapidly, and in great disorder. About 25 of the Rebels were killed, wounded and captured. Our loss was five slightly wounded, none disabled. The weather being intensely hot, the horses in the section of battery with us, became too much exhausted to move further. Their ammunition was also about exhausted. The two guns were consequently left at this place to await the arrival of the main force. Lieutenant Krebs, with Co. D, was left to support the guns, in case of an attack. There were also seven men of Co. I left here to guard the prisoners.

Immediately after crossing the creek, one company of the 10th Mo., and one of the 9th Ill., were ordered to move two miles out on our left flank, and break up a camp of the enemy said to be in that direction. Lieutenant Patterson, with Co. E of our Regiment, was ordered on that expedition. This detachment drove the rebels from their camp, toward their main body on the Tuscumbia road. This body of the enemy, 250 strong, came upon the two guns of Tamrath's Battery that we had left at Cherokee Bluffs, and before the guns could get to us, they, and all of Co. D, except three men, and the seven men of Co. I, were captured. We moved rapidly back, and succeeded in recapturing one of the guns in "Lundy's Lane."

Col. Cameron, of the 1st Alabama Regiment, (loyal,) was killed here in the charge. The Rebels fled to the timber on our left, beyond the reach of our muskets, and too far off for the effective firing of the "Mountain howitzers."

Col. Cornyn now ordered us to fall back and rejoin the main body, as we numbered only 1200, all told, while the enemy were not less than 2500 strong. Scarcely, however, had we left "Lundy's Lane," before the enemy filed out of the timber and formed a line across the open field, threatening our rear. The advance of the Infantry force being now only one mile back, we turned about and confronted our foe. The 9th Ill. Inft. dismounted, and moved around to the left flank of the enemy's line, while the cavalry charged their front. They broke and fled beyond a high ridge, and we advanced rapidly and took possession of the ridge. In the meantime, Col. Bane's Brigade, and Welker's Battery came rapidly on the field, unobserved and unknown to the Rebels. This Brigade was immediately posted as follows: The 50th Ill. behind a high grading of the Railroad and to the left of the open field, on which the Rebels had formed their line previous to being driven back by our Cavalry; the 7th Ill. Inft. were moved in the timber, around to the right of the field, and a little further advanced than the 50th; the 57th Ill. were held in reserve. The Cavalry received orders to fall back rapidly, and in apparent confusion, as soon as the enemy should appear on the ridge.

This disposition being made of the forces, the 9th Ill. Inft. fell back 100 yards, to a fence overgrown with bushes, and lay concealed behind it. The Rebels advanced with loud shouts, and planted a 12-pound Howitzer on the ridge. Our Cavalry hastily retreated, and the enemy believing victory certain, dashed gallantly ahead, when the 50th and 7th Ill. Regiments opened on them a deadly fire. About the same time, a body of the enemy appeared on the left of the Railroad on the ridge. They were opened upon by the 9th Ill. The contest was not long. In less than ten minutes, the whole body of the Rebels were in rapid retreat towards Cane Creek.

The loss of the enemy was, according to their own statement, 17 killed, 50 wounded, and 23 taken prisoners. The 9th Ill. lost 5 wounded and 59 captured (Co. D.) The entire Union loss was 3 killed, 10 wounded, and 75 captured.

Night now coming on, we bivouacked near the battle-field. On the 18th, after a reconnoisance in front, and finding the enemy in strong position near Cane Creek, our whole force fell back to Bear Creek, and went into camp.

On the 19th, Companies E and F were sent, as escort to a train, to Eastport Landing. The rest of the Regiment, with the whole mounted force, moved circuitously to "Buzzard Roost," and found the enemy, under Roddy, occupying the same position as on the 17th at Cherokee.

Bluff. Our Regiment was again deployed as skirmishers, in the same manner as before. After fifteen minutes skirmishing, we drove the enemy from his position, killing, wounding and capturing 13 of them, and losing none.

We then returned to camp at Bear Creek, taking with us a drove of cattle and sheep. On the 20th of April, the 7th Kansas Cavalry joined us, and on the next day the Ohio Brigade, Col. Fuller commanding. Our entire column moved forward on the morning of the 23d, and crossed Cane Creek without opposition; the Rebels having fallen back to Little Bear Creek. Here General Dodge offered battle, but they declined, and we bivouacked for the night. We moved forward again on the 24th, the enemy continually falling back, not even making a feeble resistance at Little Bear Creek, although the position was a very strong one.

On nearing the town of Tuscumbia, the enemy, under Forrest, left on the Decatur road. Col. Cornyn was ordered forward after them, with the 10th Mo. Cavalry, the 7th Kansas Cavalry, and the 1st Alabama Cavalry. Lieut. Col. Phillips, with two companies of Cavalry, two companies of 9th Ill. Inft., viz: A and B, and two guns of Tamrath's Battery, was ordered to move up to Florence, and capture the town. He proceeded to that place with his command. Arriving on the bank of the river, opposite the town, and observing a small force of cavalry in Florence, he called to them to send him over a boat, as he desired to send over a flag of truce. They replied, telling him to go to that place, where I suppose but few, if any, desire to go. The Col. did not feel disposed, at least to obey their orders, and thinking he had that with which he could enforce obedience to his, he placed his two rifled guns in position, and made a second demand for a boat. To this he received the same reply as before. Immediately he opened upon them with his two guns, throwing shell into the town. The cavalry on the other side broke and run. As they passed up the street, a shell was thrown among them, killing one horse. In a very short time, white flags were hung out all over the town. In the meantime, a small raft had been constructed, on which a flag of truce was sent over, and the Mayor of the town made a formal surrender. The object of demanding the surrender was, not that we might hold the place, but that we might ascertain whether the enemy had any considerable force there. The desired information being gained, the Col. evacuated it, and returned to the main force again.

The remainder of our Regiment, and the battalion of the 15th Ill. Cavalry, were ordered to move forward, within supporting distance of

Col. Cornyn. We moved forward until near night, and not being able to reach him, we returned to Tuscumbia, and bivouacked. At 10 o'clock that night, we received orders to move out rapidly and join Col. Cornyn, as he feared the enemy would come upon him, too strong, at daylight, his forces being very much exhausted. We reached him, beyond Leighton, by 2:30 A. M., on the 25th, and at daylight the whole force returned to Tuscumbia.

Our Regiment turned over 200 mules to Col. Streight, on the 26th, to complete the mounting of his force, thus dismounting Companies C, D, E, G, H and K, of our Regiment.

On the morning of the 27th April, we again moved forward, toward Decatur, to attract the attention of Forrest, until Col. Streight had moved entirely around his left flank towards Atlanta. We found the enemy posted at Town Creek, four miles beyond Leighton. Some picket skirmishing took place before night. We bivouacked near the Creek. Early on the morning of the 28th, the Rebels having discovered the position of the dismounted companies of our Regiment, opened upon us with schrapnel, compelling us to fall back hurriedly out of their range. The artillery kept up a constant firing all day, and after noon a part of the 81st Ohio and the mounted companies of the 9th Ill, crossed over, at the Railroad bridge, and drove the enemy from their position.

Col. Streight having now completely passed the enemy, our entire column moved on the return march, on the morning of the 29th April. Bivouacked for the night near Little Bear Creek. Reached Big Bear on the 30th, and were compelled to remain in camp there until the evening of the 1st of May, when a bridge having been constructed, we crossed over and proceeded up the Railroad to our old place of camping, four miles from Big Bear Creek. From there we proceeded on the main traveled road to Burnsville, reaching that place sometime after night, and bivouacked. On the morning of the 2d May, Lieut. Col. Phillips, with the four mounted companies, viz: A, B, I and F, was ordered to report to Col. Cornyn, commanding cavalry force, for an expedition to Tupelo. The rest of the Regiment moved forward, at 10 A. M., and reached Corinth by 2 P. M.

During this trip the Regiment was out from camp 18 days, and had five engagements with the enemy—two on the 17th of April, one on the 19th, one on the 27th, and one on the 4th of May. The great object of this expedition, was to divert the attention of the enemy until Col. Streight, who was fitting up an expedition for a grand raid into Georgia, should have time to complete the mounting of his men, and get well started on his way.

Lieut. Col. Phillips, with the four mounted companies of our Regiment, having been ordered on an expedition to Tupelo, separated from the remaining companies at Burnsville, on the 2d of May, and proceeded to Tupelo. Had a skirmish with the enemy there, and rejoined the Regiment at camp, May 7th.

Quartermaster Korn died of disease May 6th, 1863. Dr. Guelick and Captain Hawes were detailed on the 7th of May, the former to Fort Henry, and the latter to Memphis. Dr. Wm. A. Allen, 2d Assistant Surgeon, appointed by the Governor of Illinois, reported for duty on the 12th, and was mustered into the service, to rank from that date.

On the 13th of May, the Regiment moved into the barracks formerly occupied by the 39th Ohio, one mile sout-east from Corinth.

On the 15th of May, Brig. Gen. Thomas, Adjutant General U. S. Army, addressed the soldiers at Corinth, announcing and advocating the policy of the Government in regard to freeing and arming the negroes. His remarks met with a hearty approval by nine-tenths of the soldiers at the military post of Corinth.

May 26th, our Regiment being again all mounted, we were ordered to report to Col. Cornyn, commander of Cavalry Brigade, at 10 A. M. Moved immediately thereafter, on the Corinth and Hamburg road, toward Hamburg Landing. We reached that place and began to cross the Tennessee River about dark, the 9th Ill. crossing over first. Our Regiment all got over by 2 A. M., of the 27th, and the remainder of the force by noon of the same day. At 1 P. M., the entire column moved forward on the road towards Florence, taking the most easterly route. Halted, for rest and feed, two hours at 1 o'clock, A. M., of the 28th, and then moved forward again eight miles North-east from Florence. A detachment of the 7th Kansas Cavalry destroyed two large woolen factories, four miles from the city. We drove in the videttes of the enemy, and when we were within one hundred yards of the town, they opened on us with a battery of two guns, throwing schrapnel with great accuracy, compelling us to move from the road, by the left flank, into the timber, to avoid the deadly missiles. Col. Cornyn moved his howitzers rapidly forward, and soon silenced the Rebel guns.

The 9th Ill. was now dismounted and thrown forward as skirmishers. The 1st Battalion, (Cos. A, B and C,) Lieutenant Ruhland commanding, moving forward in column, as reserve. The opposition of the enemy did not amount to much, and we soon had possession of the town. Our loss was two wounded, and two captured. The enemy lost from ten to twelve killed and wounded, and sixty to eighty captured. After searching the town, and destroying all the stores of value to the enemy, we began our return march, taking the most westerly route, so as to destroy three large cotton mills and two more large woolen mills, all of which we succeeded in doing without loss to us. At 12 o'clock, midnight, we bivouacked until morning. The enemy disputed our entire advance from Florence to the place of bivouack, and then ceased to molest us. We reached the crossing opposite Hamburg, at 2 A. M., of the 30th May, when we bivouacked until morning.

During the day the enemy appeared in force in our rear, before we had even our baggage across, and as Col. Cornyn had moved down to Savannah to relieve the 15th Ill., Lieut. Col. Phillips assumed command, and moved out one-half mile from the river and offered battle, when the Rebels hastily fell back. We succeeded in all getting over by 2 A. M. of the 31st, without further molestation: In the skirmish on the opposite side of the river, none of our men were hurt. The enemy lost several in wounded and captured, none are known to have been killed. At 7 A. M., the 31st, the entire column move toward Corinth, and we reached camp there at 1 P. M.

During this expedition, the Regiment was out six days, and engaged in two skirmishes with the enemy. The object of the expedition seemed to be the destruction of public property and stores which would be of advantage to the enemy.

After leaving Hamburg Landing at 1 P. M., of the 27th May, the boys were in their saddles, or pack-saddles, as they then were, for about thirty-six hours almost constantly, except the few hours they were in Florence searching the houses for arms, and destroying stores that might be serviceable to the enemy. At 12 o'clock, on the night of the 28th, they halted, until early in the morning, when they were off on the march again. The result of this raid was 64 prisoners captured, over 200 negroes brought in, a large number of mules and horses captured, and about $3,000,000 worth of Factory property destroyed.

On the 3d of June, 1863, the Regiment received orders to be ready to move on the next morning, at 8 o'clock, with camp and garrison equipage. Moved on the 4th, in accordance with the above order, in a North-west direction. Passed through Cherwalla, and bivouacked for the night about ten miles west of it. The Tuscumbia and Hatchie Rivers had to be bridged, in order to cross the artillery and infantry. The entire Brigade were moving with us. These streams were bridged, the forces crossed, and we arrived at Pocahontas by 4 P. M., on the 5th of June, and bivouacked in the town for the night. On the 7th, the Regiment moved into camp one-fourth mile north of the town.

On the 8th of June, Lieut. Col. Phillips, with Companies A, B, E,

F, G and I, moved south on a scout, and returned on the 9th, at 1 P. M., bringing in a drove of cattle and sheep. The remaining companies of the Regiment went as an escort to a train of wagons, as far as the bridge on Tuscumbia Creek.

On the 11th of June, Capt. Kneffner, with Companies A, C, E, H and I, moved North-west on a scout, and returned in the evening, having marched 40 miles, bringing in three prisoners.

The Regiment, accompanied by one section of Tamrath's Battery, moved south on the Ripley road, on the 12th of June, at 1 P M., and bivouacked for the night within ten miles of Ripley. Moved forward early on the morning of the 13th, and took possession of Ripley without opposition. The town was searched, but nothing of a contraband nature was found, except a number of negroes, who were confiscated for the use of the Government. Moved on in the direction of New Albany. At Orizabo, the flankers on our left encountered a few Rebel soldiers, and after driving them off, burned the place, as it contained Rebel stores and was a place of rendezvous for them. While stopping to feed, about four miles south of Ripley, a family moving to Ripley came along. Their wagons and carriage were searched, and a Rebel mail was found in the old lady's carpet-sack. Their horses and mules were all confiscated, except one old team of mules which they were allowed to keep.

The Regiment then proceeded to New Albany, reaching that place about 4 P. M. Finding the town nearly deserted by citizens, and used as a general Headquarters for guerrillas, and a supplying point for them, it was entirely destroyed, after any stores of value that could be carried away were taken.

We then moved back toward Ripley, on a different route from the one by which we had entered, going three miles and bivouacking for the night.

At 1 o'clock, A. M., June 14th, Lieutenant Krebs and escort came into our bivouack from Pocahontas, with orders from Col. Mersy, for us to return as rapidly as possible to camp at Pocahontas, as the enemy were planning to capture us. We moved at 2 A. M. Reached Ripley at breakfast time, and camp at Pocahontas at 8 P. M. At daylight this morning, the enemy, 1500 strong, reached our last night's bivouack. But fortunately we were safe out of their reach. It was fortunate for us, for our force numbered but 300 men with two pieces of artillery.

The Regiment was out three days on this expedition. It captured, and brought in, about 25 Rebel soldiers, 50 contrabands, and 100 head of horses and mules. It marched over one hundred miles.

On the 17th of June, the Regiment again moved southward, at 8

P. M., with six days rations. The night was rainy and intensely dark. One section of Tamrath's Battery was with us, under Lieut. Bruner. Marched all night in the dark and rain. It was such bad traveling, that we only moved twelve miles by sunrise of the 18th. Halted and fed at old "Secession Hopkins'," where the Regiment had already fed four times. Reached Ripley at 1 P. M., and found no enemy, but were told that 1,500 Rebels were moving around, to get between us and Pocahontas. We moved back two miles, and halted to feed. Here we were joined by 125 men of the 5th Ohio Cavalry, Major Smith commanding, and 180 of the 18th Missouri Mounted Infantry, commanded by Lieut. Col. Sheldon. Our whole force now numbered a little over 600: 5th Ohio Cavalry 125, 18th Missouri Mounted Infantry 180, Section of Battery 50, 9th Ill. Mounted Inft. 275. Total, 630.

Lieut. Col. Phillips, senior officer present, assumed command of the whole force. We moved back five miles and bivouacked for the night. Finding no enemy, we moved forward again by daylight of the 19th. Passed through Ripley at 8 A. M., and New Albany at 2 P. M. Captured Lieut. Col. McCarly of the 23d Mississippi, below Ripley. Drove in the videttes of the enemy at New Albany, and moved forward on the Pontotoc road. When within six miles of the latter place, Lieut. Col. Phillips having gone as far as his orders permitted him, moved five miles West, and then moved North towards Rockford. Marched until after midnight of the 19th, having to cross a terrible swamp, called the Octohatchie. We bivouacked for the night on a ridge between Octohatchie and Mud Creek. Moved forward again at 7 A. M., of the 20th, 5th Ohio occupying the rear, and 18th Missouri the advance. While we were preparing a crossing of Mud Creek, the enemy, 3,000 strong, under Gen. Ruggles, made a furious attack upon the rear guard, but were most gallantly met and checked by the 5th Ohio Cavalry. Six companies of the 9th Ill. Inft. were dismounted, and deployed as skirmishers. They, and the 5th Ohio Cavalry, held the enemy in check for two and a-half hours, until the artillery had crossed the several most wretched fords of Mud Creek. One of the caissons getting stuck in the mud, we were compelled to leave one half of it there, and as it completely blocked up the crossing, we had to destroy the five baggage wagons that were behind it, to prevent their falling into the hands of the enemy; everything we could possibly save, being brought over the ford. We fell back rapidly, and got possession of Rocky Ford, before the Rebels got around, and succeded in crossing before they could molest us.

Our loss in this engagement, was 5 killed and 18 wounded. The loss of the enemy could not be definitely ascertained, but was not less than 200 in killed, wounded and missing.

The place where this battle was fought, was a dense cane-brake. Men could not see each other more than a few feet. Our men could hear every command given by the Rebel officers, but could not see the enemy.

After getting safely out of that terrible bottom, and crossing the Tallahatchie at Rocky Ford, we moved through Salem, on the 21st, and reached camp at Pocahontas, at noon of the 22d June. The Regiment was out six days, during this trip. Had to endure some very hard marching. Marched almost constantly, day and night.

On the 23d of June, 2d Assistant Surgeon Dr. Allen, was ordered to report at LaGrange, Tenn., by Surgeon Gay, Medical Director left wing 16th Army Corps, and left for that place on the 24th.

On the 6th of July, Companies A, C, E, F, G, H and I, under the command of Lieut. Col. Phillips, moved North-west on a scout, and returned on the 7th at noon, not having found any force of the enemy.

On the 8th of July, the entire Regiment moved Northward, with three days rations, 35 miles, and returned on the 9th without finding any force of the enemy. Brought in a number of citizens as prisoners, with all the horses and mules, of any value, that could be found. Rabid secessionists followed after, pleading for their animals. Col. Phillips would tell them that he was a kind-hearted man, had a number of prisoners, and did not wish to have them walk. Hence, he must have their horses and mules. He expressed sorrow for the necessity. It is a question whether that sorrow was very *deep down*, however, as he has no mercy on Rebels, and takes all the horses and mules from them, that he can place his hands upon, without much trouble of conscience.

On the 12th of July, the Regiment again moved in a North-west direction, with five days rations. Joined Col. Hatch's force from La Grange, North of Bolivar, and the combined force moved to Jackson, and on the 13th engaged a Rebel force there, under Forrest, Newsom, and Biffle. Our Regiment was dismounted as skirmishers. After brisk firing for one-quarter of an hour, we dislodged them. The cavalry then moved over the river and took the flank of the skirmish line. The right wing of our Regiment were recalled from their position on the South side of the creek, and placed in reserve of the left wing. We then moved rapidly forward, until within a few hundred yards of their fortifications, when we made a charge upon their works and drove them out, by a charge from our skirmish line. We moved forward, thinking that they had left. But when in the suburbs of the North side of the town, the Rebel cavalry came charging down on us from the North-east and East parts of the town. We quickly formed in line facing them, and went into them with a fierceness that they could not long stand. In about fifteen minutes they were driven entirely from the field, and we advanced to their position. We captured a goodly number of horses and muskets they were compelled to leave. One Rebel Captain was found dead on the field. A prisoner who was captured, said he was a notorious guerrilla chieftain, and hated by their own men. Said there would not be much sorrow for his death. The fighting in all lasted about two and a-half hours.

We captured about 70 prisoners, 30 of whom were paroled, the remainder were brought into camp. Our loss was one killed and six wounded. The enemy's loss in killed and wounded, was about two hundred. The Regiment returned to camp about 1 P. M., of the 15th, having been out four days.

On the 18th, six companies, under command of Lieut. Col. Phillips, started on a scout about dark, after a party of guerrillas who had made a dash upon some of the Home Guards at Middleton, killing and taking prisoners several of them. They pursued them all night, in the direction of Bolivar, but could not find them. Returned to camp about noon the next day.

On the 20th of July, the Regiment moved South, accompanied by two guns of Tamrath's Battery. At Hopkins we were joined by the 11th Ill. Cavalry, commanded by Major Kerr. Moved on to within three miles of Ripley, and bivouacked at the forks of the Nubbin Ridge and Ruckersville road. Two companies of Cavalry and two companies of Mounted Infantry were sent towards Ripley to reconnoiter. Discovering no enemy, they soon returned. On the 21st, the command moved back seven miles to Ruckersville, and there awaited orders from Corinth. We moved forward again on the 22d, at 3 A. M. Halted at Ripley two hours. Captured two prisoners, and then moved back to camp at Pocahontas.

The Regiment moved North-west, at daylight on the 26th of July, with eight days rations. It joined Col. Hatch's command, North of Bolivar, at 8:30 P. M., of the same day. After the Regiment was formed, before marching, a brief prayer was offered by the writer, who was then present with the Regiment. Bivouacked for the night, ten miles North of Bolivar. On the 27th, Lieut. Col. Phillips was ordered to the command of a Brigade, consisting of the 9th Ill. Inft. and 3d Michigan Cavalry, and Captain G. G. Lowe took command of the

Regiment. We joined Col. Prowitt's command at Lexington, Tenn., on the 28th. Passed through Clarksville, a Union town, to-day. Had captured a goodly number of mules and negroes, and about 100 prisoners up to this date. Among the latter were two Colonels. Passed through Huntingdon on the 29th. A strong Union town. While stopped here, two daughters of Col. Hawkins of the 2d West Tennessee Cavalry, (loyal,) paraded the streets, carrying the stars and stripes. This was cheering to our boys. We lay over most of the 29th at Macedonia. Moved to Trenton on the 31st. Passed through a very rough country, and in a poor state of cultivation. From Trenton we proceeded South, towards Jackson, passing through Jackson on the 1st of August, and reaching camp at Pocahontas on the 3d of August, about 8 P. M.

The Regiment was out, during this scout, nine days. Did not have any engagements with the enemy.

On the 6th of August, Companies A, C, D, E, G, H, I and K, under command of Lieut. Col. Phillips, moved North-west of Bolivar, and returned on the 7th, without finding any forces of the enemy.

On the 12th of August, at 10 P. M., the Regiment moved South, with six days rations. Marched all night, and halted at sunrise and fed. At 6 A. M., of the 13th, we were on the march again. Took the road through Salem, passing that place about 4 P. M., and bivouacking for the night six miles beyond it. Moved forward again at daylight on the 14th, crossing the Tallahatchie at Rocky Ford, and bivouacking for the night. Moved West on the Oxford road, early on the 15th, reaching that place at noon. Here we joined a Brigade from LaGrange. Lieut. Col. Phillips assumed command of the Brigade, and moved on six miles beyond Oxford, on the Coffeeville road, and bivouacked for the night. At daybreak, on the 16th, moved forward again. We were joined to-day, by a Brigade of Cavalry from Germantown and Collierville, under the command of Lieut. Col. M. R. M. Wallace, who being junior officer to Lieut. Col. Phillips, reported his command to him for orders. Lieut. Col. Phillips now assumed command of the whole force, consisting of two Brigades. Lieut. Col. Wallace had command of the 1st Brigade, and Major Coon of the 2d.

The whole force crossed the Tochamy River on a ferry boat, and reached Water Valley at 12 M. Here our advance captured a train of seven six-mule wagons, and a number of prisoners who were guarding the train. The 1st Brigade was so long delayed in crossing the river, that Major Coon, who had command of the 2d Brigade, did not leave Water Valley until 5 P. M. He then moved forward to within two miles of Coffeeville, and bivouacked for the remainder of the night. It was 2 A. M., of the 17th, when we reached that point.

A heavy storm of rain came on shortly after leaving Water Valley, and the night became intensely dark. The darkness made it very difficult to march at all. Often the mules, with their riders, would tumble into the ditches. The 1st Brigade, commanded by Lieut. Col. Wallace, moved only one mile from Water Valley, when the darkness became so intense, that movements were almost impossible. The Brigade was consequently ordered into bivouack for the night. On the morning of the 17th, Lieut. Col. Wallace joined the 2d Brigade at Coffeeville. The entire force now moved forward rapidly towards Grenada, the 11th Ill. Cavalry having the advance. When ten miles from Coffeeville, six or eight locomotives and 40 or 50 cars were captured, and a guard placed over them. When the advance were within four miles of Grenada, the Rebels fired the two large Railroad bridges over the Tallobusha, and before we could reach them, they were completely destroyed. The 11th Ill. Cavalry was ordered forward, as rapidly as possible, to prevent the unnecessary destruction of property; and the entire 2d Brigade moved forward at a brisk trot. When within one mile of town, the 11th Cavalry were checked by about 300 of the enemy. The 9th Ill. Inft. were dismounted and sent forward as skirmishers. Soon after, the 2d Iowa and 3d Michigan Cavalry went into the action. Orders were sent back to Lieut. Col. Wallace to hasten up his Brigade, and move forward with all possible dispatch. As soon as the Battery was placed in position, Col. Wallace was ordered to enter town, with his Brigade, by the lower ford. The enemy not replying to our Battery, Major Coon was ordered to charge across the ford, with the 2d Iowa Cavalry, and at the same time to ferry over a portion of the 9th Ill. Inft. as a support, in case the enemy pressed him too hard. This force crossed and took possession of the town, without further opposition.

The captures which we made, were as follows: 60 locomotives; 450 cars, of all kinds; considerable stores, and $8,000 in Confederate scrip.

As the enemy had burned the bridges across the Tallobusha, making it impossible to run off the rolling stock, the cars, locomotives, machine shops, depots, Commissary and Quartermaster buildings were fired, and destroyed.

At 7 P. M., reports having come in that the enemy were returning to attack us in force, our entire Division, except the Picket and Provost Guard, were ordered to recross the Tallobusha, and bivouack, ready to fall in at a moment's notice. One hour later, Col. Winslow, commanding a Brigade of Cavalry, from "Blackwater," entered the town from the South. He being the ranking officer, now assumed command of the whole force. His Brigade took possession of the place, and the whole force bivouacked for the night.

The entire loss of our Division in the fight, was one man killed and two wounded. The 9th Ill. Inft. had one man wounded.

The 1st Brigade was so far in the rear, at the beginning of the action, that it was not engaged, except Perkin's Battery of Mountain Howitzers.

The entire forces in Lieut. Col. Phillips' command, during this expedition, consisted of the following Regiments, viz: 9th Ill. Inft. (mounted) Captain Kneffner commanding, 300; 2d Iowa Cavalry, Captain ——— commanding, 200; 11th Ill. Cavalry, Major Funk commanding, 150; 3d Michigan Cavalry, Major Hudson commanding, 200; Total, 2d Brigade, Major Coon commanding, 850. 9th Ill. Cavalry, ——— ——— commanding, 250; 3d Ill. Cavalry, Major Connor commanding, 200; 4th Ill. Cavalry, ——— ——— commanding, 300; Total, 1st Brigade, Lieut. Col. Wallace commanding, 750. Total in Division, Lieut. Col. Phillips commanding, 1,600.

The force of the enemy at Grenada, was between 1,500 and 2,500, and was under command of Col. Slemmer, Gen. Chalmers being, at the time, absent. Major Leath, Gen. Chalmers' Quartermaster, was captured in Grenada, and with him the Confederate scrip mentioned above.

During the action, Col. Winslow, with his Brigade, was in bivouack, within five miles of Grenada, and had he moved on the South rapidly at that time, we would have captured most of the enemy, and his entire Quartermaster train of over 100 wagons.

Lieut. Col. Phillips insisted on pursuing and capturing, at least, their wagon train. But Col. Winslow was in command and not willing. Lieut. Col. Phillips then requested permission to pursue with his command, but was refused. Having command, Col. Winslow ordered the destruction of property to cease. Hence, two locomotives, and about a dozen cars, were left on the North side of the Tallobusha, for the Rebels to run down produce from Water Valley and the country North of them.

The entire command remained in bivouack on the 18th, and moved on the return march, at 5 A. M., on the 19th, taking the Oakland road. Bivouacked for the night, just across the Tochamy River. We moved forward again at 5 A. M., of the 20th. Ferried over the Tallahatchie, and bivouacked for the night seven miles North of it. Moved again at 5 A. M., on the 21st. Col. Winslow and his command left us to-day, for Memphis. Fed near Looxahoma. Bivouacked for the night, near Bucksnort. Moved at the same hour on the 22d. Lieut. Col. Wallace

with his command, turned to the left to-day, for his camp at Collierville.
We passed through Holly Springs about 4 P. M., to-day, and bivouacked
seven miles North-east of town. This is a nice town, on an elevated
situation, with some very fine buildings in it. Guards were placed at
each of the houses. Many ladies made their appearance, as our boys
passed along the street. Some of them looked on smilingly, while
others manifested scornful contempt, in their very looks. But what
did our boys care for their scorn? They only smiled the more.
The sight which the citizens beheld, as our forces passed, was no doubt
to them a sore one. A long train of negroes, men, women and children,
were accompanying us. At least $1,000,000 worth of property, as
slaves had formerly been rated, was leaving them. They had long been
accustomed to regard these persons as the great source of their wealth.
This war had been instigated for the purpose of riveting the chains of
bondage more tightly upon these slaves. Many of them, perhaps, had
been called upon to mourn the death of some dear friend, who had been
slain in waging this war. They had thought thus to make more secure
this species of their wealth. But now they were compelled to see it,
taking to itself *legs* and fleeing away.

Our boys arrived in camp at Pocahontas, on the 24th of August, after
having been out thirteen days. They left camp with six days rations.
Where did the other seven days rations come from? I suppose none of
the boys can tell! Perhaps, if the smoke-houses and hen-roosts of the
citizens along the way could speak, they might tell. Or, may be, even
the citizens themselves, if any one should take the trouble to travel
along and enquire of them, could tell something about it.

The expedition was certainly a grand success. Some raids, about
which much has been said and written, were of far less importance. It
was a bold dash, of more than one hundred miles, into the midst of the
enemy's country. Our forces met on their own chosen ground, at least
an equal, and it is thought, a greatly superior force of the enemy;
drove them from their position, after a smart skirmish; captured a
large amount of their stores, with about fifty prisoners. About $8,000,000
worth of public property was destroyed. Destroyed because two long
bridges on the Railroad had been burned by the enemy. About 500
head of horses and mules were captured. And at least 2,000 negroes
were brought in with our forces; thus weakening the hands of our
enemies, and obtaining that, by which to strengthen our own hands.
These, as slaves were formerly valued, were worth at least $2,000,000.
The entire Union loss was only one man killed and two wounded. Had
there been a special correspondent with our forces, it would have been

heralded in the newspapers with a flourish that might have resulted in a *star* on our worthy Lieut. Col. Phillips, who commanded the expedition. The material, at least, was there.

Charles Chevi, 2d Lieutenant of Company C, resigned, and his resignation was accepted, to take effect August 7th, 1863.

August 26th, the Regiment was paid by Major W. H. Johnston, for the months of March, April, May and June.

August 29th, Captains Kneffner and Robinson, and Lieuts. Rollmann and Cowgill, were ordered to report to Col. Alexander, at St. Louis, for duty in the Invalid Corps.

At the regular periodical muster and inspection, on the 31st of August, Captain G. G. Lowe acted as Inspecting and Mustering Officer.

September 3d, 1863, 1st Lieutenant George W. Williford, was commissioned and mustered as Captain of Company F.

September 4th, 1863, Rev. Marion Morrison reported for duty, with commission as Chaplain of the Regiment. He was mustered in as such. to date from the 4th.

On the 3d of August, 1863, 105 deserters, mostly from the 128th Ill. Inft., were assigned to duty in the 9th Ill. Vol. Inft., and were transferred to the various companies, so as to equalize the strength of those companies.

On the 6th of August, Lieutenant McClure, commanding detachment of the 128th Ill: Vol., reported his men, in compliance with orders from Headquarters 16th Army Corps, to the Regiment for duty. The detachment numbered 103 men, and were assigned, pro rata, to the several companies. Lieutenant Lenma, Adjutant of the 128th, was assigned to Company F, and Lieutenant Cooper to Company B, until further orders. In the order for consolidation, Lieutenant Lenma's name was dropped, (he having resigned,) and Lieutenant Cooper was transferred from Company B. to Company F.

On the 16th of August, 1863, 1st Lieutenant Krebs received a commission as Captain of Company D, and Orderly Sergeant H. Weber as 1st Lieutenant Company D, and both were mustered in from that date.

When the writer reported to the Regiment for duty, on the 4th of September, as above noticed, the Regiment was in command of Captain G. G. Lowe, Lieut. Col. Phillips having been summoned to Memphis, as a witness before a court martial in the case of Lieut. Col. Bowen of the 10th Mo. Cavalry. Lieut. Col. Phillips was detained there for two or three weeks, and Captain Lowe continued in command of the Regiment, with credit to himself.

After joining the Regiment, arrangements were made for regular preaching services on each Sabbath, and prayer-meetings on Sabbath and Wednesday evenings. I would here say, that we have been able, notwithstanding the great amount of scouting duty the Regiment has had to perform, to hold our regular services on almost every Sabbath, up to the present time, except the few weeks I was absent from the Regiment, on orders, in Illinois. The Regiment had been without a Chaplain for about 20 months. For several Sabbaths we held our services under the shades of the trees in front of the Colonel's quarters. Soon, however, some of the soldiers volunteered their services, and erected a comfortable chapel, 40 by 24 feet, in which to hold our meetings. We had occupied this but a few Sabbaths, when we moved from our old camp at Pocahontas.

During the first three weeks of September, from one to four companies were out scouting, almost daily. Gen. Chalmers was concentrating a force South of the Memphis and Charleston Railroad, to make a dash upon that road, and cut off communication between Memphis and Corinth.

On the 27th of September, the Regiment, under command of Lieut. Col. Phillips, who had re-joined it, moved South toward New Albany. On arriving within six miles of that place, he found the enemy too strong for a further safe advance with the force he had, and returned to camp at Pocahontas on the 29th.

On the 2d of October, the Regiment moved North on a scout. Found and engaged a small force of the enemy, on Forked Deer River. In this engagement, Private Peterson, of Co. K, was killed. Finding no more force of the enemy, the Regiment returned to camp at Pocahontas on the 4th of October.

During the latter part of September and the first week in October, there was much talk that we would be removed, and take up the march somewhere. Gen. Sherman's forces from Vicksburg, were constantly passing towards Corinth, for two or three weeks. It was reported that they would take the place of the 16th Army Corps in occupying Memphis and Corinth and the Railroad between them; and that our Corps would move into an active campaign. Thus we were kept, as soldiers often are, in suspense from day to day. Not knowing what a day might bring forth. In the meantime Sherman's forces passed on towards Chattanooga, and we were still in our old quarters.

As the weather was now becoming too cold for the airy tents, which most of the Regiment occupied, the boys went to the timber, split boards, hauled poles, &c., and put themselves up comfortable quarters. Brick chimneys, left where houses had been burnt through the country,

[5]

were torn down and brought into camp, and neat little chimneys built to their shanties. Thus the boys were preparing for comfortably spending the winter in their camp.

On the 4th of October, commissions arrived, as follows: 2d Lieut. John Mallmann, to be Captain of Company B; 2d Sergt. L. Grieser, to be 1st Lieut. Company B; 1st Lieut. I. Clements, to be Captain Company G; 2d Lieut. N. G. Perrine, to be 1st Lieut. Company G; 1st Lieut. S. T. Hughs, to be Captain of Company I; 2d Lieut. Wm. Paden, to be 1st Lieut. Company I; Com. Sergt. C. A. Spatee, to be Regimental Quartermaster. Of the above, the following were ordered on duty, in their new rank, viz: Grieser, Clements, Perrine and Spatee.

On the 6th of October, the Regiment, under command of Lieut. Col. Phillips, moved South towards Ripley, on the Jonesborough road, and bivouacked for the night at Ruckersville. Moved forward again at daylight on the 7th, and reached Ripley at 8:30 A. M., and at 9:30 moved North-west towards Salem. When within five miles of that place, an advance was sent out, which ascertained that the enemy were in Salem about 3,000 strong. It was determined by Lieut. Col. Phillips, to attack them on the morning of the 8th, although his force did not exceed 400 men. Hence, early in the morning, one company was sent rapidly forward, and drove in their pickets and developed their forces. This done and they fell back. Soon after, the Regiment move forward in force. Arriving at the town, it was found that Col. McCrillis was there with his Regiment of cavalry, and that the Rebels had fallen back out of town. It was soon ascertained, however, that their falling back was not a retreat, but a pretense, and that they were preparing to attack us. Hence, the 9th Ill. Inft. was dismounted and deployed as skirmishers, and the two guns of Tamrath's Battery accompanying the Regiment, were placed in position, and opened upon the enemy. In a very short time the enemy made a vigorous effort to drive us, but failed. After engaging this vastly superior force for three hours, and our ammunition failing, we fell back on to the Railroad at LaGrange, and were reinforced. Five of our men were killed and twenty wounded in this engagement.

After reaching LaGrange, a dispatch was sent into camp, for all the men in camp fit for duty, to join the Regiment at that place. Reinforcements were now secured and preparations made for driving the enemy back, or cutting off his retreat. On the 11th of October, the Regiment, together with Col. Hatch's mounted force, moved South-west. Had an engagement with the enemy at Graham's Mills, and another at

Wyatt's, defeating them in both engagements and driving them Southward, after severe skirmishing.

Our entire mounted force was commanded by Col. Hatch, the Brigade by Lieut. Col. Phillips, and the Regiment by Captain A. G. Hawes. In these two last engagements, the 9th Ill. lost one man killed and five wounded.

The following is a list of the killed and wounded in the various engagements, since the Regiment was mounted on the 20th of March, 1863.

COMPANY A.—At Jackson, Tenn., *Killed*, Konrad Schaeffer; *Wounded*, Sergt. Michael Hartweek, Privates Charles Harris and George Heiler.—1 killed and 3 wounded.

COMPANY B.—Cherokee Bluffs, Miss., *Wounded*, Gustar Blank; Mud Creek, Miss., John Snider; Salem, Miss., James Luston; Wyatt's, Miss., *Killed*, William Toliver; *Wounded*, 1st Lieut. Louis Grieser, Private Wm. Crum. In all, 1 killed and 5 wounded.

COMPANY C.—Mud Creek, Miss., *Killed*, Sergt. Charles Ehrlich, Private George Valler, *Wounded*, Sergt. Wm. Heser, and Private Eilb Menson; Jackson, Tenn., Sergt. Engen A. Hauke; Salem, Miss, Corp. Wm. Striegal, and Private G. M. Smith; Athens, Ala., Samuel Spring. In all, 2 killed and 6 wounded.

COMPANY D.—Salem, Miss., *Killed*, G. W. Hatfield, *Wounded*, Chrst. Lambe. One killed and one wounded.

COMPANY E.—Mud Creek, Miss., *Wounded*, Charles B. Fleming, Wm. M. Gery and Ephraim J. Tyler; Salem, Miss., Jas. Stewart and Wm. Mock. In all, 5 wounded.

COMPANY F.—Salem, Miss., *Killed*, Thos. Ellison.

COMPANY G.—Mud Creek, Miss., Henry Brown and Jonathan Hampton; Salem, Miss., Wm. Cheneworth and Jas. M. Newton. In all, 4 wounded.

COMPANY H.—Salem, Miss., Francis M. Strickle, Ahiron D. Simons, Benj. R. Felts; Florence, Ala., Wm. H. Neal. In all, 4 wounded.

COMPANY I.—Mud Creek, Miss., *Wounded*, Lieut. S. T. Hughs, Chas. S. Patton; Grenada, Miss., S. P. Irwin; Jackson, Tenn., Oliver Hays; Salem, Miss., *Killed*, E. K. Richards, *Wounded*, Richard Jordon ; Wyatt's, Miss., John Graham; Athens, Ala., M. D. Holcomb. In all, 1 killed and 7 wounded.

COMPANY K.—Montazuma, Tenn., *Killed*, John M. Peterson; Salem, Miss., John Q. Martin, *Wounded*, Lieut. Ulen and Peter Hall. In all, 2 killed and 2 wounded.

A number of incidents of interest, occurred during the period covered by this chapter.

When on a scout to Tupelo, the boys were feeding near the house of a citizen. A woman came to Col. Phillips to make complaints that one of her horses had been taken, and a negro man or two had left her and was following our forces away. The Col. very politely told her, (for he is always polite to the ladies, unless they cease to act the lady,) that he was sorry for her, but that it was his business to keep the Rebels out of that country, so that they might not molest peaceable citizens like her. In order to do this, he must have horses to mount his men. Hence, from military necessity he must take her horse. That more effectually to accomplish the work of clearing the Rebels out of the country, the Government had resolved to arm the negroes and make soldiers of them. Hence, he must take her negroes also. Finding she could accomplish nothing by her entreaties with the Col., she was returning to the house, when she saw that they were taking her corn to feed their animals. Some of the boys were also chasing her chickens, and they were rapidly decreasing in numbers. She now set up a terrible lamentation, and commenced praying that God would send the Yankees out of the country. In the warmth of her petitions, she used the following forcible language: "O, Lord, if you can't come yourself, just now, do send General Price with his great army, to drive these miserable Yankees out of the country." Until this petition was uttered, some of the boys felt a sympathy for her. But the utterance of it, seemed to drive away both their sympathy and their gravity. The Col. finally sent an orderly, telling her to go into the house ånd finish her prayers.

Another. When on a scout near Ripley, Miss., the Regiment were in camp, and, as usual, helping themselves to the contents of a corn-crib, that thereby they might strengthen their mules for the heavy duties laid upon them. A woman appeared, with the usual cry, that she was a "poor lone widow, with six orphan children," and requested the Col. to leave her corn enough to make her bread until she could raise more. The Col. assured her that they would leave her some corn. In a short time, one of the girls came out, with the cry, "O, Col., the soldiers are taking every bit of our corn, and we will all starve." The Col. gave orders to the Adjutant to have a guard placed at that woman's corn, and instruct it to see that *some* of that corn was left. The Adjutant detailed a guard. In the meantime, it had been ascertained that the family had a lot of wheat; and although it might be hard for a Southern family to live without corn-bread, still it was supposed that if they had wheat-bread, they would not *starve*. Hence, as corn to feed upon was scarce, the Adjutant, in instructing the guard to see that *some* of that corn was left, gave him a knowing wink, which he well understood. *Some* of the corn was left. But it was simply a little shelled corn in the bottom of the crib. One of the girls having made a reconnoisance to the corn-crib, to see how things were getting along there, and made the discovery that it was all gone, came back running and crying, "Oh, mother, mother; they have taken every bit of our corn, and now we will have nothing to eat but wheat-bread. What will we do.''

Still another. It was almost a daily, and often an hourly occurrence, for citizens to visit the Col. at his Head Quarters, to endeavor to get back a horse or mule that had been captured. One day two ladies had visited him for that purpose. While they were engaged in reasoning the matter with him, dinner was announced. He invited them to go out and eat dinner with him. The invitation was accepted. The cook, or Doctor, or some one, expecting that they would be there for dinner, set a bottle of liquor on the table. After dinner was over, the Colonel politely invited them to take a drink. After some little hesitation, they each took their glass of liquor. The Colonel, always supplied with cigars, took his cigar-case from his pocket, and reached it to them. They each took a cigar, lit it at the cook's fire, and sat down and deliberately smoked it. In the North, to smoke in the presence of ladies is considered the greatest impoliteness. Not so in the South, however.

One more. When on the return from the raid to Grenada, Miss., the Regiment passed through Holly Springs. There was some apprehension that there might be a disposition on the part of some of the soldiers to fire the town, owing to treatment received from the citizens on a former occasion. Hence, a guard was placed at each house, until the forces should pass through. Surgeon Gulick desiring some water for sick men, started to go into a yard to get it, but the guard would not allow him to pass in. He handed his canteen to a colored man in the yard, requesting him to fill it with water. While he was doing it, a woman came from the house, much excited. Coming towards the Doctor, she inquired, "Is there a Mason here?"

Doctor.—"Why, madame, what do you wish?"

Mad. M.—"I am the widow of a Mason. I wish to know if there is a Mason here. I wish protection."

Doctor.—"Madame, you had better go into the house. You do not need protection. There is a guard around your house."

During this conversation, a chicken, from some cause ran through the fence into the street. A soldier started after it, to catch it. The Doctor's companion seized a long club, and quickly got over the fence and after the soldier. Unobserved, she came upon him, when about to catch the chicken, and struck him a heavy blow over the head. This he did not resist, as it was from a woman. But after the second blow, he supposed that "forbearance ceased to be a virtue," even if a woman was involved. The Doctor says he was scared when he saw her seize the club and climb the fence. He supposed she was coming at him.

Still another. At the same time and place with the last, a lady whose horse had been taken, came out to Col. Phillips, very pleasant, and announced herself as a daughter of Gen. Bradshaw; took the Colonel's horse by the bridle, and told him that she would be servant for him, and he had to submit to having her lead his horse up to her gate. She invited him to go in and have something to drink. He could not well refuse her invitation, even if he had desired to. Once in the house, she told him that she had both wine and whisky. Said she did not know how it was with our officers, but theirs all preferred the whisky. The Colonel told her that he would not be an exception, and so helped himself to a portion of the whisky.

Another one yet. During the raid on Florence, when the town was being searched, and contraband goods taken, tobacco and wine were both regarded as contrabands of war. Considerable quantities of both were found in the town. Dr. Allen tells of one soldier whom he saw with three boxes of tobacco on his mule before him. Having more than he could well carry, and meeting a citizen on the street, proposed to give him a box. Another, whom he met, had three or four boxes of bottles of wine on before him. Being rather overburdened, he made a present of one box to the Doctor, which he accepted, I suppose, as *hospital stores*.

Another on Dr. Gulick. I hope the good natured Doctor will pardon me for using his name so frequently in this connection. When on the return march from the raid to Grenada, Miss., as has been stated, there was a drove of about 2,000 negroes followed the returning column. They were of all ages, and both sexes. Old grey headed grandfathers and grandmothers were there. Men and women in the vigor of life were there. Prattling little boys and little girls were there. Suckling babes were there also. This great crowd of colored people were there, some of them pretty well clad, others almost naked. It is described as a sight sufficient to touch the heart of any one. Mothers were there, traveling on foot a journey of 75 to 100 miles, carrying their infant children. Two or three of these mothers, overcome with traveling to keep up with a mounted force, carrying their children, actually laid them down by the road side, and pressed on to liberty. "Can a mother forget her sucking child?" Some of these poor creatures seemed willing to leave their children behind, rather than be left themselves, hoping, perhaps, that some "good Samaritan" would care for them. The Doctor, kind-hearted man, finding one of these little ones, alighted and picked it up, and as some of the boys passed him, was dandling the child. He placed it in his ambulance, and when they halted, he found its mother. All praise to the Doctor for this humane act.

Another fact, closely connected with this rebellion, for the suppression of which our Regiment has so nobly contended. While in camp at Pocahontas, the writer took the pains to ascertain some facts with reference to the education of the citizens. When we had been in camp about three months, I called at the Provost Marshal's office, and ascertained that 1,520 citizens had taken the oath of allegiance, that they might make purchases of coffee, salt, &c., from our Commissary. Of the above number, just 300 could write their own names. The other 1,220 had to have their names written and make their mark. At another point where the Regiment was in camp, on the Tennessee River, out of 313 who took the oath in one day, only 13 could write their own names. The remaining 300 had to make their mark.

Now, looking at these facts, and if they are anything like an approximation even, to the state of society in the South, need we any longer wonder at this rebellion? A few well informed and designing leaders can go into a community, such as the above facts indicate, and influence its inhabitants to almost any course of action they may desire.

CHAPTER VII.

FROM THE TIME OF LEAVING POCAHONTAS TO THE PRESENT.

Orders to move camp—March to Eastport—Regiment detached for scouting duty—From Eastport to Pulaski—Pulaski to Athens—Scouting along the Tennessee—Going into quarters—Roddy's Raid—Scout below Florence.

As stated in the preceding chapter, there had been much said about our Regiment leaving camp and being thrown out into an active campaign; that that exitement had passed away, and the boys had prepared themselves with comfortable quarters in which to spend the winter.

When thus comfortably fixed for living during the winter, orders came for the Regiment to be ready to move on the morning of October 30th. Thus the comfortable little dwellings prepared by the boys; the chapel prepared for our religious services; the new hospital just finished, and such like comforts were all left behind. But such is the common lot of soldiers. They have a very uncertain life before them. They know not to-day, where they shall be on to-morrow. The order was to conduct a Battery to Corinth. Whence, from there, we knew not.

The morning of October 30th came, and with it heavy clouds, threatening rain. Baggage must be packed up. Tents must be struck. Wagons must be loaded. By about 8½ A. M., all was ready, and we were on the march. About the time we started, it commenced raining, and rained heavily all day. This made it difficult for the Battery wagons to proceed rapidly. Came to Cypress Creek and bottom. The stream was very difficult to cross. There was a swampy bottom, of three miles, which we had to cross. The Battery did not get through it that night, but camped in the bottom. The right wing of the Regiment moved out to the ridge beyond, and there awaited the arrival of Battery and left wing. It being found they could not get through that night, all went into bivouack until morning. At an early hour on the morning of the 31st, the Regiment and Battery were on the move. We reached Corinth about 1 P. M., of the 31st. Here we were relieved as escort to the Battery. Went into camp in the barracks lately occupied by the 50th Ill. Regiment. Here we remained until the morning of the 3d of November.

On the 2d of November, we were mustered for pay. Received orders on the 2d, to move the next morning, as escort to a train, to Iuka. Orders were issued regulating the order of march. There was a train of about 200 wagons and ambulances. The advance was ordered to move at 4 A. M., and the rear at 6 A. M. The whole was under command of Lieut. Col. Phillips. Such was the promptness with which he had each part of the column to occupy its position, that when the rear moved, and he went to the telegraph office to dispatch to Gen. Dodge that all were moving, it lacked ten minutes of six o'clock. Moved on steadily until noon. Halted one hour to water and rest. At 5 P. M., we reached Iuka, a distance of 25 miles. It was regarded a very speedy trip for so long a train. We bivouacked for the night, near Iuka. On the morning of the 4th of November, we moved at 10 A. M., as escort to a train of 150 wagons, to the crossing of the Tennessee River at Eastport. We arrived at Eastport at 2 P. M.

Gen. Dodge's orders to Lieut. Col. Phillips, commanding the 9th Ill. Inft., was, that immediately upon his arrival at Eastport, he should leave the train, together with his own Regimental teams on this side, and ferry the Regiment across the river, so as to be ready to move as early as practicable on the following day. The Regiment was all across by about sundown, and bivouacked one half mile from the river.

Our Regiment, Lieut. Col. Phillips commanding, was ordered on detached duty, and thus separated from the 2d Brigade, to which it properly belonged.

I might here state that the whole of the 2d Division of the 16th Army Corps, under command of Gen. Sweeney, Gen. Dodge being the department commander, had taken up the march from Corinth on the 2d and 3d of November, and was engaged in being ferried across the Tennessee River at Eastport.

Gen. Dodge's order, detaching the 9th Ill. Inft., assigned it to *scouting* and *foraging* for animals. The Division teams needed recruiting. Horses and mules must be procured in the country through which we were about to march, for this purpose. Gen. Sherman had lately marched his army through the same country, and it was very naturally supposed that animals would be scarce. Hence, a part of the order to our Regiment was to gather up all the horses, mules, cattle and sheep that could be found in the country. It was further ascertained that portions of Rebel cavalry had crossed North of the Tennessee River, to annoy our forces on their march. Hence, an additional duty assigned to the 9th Ill. was to make reconnoisances and watch the movements of the enemy.

On the night of the 4th, Lieut. Col. Phillips issued orders to be ready to move at 6 A. M.; the next morning. He also issued orders detailing one non-commissioned officer and six men from each company for foraging purposes, and instructing the foragers to bring in all horses, mules, cattle and sheep that could be found on our route. All soldiers were forbidden to leave the ranks, except such as were detailed for that purpose.

On the morning of the 5th of October, the Regiment was on the march by daybreak. Took the Florence road, for about three miles· Turned North, and traveled about ten miles through a poor, rough, broken country. Halted to make inquiry as to the country. Found a good Union man, with a clever family. Had the old man to go with us, as a guide. The Regiment here separated and traveled two different roads. About noon the flankers of the right wing were fired on, near a house. A number of shots were fired. Several horses and some cattle were taken. Halted to feed, two hours. During that time the left wing came in. All having fed, we took up the march again. Proceeded in the direction of Florence. Bivouacked for the night, after dark, about 14 miles from Florence. It had rained almost constantly during the day. Was still raining some when we halted. There was a fair prospect for a disagreeable night for laying out. But it did not rain much during the night. We brought in two men as prisoners, and about forty head of horses and mules, with some cattle.

November 6th, the Regiment moved at sunrise, bearing South. At 2 P. M., we came into a rich country. Plantations large; abundance of negroes; stock was plenty, which was gathered up. At many of the plantations we would collect 20 or 25 mules. Halted two or three hours and gathered up stock and fed. We then moved five or six miles West, and bivouacked for the night near a house owned by a large planter. The woman applied for protection. No one was allowed to enter the house. Negroes came in from different plantations. Through them we gathered much information as to the whereabouts of stock. Did not leave camp until about 11 A. M., of the 7th November. Sent out companies in different directions, to forage for stock. Succeeded in gathering a large amount of it. We were here South of the road leading from Eastport to Florence. We had crossed that road on the afternoon of the 6th.

During both the days we were out, we could frequently hear of forces of the Rebel cavalry on the North side of the river. They were often very near us, but always kept out of our way.

November 7th, at 11 A. M., we took up our march to strike the Florence road, hoping to meet the Brigade. We met them, and reported 300 head of horses and mules, 250 head of cattle, and 200 head of sheep, which we brought in and turned over. We met the column about 2 P. M., and bivouacked near a large brick house, residence of Captain Boggs.

The Regiment was now ordered to draw five days rations, and scout on the left flank of the advancing column. The main column, consisting of the 2d Division, 16th Army Corps, proceeded in the direction of Pulaski, Tenn., leaving Florence about eight miles to the right. On the march Col. Mersy, commanding 2d Brigade, had orders to burn a large Cotton Factory, which was being run by orders from the Southern Confederacy. The factory, together with the raw cotton, was worth about $100,000. The whole establishment was consigned to the flames on the morning of the 10th of November.

When the 9th Ill. Inft. left the advancing column, on the morning of the 8th, it proceeded in the direction of Waynesboro, and bivouacked twelve miles North-east of Waynesboro, and twenty miles from Gravelly Springs. Moved forward again early on the morning of the 9th, and marched thirty-five miles, bivouacking near Lawrenceburg. We moved again on the morning of the 10th, traversing the country to see that no Rebel forces were there to molest the column. We passed through

Mt. Pleasant. Bivouacked for the night five miles from Columbia, near the residence of Bishop (now Rebel General) Polk's residence. On the morning of the 11th, moved into Columbia, and proceeded in the direction of Pulaski, Tenn. Bivouacked two and a half miles from Pulaski. On the morning of the 12th, moved into Pulaski, and joined the column.

During this scout of four days, part of our business still being to collect stock, we brought in 500 head of horses and mules. Passed through some very fine and well improved country. There was no opposition met from the enemy, worth noting.

From the time of leaving camp at Pocahontas, up to our arrival at Pulaski, we supposed (at least the uninitiated) that our whole force was moving on in the direction of Chattanooga, and that was our destination. We expected soon to reach that place and take part in the great battle pending there. But on arriving at Pulaski, Gen. Dodge established his Head Quarters there, and his command were stationed along the Railroad running from Nashville to Decatur, to repair the road for use. The 2d Brigade, with the exception of the 9th Ill. Inft., went into camp at Pulaski. The 9th was still ordered on detached duty, and sent to establish a post at Athens, Alabama.

On the afternoon of the 12th of November, we moved South of Pulaski, along the line of the Railroad, and bivouacked nine miles from Pulaski, near where the Ohio Brigade were in bivouack. Here the men were ordered to draw five days rations, in their haversacks. They were also notified that our train and baggage would be left behind, and to make a change of clothing if they desired it.

On the morning of the 13th of November, we moved at daylight, Southward, leaving our wagons, baggage, and hospital to proceed with the Ohio Brigade to Prospect, where that Brigade was to be stationed. At Prospect, we forded the Elk River. When the advance reached the river, and were looking for a ford, some Rebel soldiers were seen on the opposite side, and fired upon. They interposed no obstacle to our crossing, however. After crossing the river, one battalion, under command of Captain Lowe, proceeded by a circuitous and Westerly route. The remainder of the Regiment proceeded by the direct route to Athens, Ala., arriving there before sunset. A few miles North of the town, one man of Company G, was taken prisoner when out foraging, by a few Rebel soldiers who were in the neighborhood. A small force of Rebel cavalry had occupied Athens on that day, but they speedily left on our arrival. The advance of our column came very rapidly into town, pursuing the party who had captured our man. They were pursued some distance through the town. On our arrival, Lieut. Col. Phillips, who was in command of the Regiment during the entire march, took possession of the town. Captain I. Clements was appointed as Provost Marshal, with his Company (G) as Provost Guard. Captain Lowe, with his battalion, reached Athens sometime after dark.

The Regiment went into bivouack in different parts of the town. Col. Phillips made his Head Quarters in the Court House.

On the morning of the 14th of November, the entire Regiment, under command of Lieut. Col. Phillips, moved South towards Decatur. Proceeded to the bank of the river opposite Decatur, and reconnoitered the position. Found the Rebels were occupying the town, and had a Battery of two guns. We moved back two miles, halted and fed. Parties were sent in different directions to reconnoiter. The entire Regiment returned to Athens the same evening, and bivouacked as on the previous night.

On the morning of the 15th of November, the Regiment moved out one mile North-east of town, and went into camp. Here we remained until the morning of the 18th, simply sending out single companies each day to reconnoiter.

One object of our expedition was to examine the condition of the Railroad and telegraph line. On leaving Pulaski, Lieut. Oats, with twelve men, was detailed for that purpose. He proceeded along the line of the Railroad from Pulaski to Decatur, examining carefully its condition. The writer was requested by Lieut. Col. Phillips to accompany him, and report the condition of the telegraph. We were often separated two or three miles from the main column.

On the evening of the 17th, a portion of the teams came down from Pulaski, with five days rations, and returned to Prospect the next morning.

On the morning of the 18th November, the entire Regiment moved West, in the direction of Florence. Crossed Elk River, fifteen miles West of Athens, and halted to feed. During the afternoon of this day, when near Rodgersville, the advance were fired upon by a squad of Rebels, who broke and ran. No one hurt. Two companies moved rapidly down to the Tennessee River, at Lamb's Ferry, hoping to capture the boat. But it was on the other side of the river. Moved West on the Florence road, and bivouacked for the night nine miles West of Rodgersville.

November 19th, we moved at daylight, Westward on the Florence road. At Shoal Creek bridge the advance encountered and chased some Rebels, who seemed to be guarding the bridge. Proceeded rapidly with two companies, to Bambridge Ferry, six miles above Florence, and captured the ferry-boat. The Rebels opened fire from the opposite side of the river. Our two companies were deployed as skirmishers, and returned the fire. A brisk fire was kept up for one hour, until the boat was destroyed, when we started on our return march. Re-crossed Shoal Creek. Halted and fed. Mounted and continued our return march. Bivouacked for the night West of Elk River.

We moved again early on the morning of the 20th of November, and returned to Athens about 12 M. Proceeded through town, on the Decatur road, about six miles, halted and fed. From this point four companies returned to Athens, and occupied our old camp. The remainder of the Regiment proceeded to Moorsville. Found a force occupying that place, and returned to camp at Athens on the 21st. On the afternoon of this day, we moved our camp South-west of town.

The country having been completely explored, and considering there was no immediate danger from the enemy, the Col. sent for our teams and baggage. They arrived on the evening of the 21st, and the boys were glad to have a change of clothing.

I would here say, that upon our first coming to Athens, it was not deemed prudent to remove any baggage here, except such as could be carried on our animals. Our Regiment was sent down here all alone, in the midst of an enemy's country. No one knew the exact strength of the enemy. It was fifteen miles to Prospect, where our nearest forces were. The Elk River intervened, and was often past fording. At that time there was no way of crossing it, except on a very small boat which would only carry one wagon. It was a hazardous position we occupied, at best. There was a heavy force of Rebels South of the Tennessee River. There were a number of ferries for crossing at different points. But having reconnoitered the country, and destroyed several of the enemy's ferries, it was thought our train might be brought down with safety.

From the time we left camp at Pocahontas, until our train was brought down, we had been out 23 days, and on the march nearly all the time. During this time, we had with us no tents or covering of any kind, except such as we carried on our animals. We would march all day, often making 40 and 45 miles, and then lay down on the ground at night, with no covering but our blankets. During this time, we marched over 400 miles.

When our train arrived, and our camping ground was determined we had no tents, which could be quickly spread for a shelter. Most of the boys were under the necessity, for several nights, of doing as they had done, sleeping in the open air. Soon lumber was procured, from the fence around the Fair Grounds and the buildings it contained, and unoccupied stables and fences, with which to build shanties. But we had no nails, and this country could furnish none. But where there were buildings and fences, there were nails, and the old nails were preserved, and thus the boys built their houses. After a time, they were quite comfortable in them. The work of building "New Athens" was, however much retarded by the fact that several companies of the Regiment were almost constantly out on scouting duty. But ere long their houses were finished, with comfortable fire-places attached.

As I have stated above, Lieut. Col. Phillips, with the 9th Ill. Inft., was detached, and sent to Athens to establish a post. It was a strange kind of *post* for two or three weeks. Much was said about "Col. Phillips' circulating post." After we were settled down in our camp, however, Col. Phillips formally assumed command of the post, with his Head Quarters in town, leaving Major Kuhn in command of the Regiment. Still the *post*, or its head, was rather circulatory; for whenever the Regiment was out on a scout of any considerable importance, the Col. was sure to go along.

It devolved upon our Regiment not only to hold its post at Athens, but to guard the crossings of the Tennessee River for a distance of not less than fifty miles in length. Consequently, there was a great amount of scouting duty to perform. Almost daily, the various crossings of the Tennessee River, between Decatur and Florence, were visited by portions of our Regiment, and the ferry-boats either destroyed or captured.

On the 28th of November, three companies, under command of Lieut. Col. Phillips, moved West at 11 P. M., on the Florence road, and crossed Elk River, in search of some Rebel cavalry said to have crossed the Tennessee River that evening. He came upon and captured a squad of fifteen of them. Not finding any more force, he was returning to camp the next morning with his prisoners, when he was met by a dispatch from Gen. Dodge, stating that a large body of Rebels had crossed about Florence, and ordering him to reconnoiter and watch their movements, and develop their strength. A squad of men were sent in with the prisoners, with orders for one company more to join him. He had gone out with only one days' rations. The company that joined him could not carry rations to him, for we were short in camp. Our teams had gone to Pulaski for rations. The Division teams from Columbia had not arrived with rations, as expected. Our teams were detained there several days. But the boys of the 9th are not likely to starve, when there is anything in the country around them to eat.

The first night they camped near the town of Rodgersville. The Col. sent orders to the different houses in town, requiring each to supply a certain number of rations of corn bread. Some demurred, saying they had nothing of which to make bread. A second order was sent, that if it was not provided in such a length of time, he would burn their houses. This brought corn bread in abundance, but not of a very fine quality. The next night they camped near a good supply of sweet potatoes, to which they helped themselves. The following day they came across a store of Rebel commissaries, and were thus further provided. They were out four days. Came upon a body of Rebels, of whom they captured about thirty. When pursuing them, Col. Phillips was chasing his man, and made a sabre stroke at him, cutting him over the head. About that time, the Col.'s horse fell, and threw him on his face on the frozen ground. He captured his man, however.

On the 25th of January, 1864, Companies B, C, D, F, H, I and K, under command of Lieut. Col. Phillips, moved out on a reconnoisance West. This left but three companies in camp. Company A was doing picket duty. Company G was acting as Provost Guard, and stationed in town. This left Company E in camp alone. News of the weakness of our force was immediately carried over the river, and Gen. Roddy notified of it. Consequently, early on the morning of the 26th of January, about 4 A. M., our camp was attacked by Gen. Roddy, with 700 men and two pieces of artillery. The pickets on the West of our camp were fired upon. Company E moved out promptly to support the pickets, when they met the overwhelming force of the enemy. After a brief engagement, and finding the strength of the enemy, this company fell back into town, to co-operate with Company G. This gave the Rebels possession of our camp. They plundered it of all the baggage and valuables. Our men were pursued into the town, the Rebels occupying the Southern part of the town, and our boys the Northern part. The Rebels also placed their artillery in position, and began to shell the town. After a smart skirmish of about forty minutes, the enemy retreated, and returned towards the river. This they did, although they numbered ten to our one.

The loss of the 9th, in this engagement, was two men wounded, viz: Spring, of Company C, (since dead,) and Holcomb, of Company I. One man, not a soldier, but an employe of our Surgeon, was shot in the hospital yard, although entirely unarmed. The enemy admit a loss of six killed and eighteen wounded. Three of our boys pursued them, and fired upon them when a short distance from the river, killing one and wounding two. They returned to camp safely, except that they lost their horses.

The officers lost all their baggage and effects, except such as they had with them. So with the men.

On the 28th, seven companies, under command of Lieut. Col. Phillips, moved West on the Florence road. Bivouacked for the night, eight miles East of Florence.

Early on the 29th, moved into Florence, chasing some Rebel soldiers from the town. Passed on twelve miles West of Florence, to Pride's Ferry. Here we had a sight of some Rebels, but they made good their escape. We destroyed a factory and mill in this region. Captured a train of about twenty wagons with their teams.

Near this Ferry lives a man named Woods, who is living with a negro woman as his wife. To this woman he had a large number of children, whom he was holding as slaves. He was holding about forty of his own children as slaves. The Regiment foraged heavily upon him. About 3 P. M., we started on the return march, and bivouacked four miles from Florence. In this region, large numbers of negroes came in, and followed the Regiment on its return march to Athens.

On the morning of the 30th, moved towards Athens, and bivouacked for the night, West of Elk River. On the 31st, reached camp at Athens.

The Regiment was out, during this expedition, four days. It brought in about 500 negroes, men, women and children; 150 head of horses and mules, and 100 head of cattle, besides a train of 20 wagons.

On the 15th of February, the Regiment, under command of Lieut. Col. Phillips, moved to the Tennessee River, at Lucas & Brown's Ferry. The Regiment remained in bivouac during that entire week. Their work was patroling the river for ten or fifteen miles above and below Decatur, capturing flat-boats and ferry-boats, constructing canoes, &c. The weather was very cold. They had no shelter. Had to work much about the water, and withal, it was a very hard week's duty. The Rebels were occupying the other side of the river, and there was almost constant firing at each other across the river. Lieut. Oats, of Co. K, was in a flat-boat with fifteen men, when he was fired upon by about twenty Rebels, at close range. One man of Co. I was severely wounded. The fire was returned, and it is thought, from the noise, several of the enemy were killed and wounded. The Lieutenant captured four Rebel prisoners.

The Regiment returned to camp on the 20th, leaving two companies to patrol the river and guard our boats. During the week of boat capturing, one flat-boat captured above Decatur "ran the blockade" past the town, with three of our boys in it. They lay down flat, and let it float. Many incidents of interest occurred during this week, but I have not room to note them here.

On the 22d of February, the 39th Regiment Ohio Infantry arrived at Athens, and went into camp. Col. Noyes, of the 39th Ohio, assumed command of the post, relieving Lieut. Col. Phillips, who again assumed command of the Regiment.

From the 20th of February, up to the 7th of March, two companies of the 9th Ill. was kept constantly at the Tennessee River, patroling it for several miles below Decatur. These companies were relieved every two days, by others. In the meantime several other regiments passed through Athens, on their way towards Decatur. These were the 63d Ohio, 27th Ohio, 43d Ohio, and 111th Illinois, with the 4th Michigan Battery.

The Railroad was completed about the last week of February, and the cars commenced running through from Nashville. Soon boats to construct a pontoon bridge at Decatur, commenced passing on the cars. Gen. Dodge, who commands the department, was below. Active preparations were being made for occupying Decatur. To do this, the Tennesse River must be crossed, in the face of an opposing foe. The enemy was occupying Decatur, and the South bank of the river at the various ferries below.

The Regiment was paid, by Major Gregory, on the 2d of March, 1864, for the months of November and December. It had been paid on the 16th of December, 1863, by Major Hinkley, for the months of September and October, 1863.

On the morning of the 7th of March, the 9th Ill., together with a detachment of 60 men of the 18th Mo., and two sections of a U. S. Battery, stationed at Athens, received marching orders, and moved at 10 A. M., on the Lucas Ferry road. Arriving within two miles of the river at 2 P. M., they halted and fed, remaining until near dark, when they moved on to the river under cover of darkness.

It was known that an attempt would be made to cross the Tennessee River that night or early the next morning, both at Lucas Ferry and Decatur. The flat-boats, canoes, &c., which the 9th Ill. had for the past two or three weeks been collecting at Lucas Ferry, would now be brought into use. At Decatur, the boats intended for the construction of the pontoon bridge, would be used for crossing. Gen. Dodge was at Decatur superintending the crossing in person. Lieut. Col. Phillips,

[6]

of the 9th Ill., was in charge of the expedition at Lucas Ferry, which is three miles below Decatur.

The Regiment went into bivouac, after dark, about one hundred yards from the river. The flat-boats and canoes had been moved up the river one mile, so as to have the advantage of the current. Several pontoon boats had been floated down a stream running from the Railroad to a point within a mile or two of the Ferry. These had to be taken across on wagons to the river and up to the point from which the boats were to start. This occupied a portion of the men during the greater part of the night.

Details were made, of three men from each company, who could man a canoe, and four men from each company for boatmen. During the night there was a heavy rain, after which it cleared up, and the stars shone brightly. Before day, however, a very heavy fog settled over the water and surrounding country. This was favorable to our crossing, as a man could not be seen, on the water, only at a very short distance.

About 2 A. M., the artillery was placed in position on the river bank. The forces were ordered into line. The details for canoe men and boatmen received their orders. The advance were to pass over in canoes. They were placed under the command of Lieut. Rollmann, and were instructed to proceed directly across, as rapidly as possible. When they struck the opposite shore, they were to abandon their canoes, and hold the positions until the boats would get over.

The flat-boats and pontoons were placed under the command of Lieut. Oats. All were marched up the river to the boats, and at 4:30 A. M., the boats and canoes were loaded and started over. When the advance was within about 30 yards of the shore, the enemy fired a few shots, and retired rapidly in the direction of Courtland. The entire command crossed over in one and a half hours, and reported at Decatur. During the day and night following, the animals and teams were crossed over. Capt. Lowe, who had the crossing of the animals in charge, was attacked by a party of Rebels, and one man was taken prisoner.

The Regiment moved East, on the Courtland road, at 9:30 A. M., March 9th, and reached Courtland at 4 P. M., without meeting any body of the enemy. We bivouacked for the night on the Moulton road, three miles South of Courtland.

On the morning of the 10th of March, we moved into Moulton. The enemy had left the place three hours before our arrival. They moved from Moulton at daylight, on the Russelville road. We captured, at Moulton, several prisoners, one flag, a quantity of ammunition, and hospital and commissary stores. From Moulton, we moved towards Decatur, reaching that place at sundown. There the Regiment was ordered into camp, to be quartered in houses in town.

On the morning of the 11th of March, Adjutant Klock was ordered to Athens with a squad of men, to have the camp and garrison equipage moved to Decatur, which is being done at present writing, March 12th, 1864.

How long we will remain in Decatur, or where we shall go next, or how we shall be employed during the remaining four months of our service, are all matters in the future, and, in any department of life, uncertain, but especially in military life.

There are some incidents of interest, which occurred during the period of this chapter.

The first day after crossing the Tennessee River, while making for a place to camp for the night, where we learned there was forage for our animals, it began to get dark before we reached the point. The Col. drew up before a house near the road, to make some inquiry. A man came to the gate. Inquiry was made as to the distance to the point we wished to reach. These inquiries were followed by others as to whether there were any soldiers in the neighborhood. The reply was that there were.

Col.—"Were they Yanks?"

Citizen.--"Yes."

Col.—"How many was there of them?"

Citizen.—"Oh, there was a great many of them. At least 1,000."

Col.—"Was that all? I can easily whip twice that number. But I guess, my friend, you must go along and show us the road to their camping ground."

The poor man, thinking that we were Rebel soldiers, called to one of the boys to bring him out his horse until he would go with those men. But when the boy went to the stable to get the horse, it was not there. Our foraging parties had visited the stable, and relieved him of his horse. He went into the house to get his coat. There, I think, he began to realize that he was *sold*. Some of our boys had been in to get "corn bread," and the old lady, I suppose, had noticed the blue uniform, and reported us as "Yanks." When he came out he did not seem near so willing to go along. But he went with us, and when we got into camp, he waked up to the fact that he was a "prisoner of war." He had been in the Rebel army, and was detailed as a blacksmith, to shoe the horses through the country, that they might be ready for government use. He was taken with us, as a prisoner. I saw him a week later, when on our march, still a prisoner.

Another. On the next evening, an old negro man was with us when we bivouacked. He was a preacher, and quite an oracle among the darkies in that region of country. As we were gathered around our camp-fire, the old man was called up to be questioned by the Colonel. After giving all the information he could, he told us of his visions and spiritual communications. Says he, "I sees all dis trouble seben years ago. I sees *you alls* a comin down from the Norf. I sees dese two great armies, with dah uniforms on, and all dis fitin and killin one anoder." On being asked how he saw all this, he replied, "I sees it spiritually." He was asked if he saw which was going to whip, he said, "Lor, massa, yes; I sees de Norf a whippin."

Still another. During the march from Corinth to Pulaski, Colonel Mersy of the 9th, commanding Brigade, being in camp, sleeping near his camp-fire, which was made of Chestnut rails, noted for their *popping* propensities when burning, the fire flew out and set his clothes or blankets on fire. The Head Quarters guard seeing it, went and awoke him, telling him that he was on fire. His reply was, "Adjutant! Adjutant!" But the Adjutant was sound asleep, and did not answer his call. The Col. being scarcely awake, was soon asleep again. The guard awoke him a second time, and told him he was on fire. "I tink dat no my business; you wake de Adjutant." The Col., so full of military life, and wishing everything to go through its proper military channel, felt, in his half.sleeping condition, that his Adjutant General must be honored with the permission of getting up and putting out the fire.

Another one, in which our good Colonel is concerned. During the march, just before going into camp, Rebel uniforms and other accoutrements of war, were found at a house near the road. The soldiers made a pretty general *red up* of the establishment. After we were in camp, the woman of the house came to Col. Mersy, with her complaint. She represented, among other things, that she had been a widow for fifteen years. Soon Surgeon Gulick, of the 9th, who was with the Col., heard him call, "Doctor! Doctor!" The Doctor having arrived and awaiting orders, the Col. addressed him: "Now, my dear Surgeon, you does tell me if dis widow has been not married dese fifteen year."

Another one, which illustrates something of the habits of Southern women. They nearly all use tobacco, in some shape. Some of them in the various forms, of smoking, chewing, and *dipping*. When the Regiment was on its march from Pulaski to Athens, the writer was with a squad of men, who were traveling along the Railroad examining its condition. Being separated from the column, the boys becoming hungry, and desiring something to eat, rode up to a house where there were three or four women standing at the door. One of them inquired if they could get something to eat. The corn bread was produced. He then asked for some butter, which was also produced. One of the girls, thinking, I suppose, that one favor deserved another, very smilingly addressed one of the soldiers, saying, "Could you give me a chew of tobacco?" "Oh, yes," says he, taking a large plug of tobacco from his pocket and handing it to her. She took a chew, and then reached it back, thanking him. "Oh," says he, "you may just keep that, I can get more." She thanked him very kindly. I suppose she thought she was pretty well paid for her corn bread and butter.

Another. Capt. Krebs, of Company D, with a squad of 25 men, was detailed to go with the telegraph repairer along the line between Huntsville and Decatur. At a station between those two points, a small town, there were two telegraph posts down, the line on each side being perfect for two or three miles. The Captain and operator rode up to some citizens who were on the street, and politely asked them if they could not have those two posts set by the next day, stating that it would save them the trouble of bringing their team and men several miles, and would be a very great accommodation. One old man replied, "We can't do it, sir. You have taken all our negroes from us, and we have nobody to work for us." The Captain insisted that it was but a small job, and it would save him a great amount of trouble, if they would do it. The old man persisted that they could not do it. The Captain then addressed them as follows: "Gentlemen, I will be' here to-morrow evening, with fifty men to do that work. You will have supper provided for that number of men." Then turning to his command, he gave the order, "Two right, march!" and moved off. When he had gone a mile or two, a runner came up and handed him a note, saying that the citizens would have those posts set by to-morrow morning. The "supper for fifty men" had been a more powerful argument than the Captain's pleadings. I suppose it led them to conclude, that if they had no darkies to do it, they would condescend to do it themselves.

One more. Major Falconet, of the Rebel army, and who was stationed at Decatur for some time, it is said, had come to the conclusion to take to himself a wife. He had gone to Florence to get married. While on the floor, having the marriage ceremony performed, Lieut. Col. Phillips, with the 9th Ill., made a dash into Florence. Some one came into the room and cried out, "The Yanks. are coming!" The brave Major left his fair companion, broke from the house, and over the garden fence, tearing down about twenty feet of it, dashed to his boat and was off. I suppose he did not fancy being captured just then.

How his partly constituted bride felt, at his rapid exit, and whether he has ever returned for the completion of the ceremony, "deponent saith not."

Still another, showing something of the horrors of Slavery. During the recent scout to Courtland and Moulton, when in camp near the former place, the orders of Lieut. Col. Phillips were to be ready to move by daylight. The guard were instructed to wake them two hours before day. The orderlies were waked at the proper time. When Adjutant Klock had gotten up, he was informed by an orderly that there was a lady wishing to see the Colonel. The Colonel was called. In a half-sleeping condition, he told the Adjutant to see what she wished. The Adjutant went around to see her. He saw there a very decently, but plainly dressed lady. He asked her what she wished. He was perfectly amazed at her reply. She said her master was going to sell her, and she wished to know if she could not go with them. The Adjutant replied, that he would speak to the Colonel about it, and that he thought they could make arrangements for her to go with us. The Colonel having dropped asleep in the meantime, the matter was referred to Major Kuhn. He told her at once that she could go along. She accordingly came into Decatur with our Regiment. To Northern men, unaccustomed to the evils of the system of Slavery, such scenes are revolting. Here was a woman, so nearly white, that she was mistaken for a white woman. She was, in all probability, her master's daughter or sister.

BIOGRAPHICAL SKETCHES
OF THE
FIELD AND STAFF OFFICERS.

BIOGRAPHICAL SKETCHES.

I propose to add to this history of the Regiment, a Biographical Sketch of the present Field and Staff Officers.

COL. AUGUST MERSY.

Was born in Germany. He entered the military service, in 1838, as Cadet, in Karlsrhue, Grand Duchy of Baden. He graduated in 1840, as Lieutenant. He was promoted to the position of 1st Lieutenant, in 1842. In 1844, he was assigned the position of Adjutant and staff officer. In 1847, he was appointed Regimental Adjutant. A European Regiment consists of from 2,400 to 3,000 men. In this position he acted until 1849. At the outbreak of the Revolution, he consequently acted against that Revolution. In 1849, however, he joined the Revolutionary party, and was promoted to the position of Colonel. After joining the Revolutionary party, he acted for some time as Provisional Secretary of War. He soon, however, joined the army, and assumed command of the Second Brigade. Whether he had the rank of General, or only acted as such in commanding a Brigade, the writer is unable to say. He went with his Brigade, through all the battles and skirmishes of the year 1849. He was under the necessity of crossing the Rhine for Switzerland, and concluded to emigrate to America. He arrived in the United States, in November, 1849. Went West, and settled in Bellville, St. Clair County, Illinois. He was for some time Clerk, and afterwards Cashier, of the "Bank of Bellville." He also acted as Notary Public.

On the uprising of the rebellion, his war spirit was aroused. I think he had for some time previous had command of a volunteer military company. He enlisted, with his company, in the "Three months'" service. He enlisted as Captain of Company A, 9th Regiment Illinois Infantry, on the 19th of April, 1861. He was elected Lieutenant Colonel, April 26th, 1861. This position he held during the "Three months'" service. He was mustered out of the service, at the end of the three months, on the 25th of July, 1861, and again immediately mustered in, for three years, as Lieutenant Colonel of the 9th Illinois Infantry.

He was promoted to the position of Colonel, and received his commission as such, December 2d, 1861. As Colonel and commander of the Regiment, he passed through the terrible battles of Fort Donelson and Shiloh, and the "siege of Corinth." He was wounded twice at the battle of Shiloh; but notwithsthanding his wounds, he persisted in keeping the command of his Regiment. During the battle of Shiloh, Col. McArthur, commanding our Brigade, was severely wounded, in the latter part of the action, and Col. Mersy assumed command of the Brigade.

During the battle of Corinth, he assumed command of the Brigade, General Oglesby having been wounded. Since that time, he has had command of the 2d Brigade, 2d Division, 16th Army Corps. During the Summer and Fall of 1863, he was stationed with his Brigade Head Quarters at Pocahontas, Tennessee. Since November 12th, 1863, his Brigade Head Quarters have been at Pulaski, Tennessee.

LIEUT. COL. JESSE J. PHILLIPS.

Was born in Montgomery County, Illinois, May 22d, 1837. He was appointed Route Agent on the Terre Haute, Alton and St. Louis Railroad, June 26th, 1856. Resigned in May, 1857.

He read law with the Hon. James M. Davis, of Hillsboro, Illinois. He was admitted to the bar in the Spring of 1860, and opened an office in Hillsboro, the county-seat of Montgomery County, Illinois. He was prosecuting his practice when the first call was made for volunteers to serve for three months.

In politics, he was a Breckenridge Democrat. Had stumped it, for Breckenridge, in 1860. He had had a strong desire to engage in a military life. When the call was made, he at once went to work to raise a Company. Raised his Company, and was elected Captain, April 17th, 1861. The Company was accepted and ordered to Springfield, Illinois, on the 23d of April, 1861.

On the organization of the 9th Regiment Volunteer Infantry, for the three months' service, he was elected as Major of the Regiment. He acted in the capacity of Major in the Regiment during the three months' service. At the expiration of that service, he was mustered out, and immediately mustered in again for three years, unless sooner discharged, retaining still the rank of Major.

He received a commission as Lieutenant Colonel in the 9th Regiment Illinois Infantry in December, 1861, which position he still occupies. He had charge of a detachment of the Regiment, which made a successful expedition from Paducah to Saratoga, Ky. This was the first fight in which our boys were engaged. He was with the Regiment as Lieutenant Colonel, through the battles of Fort Donelson and Shiloh.

At Shiloh, he received a very severe wound from a schrapnel. He was wounded in the hand and leg. The wound in his hand was a very painful one. He was unfitted for the service by it, for several months. At the battle of Corinth, on the 3d and 4th of October, he had not yet been able to join his Regiment. He joined it soon afterward, although still suffering much from the pain caused by his wound.

During the Fall of 1862 and Winter of 1863, he was much of the time in command of the Regiment, Col. Mersy being called to the command of the Brigade. In March, 1863, he made application to have the Regiment mounted for scouting purposes. The Regiment was mounted on the 20th of March, 1863. During the year that the Regiment has been mounted, he has led it through 23 battles and skirmishes.

He has frequently been placed in command of a Brigade of mounted forces, and in one or two instances, of a Division. He had command of two Brigades of Cavalry and Mounted Infantry, with which he made a raid in August, 1863, to Grenada, Mississippi. It was one of the most successful raids of the war. From $8,000,000 to 10,000,000 worth of public property was destroyed; 2,000 negroes, and a large number of horses and mules were brought in. But little was said about it at the time. Many a less brilliant raid has brought forth a star.

He was in command of the post at Athens, Alabama, for two or three months during the past Winter. He has lately been assigned to the command of all the mounted forces at Decatur, Alabama. There is a great amount of *dash* and daring about the Colonel, and yet he always manages to get his boys out of any place, into which he leads them.

MAJOR JOHN H. KUHN.

Was born in St. Gallen, Switzerland, May 26th, 1833. Emigrated to the United States, and landed in New York, in June, 1849. He was, by occupation, a laborer. Hired with a farmer near Pittsburgh, Pennsylvania, during the first summer. He removed to East Tennessee, where he spent three years, part of the time in a glass factory in Knoxville, and part of the time boating on the Tennessee River. He moved to Alton, Illinois, in 1854. Was engaged for a time in the lumber business, and afterwards in a banking house. He had served for about six years in the State Militia, and entered the service of the United States, on the call for volunteers for three months. He enlisted with his company of "Alton Jagers," as their Captain, April 19th, 1861, and was attached to the 9th Illinois Infantry. He re-enlisted at the expiration of three months, for three years. Served, for sometime, as Provost Marshal of Paducah, Kentucky. He received his commission as Major of the 9th Illinois Infantry, December 2d, 1861. He was detailed during some months in the Summer and Fall of 1863, in charge of convalescent camp in Memphis, Tennessee. Rejoined the Regiment at Athens, Alabama, November 21st, 1863. At present writing, he has command of his Regiment, Lieut. Col. Phillips being assigned to the command of the mounted forces at Decatur, Alabama.

SURGEON EMIL GULICK, M. D.

Was born in the city of Schleswig, Dutchdom Schleswig, on the 29th of November, 1828. After finishing his school education, he commenced the study of Chemistry in particular, but with it the other branches of the medical science. While quietly pursuing his studies, the sound of the drum rang through the land, calling all able-bodied citizens into the field to fight for the independence of the Dutchdoms from the Kingdom of Denmark. This call was in March, 1848. The Doctor was then in his 20th year. Obeying his country's call, he enlisted to do battle for liberty. He enlisted as a private. He was afterwards engaged as an Assistant in the Medical Department. He was connected with the army in these capacities until 1851. He emigrated to America in 1853. He re-commenced his Medical studies, and graduated in the St. Louis Medical College, in 1859. He commenced the practice of medicine during the same year, in Alton, Madison County, Illinois. When the Rebellion broke out, and there was a call for men to defend the government of his adoption, he offered himself for that purpose. He enlisted, in the three months' service, as a private, in Company K, 9th Regiment Volunteer Infantry, on the 26th day of April, 1861. He re-enlisted, at the expiration of three months, for three years, July 26th, 1861, and was promoted to the position of Assistant Surgeon of the 9th Illinois Volunteer Infantry. On the 28th of April, 1862, he was again promoted to the position of Surgeon. He has served in that position ever since. He has been almost constantly with his Regiment. He was on detached duty in the Hospital at Paducah, Kentucky, during the months of September and October, 1863.

ASSISTANT SURGEON W. D. CRAIG, M. D.

Was born in Montgomery County, Indiana, March 27th, 1828. He was raised on a farm. Was educated at Crawfordsville, Indiana. He moved to Illinois in 1849, and graduated at Rush Medical College, Chicago, Illinois, in the Spring of 1852. From that time, up to the Summer'of 1861, he was engaged in the practice of Medicine. Was living in Aledo, the county-seat of Mercer County, Illinois, and engaged in the duties of his profession, at the time of his enlisting in the service of his country. He recruited a large portion of a Company in Mercer County. Was mustered into the service of the United States, as 1st Lieutenant Company E, 9th Regiment Volunteer Infantry, August 6th, 1861. Served in that capacity until May 12th, 1862. During the time he served as a line officer, he passed through the terrible struggles of Fort Donelson and Shiloh. He was slightly wounded at Shiloh, in the left shoulder, by a spent ball. He was assigned to the Medical Department of the Regiment, in the capacity of Assistant Surgeon, on the 12th of May, 1862. Continued with the Regiment in this capacity, until the last of December, 1863, when he was assigned to duty in Pulaski, Tennessee. During the past Winter, he has had charge of the U. S. General Hospital of the left wing, 16th Army Corpse, at Pulaski, Tennessee. He has under his charge there, about an average of two hundred patients, including a Small-Pox ward of from ten to fifteen patients.

SECOND ASSISTANT SURGEON W. A. ALLEN, M. D.

Was born in Jacksonville, Illinois, March 5th, 1830. Read Medicine with Dr. Haskall, Hillboro, Montgomery County, Illinois, 1850, 1851 and 1852. He graduated at St. Louis Medical College, in 1856, and commenced the practice of Medicine in Greenville, Bond County, Illinois, during the same year. Was engaged in pursuing his practice at that place, until January, 1863. He received a commission as 2d Assistant Surgeon in the 9th Illinois Volunteer Infantry, and entered upon his duties as such, January 16th, 1863. He was detailed, for some time, to take charge of the Medical Department of the Contrabands at LaGrange, and afterwards at Corinth. Has been constantly with his Regiment since the 1st of September, 1863, having been relieved from his duties in Corinth at that time.

HENRY H. KLOCK, LIEUTENANT AND ADJUTANT.

Was born in Manheim, Herkimer County, New York, November 27th, 1835. Received a common school education. Removed to Illinois in 1854. Was engaged in teaching public school in Madison

County, Illinois, when he enlisted. Enlisted in the 9th Illinois Infantry, Company F, and was mustered in as a private, July 28th, 1861. Was detailed as Clerk in the Adjutant's office, from September 1861. Was commissioned as 1st Lieutenant and Adjutant January 31st, 1862, to rank from October 3d, 1861. Has been with the Regiment through most of its battles. Was wounded at Shiloh and Corinth. Is still acting as Adjutant for the Regiment, and is devoted to the duties of his office.

CHARLES A. SPATEE, REGIMENTAL QUARTERMASTER.

Was born in the Dukedom of Saxony, Altenburg, in the year 1836. He was trained for the profession of Architect. He emigrated to the United States in 1855. After his arrival in this country, he was engaged principally in working upon Railroads and Saw Mills, previous to his entering the service of his adopted country. He enlisted in the "Three months' service," as a private in the 10th Regiment Illinois Volunteer Infantry. He re-enlisted, for three years, as a private in the 9th Regiment Volunteer Infantry, Company K. He was afterwards promoted to the position of a Sergeant. In December, 1861, he was appointed Commissary Sergeant. He was commissioned as 1st Lieutenant and Regimental Quartermaster, October 4th, 1863. He continues to occupy this position at the present time. Lieutenant Spatee was not in the military service in the old country.

MARION MORRISON, CHAPLAIN.

Was born in Adams County, Ohio, June 2d, 1821. He was trained as a farmer, receiving a common school education. In the Spring of 1841, he commenced the study of Latin, preparatory to the ministry. In October, 1842, he entered the Freshman class in Miami University, Oxford, Ohio, and graduated August, 1846. He studied Theology, at the A. R. Presbyterian Theological Seminary, Oxford, Ohio, and was licensed to preach, by the A. R. Presbyterian Presbytery of Chillicothe, Ohio, in the Spring of 1849. He was ordained and installed Pastor of the A. R. Presbyterian Congregation of West Fork, Adams County, Ohio, in the Spring of 1850. Was elected Professor of Mathematics and Natural Science in "Monmouth College," June, 1856. Resigned the charge of his Congregation, and removed to Monmouth, Illinois, in the Summer of 1856, and entered upon his duties as Professor, September of the same year. He had the financial charge of "The

Western United Presbyterian," published in Monmouth for several years. In June, 1861, he assumed the entire responsibility of that paper, financial and editorial, and soon after united it with "The Christian Instructor," published in Philadelphia. He continues an Associate Editor to the above paper. . In the Summer of 1861, he resigned his position as Professor in Monmouth College, and was engaged as Financial Agent of the College, until July 30th, 1863, when he was commissioned as "Captain of Cavalry, and Chaplain of the 9th Illinois Volunteer Infantry." Was mustered into the service, and entered upon the duties of Chaplain, September 4th, 1863. Has been with his Regiment ever since, except during January, 1864, when he was sent to Illinois on orders. Rejoined his Regiment February 1st, 1864.

EXCERPTS FROM THE
ADJUTANT GENERAL'S REPORT

REGIMENTAL ROSTER.

NINTH INFANTRY REGIMENT.

THREE YEARS' SERVICE.

FIELD AND STAFF.

Name and Rank.	Residence.	Date of rank or enlistment.	Date of muster.	Remarks.
Colonels.				
Eleazer A. Paine......	Mercer county..	July 26, 1861	July 26, 1861	Pro. Brig. Gen. Sept. 3, 1861
Augustus Mersy	Belleville.......	Sept. 3, 1861	Nov. 15, 1861	Mustered out Aug. 20, 1864.
Lieutenant Colonels.				
Augustus Mersy	Belleville.......	July 26, 1861	July 26, 1861	Promoted...................
Jesse J. Phillips	Hillsboro	Sept. 3, 1861	Nov. 14, 1861	Trans. as consolidated....
Majors.				
Jesse J. Phillips	Hillsboro	July 20, 1861	July 26, 1861	Promoted...................
John H. Kuhn.........	Alton	Sept. 3, 1861	Nov. 14, 1861	Mustered out Aug. 20, 1864.
Adjutants.				
Thomas J. Newsham.	Edwardsville ..	July 26, 1861	July 26, 1861	Pro. to Gen. Paine's staff.
Henry H. Klock.......	Alhambra	Oct. 3, 1861	Nov. 29, 1861	Mustered out Aug. 20, 1864.
Quartermasters.				
William G. Pinckard..	Edwardsville ..	Aug. 21, 1861	Sept. 5, 1861	Pro. Capt. and Ass't Q. M. Killed, Virginia, Feb.14,'64
Gustav Korn	Alton	June 30, 1862	....	Died May 6, 1863...........
Charles A. Spatee.....	....	May 6, 1863	Oct. 1, 1863	Mustered out Aug. 20, 1864.
Surgeons.				
Samuel M. Hamilton..	Monmouth......	July 26, 1861	July 26, 1861	Prom. Surgeon U.S.Vols.
Emil Gulich	Alton	Apr. 28, 1862	June 5, 1862	Mustered out Aug. 20, 1864.
First Ass't Surgeons.				
Emil Gulich	Alton	July 26, 1861	July 26, 1861	Promoted...................
William D. Craig......	Aledo	June 8, 1862	Aug. 12, 1862	Mustered out Aug. 20, 1864.
Second Ass't Surgeon.				
William A. Allen......	....	Jan. 15, 1863	May 12, 1863	Mustered out Aug. 20, 1864.
Chaplains.				
James J. Ferree.......	Waukegan......	July 26, 1861	....	Resigned Dec. 1, 1861 ......
Marion Morrison......	....	July 30, 1863	Sept. 4, 1863	Mustered out Aug. 20, 1864.

NON-COMMISSIONED STAFF.

Name and Rank.	Residence.	Date of rank or enlistment.	Date of muster.	Remarks.
Sergeant Majors.				
Phelps Paine..........				
Sidney B. Phillips	Hillsboro	Aug. 2, 1861	....	Died of wounds June 8, '62.
Francis Wagner.......	Fayetteville	Aug. 15, 1861	Aug. 15, 1861	See Sergt. Major Reg. as consolidated.............

Name and Rank.	Enrolled at.	Date of rank or enlistment.	Date of muster.	Remarks.
Quartermaster Sergts.				
Gustav Korn	Alton			Prom. Quartermaster
William J. Johnson		Aug. 6, 1861	Aug. 6, 1861	Mustered out Aug. 20, 1864.
Commissary Sergts.				
Eben M. Burgess				
Charles Spathe	Ullin	Sept. 5, 1861		Promoted Quartermaster.
Hospital Stewards.				
William Manchester				
Frederick Benkeman	St. Louis, Mo			Mustered out Aug. 20, 1864.
Principal Musicians.				
John Olinger		Aug. 14, 1861	Aug. 14, 1861	Mustered out Aug. 20, 1864.
Herman Wetter	Mascoutah	Aug. 8, 1862	Aug. 8, 1861	" "

COMPANY A.

Name and Rank.	Residence.	Date of rank or enlistment.	Date of muster.	Remarks.
Captains.				
John H. Kuhn	Alton	July 26, 1861	July 26, 1861	Pro. Major Sept. 3, 1862
Emil Adam	"	Sept. 3, 1861	Nov. 14, 1861	Mustered out Aug. 20, 1864
First Lieutenants.				
Emil Adam	Alton	July 26, 1861	July 26, 1861	Promoted
Ernest J. Weiyrick	"	Sept. 3, 1861		Resigned Dec. 24, 1861
George Ruhland	St. Louis, Mo	Dec. 25, 1861	Mar. 20, 1863	Mustered out Aug. 20, 1864.
Second Lieutenants.				
Ernest J. Weiyrick	Alton	Aug. 31, 1861		Promoted
Theodore Gottlob	"	Sept. 3, 1861	June 2, 1862	Mustered out Aug. 20, 1865.
First Sergeant,				
George Ruhland	St. Louis, Mo	July 28, 1861	July 28, 1861	Promoted 1st Lieutenant.
Sergeants.				
Theodore Gottlob	Alton	July 28, 1861	July 28, 1861	Promoted 2d Lieutenant.
Andreas Bustian	St. Louis, Mo	"	"	
Friederick Oberbick	Alton	"	"	Mustered out Aug. 20, 1864.
Gustav Korn	"	"	"	Pro. Q. M. Sergeant
Corporals.				
Anton Hund	Alton	July 28, 1861	July 28, 1861	Pro. Sergt. M. O. Aug. 20, '64
Anton Reiss	Belleville	"	"	Mustered out Aug. 20, 1864.
John Golbart	Alton	"	"	" "
Peter Schoppat	"	"	"	Killed at Shiloh. Apr. 6, '62
Adam Stachr	"	"	"	Died March 26, 1862
Henry Vetter	"	"	"	
Anton Schwertner	"	"	"	Pro. Serg. M. O. Aug. 20, '64
Joseph Braun	"	"	"	Killed al Shiloh, Apr. 6, '62
Musician.				
Henry Hill	Alton	Aug. 7, 1861	Aug. 7, 1861	Mustered out Aug. 20. 1864.
Privates.				
Andrae, George M	Cook county	July 28, 1861	July 28, 1861	Killed at Shiloh, Aug. 6, '62
Bauer, Henry	Alton	"	"	Mustered out Aug. 20, 1862.
Bremenkamp, Ferd	"	"	"	
Burmeister, Henry	"	"	"	
Benkeman, Frederick	St. Louis, Mo	"	"	Trans. as Hosp'l Steward.
Brenner, Henry	Alton	"	"	Re-enlisted as Veteran See Co. D, as consol.
Berger, John	"	"	"	Mustered out Aug. 20, 1864.
Bieber. John	Lincoln	"	"	M. O. as Serg't, Aug. 20, '64
Baechly, Theodore	Chicago	Aug. 1, 1861	Aug. 1, 1861	Pro. Lieut. 2d Ala.. C. T. Jan. 26, 1864.
Braun, Michael	Summerville	Aug. 16, 1861	Aug. 16, 1861	Trans. to Invalid Corps, Mar. 29, 1864
Bunze, William	Alton	Aug. 7, 1861	Aug. 7, 1861	See Co. D, as consolidated
Becker, Adam	Mascoutah			Mustered out Aug. 20, 1864.
Bauer, John	Alton	Aug. 30, 1861	Aug. 30, 1861	
Dammier, Christian	Edwardsville	July 28, 1861	July 28, 1861	Mustered out Aug. 20, 1864.
Duttenhofer, Jacob	Mascoutah	Aug. 7, 1861	Aug. 7, 1861	" "

Name and Rank.	Enrolled at.	Date of rank or enlistment.	Date of muster.	Remarks.
Deitz, Louis..........	Mascoutah......	Aug. 7,1861	Aug. 7,1861	Mustered out Aug. 20,1864.
Ellmer, Friedrich.....	Belleville.......	"	"	Died June 10, 1862. in Hospital at Quincy...........
Fries, Erasmus........	Mascoutah	July 28,1861	July 28,1861	Mustered out Aug. 20,1864.
Frank, Nicholas.......	Alton...........	"	"	
Frank, Charles........	Trenton	"	"	Mustered out Aug. 20,1864.
Frey, William	Mascoutah	Aug. 7,1861	Aug. 7,1861	"
Fisher, Andreas.......	Alton...........	Aug. 27,1861	Aug. 27,1861	....
Gilrich, Charles	"	July 28,1861	July 28,1861	Killed at Corinth, Miss., Oct. 4, 1862..............
Gaulocher, Anton	Lincoln.........	Aug. 7,1861	Aug. 7,1861	....
Glenk, Henry..........	St. Louis, Mo...	Aug. 27,1861	Aug. 27,1861	Killed at Shiloh Apr. 6,'62.
Haber, Jacob	Alton...........	July 28,1861	July 28,1861	Mustered out Aug. 20,1864.
Haas, Ferdinand......	St. Louis, Mo...	"	"	....
Hall, William.........	Alton...........	"	"	....
Hertweek, Michael....	"	"	"	Trans. to Invalid Corps, March 29, 1864 ....
Harter, Bernhard	"	"	"	Mustered out Aug. 20,1864.
Horn, Henry..........	"	"	"	"
Habman, John	Milwaukee, Wis	"	"	Discharged July 21, 1862...
Herrman, Charles.....	St. Louis, Mo...	Aug. 27,1861	Aug. 27,1861	....
Herrman, William	"	"	"	Killed at Shiloh Apr. 6,'62.
Harris, Charles	Jerseyville	Sept. 6,1861	Sept. 6,1861	See Co. D, as consolidated.
Janke, Henry.........	Alton...........	July 28,1861	July 28,1861	Mustered out Aug. 20,1864.
Jebe, Thomas	Lincoln.........	"	"	Deserted Feb. 21, 1862...
Kahl, Frank	Belleville.......	"	"	Mustered out Aug. 20,1864.
Klein, Christian......	Fayetteville	Aug. 7,1861	Aug. 7,1861	"
Koch, Friedrich.......	Alton...........	Sept. 1 1861	Sept. 1,1861	Re-enlisted as Vet. See Co. D, as consolidated...
Kortkamp, William ...	"	"	"	
Linsig, Gottlieb.......	"	July 28,1861	July 28,1861	Died Nov. 5,'62, at St. Louis
Luehr, James H	"	"	"	
Lauber, Ambrois......	Lincoln.........	"	"	Killed at Shiloh Apr. 6,'62.
Miller, Charles........	Alton...........	"	"	Disch. Oct., 1862; wounds.
Mangels, Peter........	"	"	"	Mustered out Aug. 20,1864.
Miller, Henry.........	Moro	"	"	Re-enlisted as Vet. See Co. D, as consolidated...
Meyer, August	Chicago	"	"	Mustered out Aug. 20,1864.
Nicholas, Jacob	St. Louis, Mo...	"	"	Re-enlisted as Vet. See Co. D, as consolidated...
Ott, Andreas	Alton	"	"	Mustered out Aug. 20,1864.
Renandin, Piere.......	Belleville......	"	"	" "
Rebuss, John..........	"	"	"	" "
Schuchman, Andreas.	St. Louis, Mo...	"	"	" "
Schoppet, John........	Alton...........	"	"	" "
Schaefer, George......	"	"	"	
Schuch, Paul	"	"	"	....
Schaefer, Conrad.....	St. Cloud, Minn.	"	"	
Scharff, Ephraim	Edwardsville ..	"	"	Disch July 21,'62; disabil..
Schmid, John.........	St. Louis, Mo...	"	"	Mustered out Aug. 20,1864.
Scherrer, Friedrich...	Mascoutah	"	"	Died April 16, 1864.........
Seibert, Charles.......	St. Louis, Mo...	"	"	Re-enlisted as Vet. See Co. D, as consolidated...
Schmid, Christian.....	Madison co.....	"	"	Trans. Jan. 14, 1864, by G. O. 21, A. G. O.
Wolter, William.......	Belleville.......	"	"	Mustered out Aug. 20,1864.
Wehrli, Jacob	Alton...........	"	"	"
Weis, Martin	"	"	"	
Weiler, George	Madison co.....	"	"	Mustered out Aug. 20,1864.
Weber, John..........	St. Louis, Mo...	"	"	"
Recruits.				
Brakebusch, Henry...	Alton...........	Feb. 6,1864	Feb. 6,1864	See Co. D, as consolidated
Bullion, John..........	Fosterburg	Feb. 3,1864		" "
Crain, George W	....	Apr. 15,1862	Nov. 5,1862	" "
Elliott, William D	....	"	"	" "
Ekols, Thomas........	....	"	"	" "
Felts, William........		"	"	" "
Hess, John	Alton...........	Mar. 18,1864	Mar. 18,1864	" "
Hill, John A	Belleville.......	Aug. 15,1862	Nov. 5,1862	" "
Hartwell, John L.....		"	"	" "
Hunter, William B	....	Aug. 1,1862	Nov. 4,1862	See Co. F, as consolidated
Jargner, August	Fosterburg	Feb. 3,1864	Feb. 3,1864	See Co. D, as consolidated
Jackson, Josiah	....	Aug. 15,1862	Nov. 5,1862	" "
Lemaster, James		"	"	" "
Lemaster, William C..		"	"	" "
Meyer, Jacob	Alton..........	May 29,1862	May 29,1862	Died Aug. 24,'62, at Corinth
Miller, Friedrich......	Mascoutah	Aug. 7,1862	Aug. 7,1862	Mustered out Aug. 20,1864.
Morgenstern, William.	Belleville.......	Jan. 17,1864	Apr. 16,1864	See Co. D, as consolidated
Mitz, Henry	Shipman	Jan. 22,1864	Jan. 22,1864	" "

Name and Rank.	Residence.	Date of rank or enlistment.	Date of muster.	Remarks.
Moore, James..........	....	Aug. 15, 1862	Nov. 5, 1862	See Co. D, as consolidated
Moore, John S	....	"	"	" "
McAnally, Mathias....	....	"	"	" "
O'Daniel, James H....	....			
Quast, John M........	Alton	Sept. 6, 1862	Sept. 6, 1862	Disch. Oct. 19, '62; disabil.
Rose, Christian........	"	Aug. 10, 1862	Aug. 10, 1862	Vet. See Co. D, as consol.
Ribke, Charles	Fayetteville	Sept. 10, 1862	Sept. 10, 1862	....
Rector, George W	....	Aug. 15, 1862	Nov. 5, 1862	See Co. D, as consolidated
Rusehing, Hugh.......	....			
Sosal, August	Alton	Aug. 10, 1861	Aug. 10, 1861	Mustered out Aug. 20, 1864.
Schalter, Adam........	Lebanon.........	Aug. 7, 1861	Aug. 7, 1861	" "
Straubinger, Benedict	Fayetteville			
Stahl, William.........	St. Louis, Mo...	"	"	
Sultan, Henry	"	Aug. 27, 1861	Aug. 27, 1861	Deserted June 22, 1862.....
Slater, William H	....	Aug. 15, 1862	Nov. 5, 1862	See Co. D, as consolidated
Stroutt, William.......	....	"	"	
Thoma, Stephen.......	Alton	Aug. 12, 1861	Aug. 12, 1861	Mustered out Aug. 20, 1864.
Vanburg, Nicholas....	Belleville.......	Aug. 14, 1861	Aug. 14, 1861	....
Valentine, Louis	Mascoutah......	Jan. 26, 1864	Jan. 26, 1864	See Co. D, as consolidated
Winter, George.......	"	Aug. 7, 1861	Aug. 7, 1861	Mustered out Aug. 20, 1864.
Weber, Benedict	Fosterberg	Feb. 3, 1864	Feb. 3, 1864	See Co. D, as consolidated
Woolsey, Singleton ...	....	Aug. 15, 1862	Nov. 4, 1862	See Co. B, as consolidated
Zercher, Wendel	Mascoutah......	Aug. 7, 1861	Aug. 7, 1861	Mustered out Aug. 20, 1864.
Under Cooks.				
Husten, F.............	....	Dec. 10, 1863	Jan. 24, 1864	Deserted May 1, 1864, at Decatur, Ala................
Kimbell, Pleasant	....	"	"	See Co. D, as consolidated
Polk, James..........	....	Dec. 7, 1863	"	" "
Sour, Allex	....	Dec. 18, 1863	"	" "

COMPANY B.

Name and Rank.	Residence.	Date of rank or hn-listment.	Date of muster.	Remarks.
Captains.				
William C. Kueffner..	St. Louis, Mo...	July 26, 1861	July 28, 1861	Resigned Nov.1,'63. Transferred to Inv. Corps.....
John Mallman........	Summerfield ...	Aug. 25, 1863	Oct. 2, 1863	Mustered out Aug. 20, 1864.
First Lieutenants.				
Hamilton Lieber......	Lebanon........	July 26, 1861	July 28, 1861	Resigned May 4, 1862.......
Louis Grieser	Belleville.......	Aug. 25, 1863	Oct. 2, 1863	Mustered out Aug. 20, 1864.
Second Lieutenants.				
Frederick E. Vogeler.	Belleville.......	July 26, 1861	July 28, 1861	Killed in battle Apr. 6, 1862
John Mallman.........	Summerfield ...	Apr. 7, 1862	June 2, 1862	Promoted...................
Louis Fischer	Belleville.......	Aug. 25, 1863	Mar. 6, 1864	Mustered out Aug. 20, 1864.
Sergeants.				
John Mallman........	Summerfield ...	July 28, 1861	July 28, 1861	Promoted 2d Lieutenant ..
Julius Hofmann	Belleville.......	"	"	Mustered out Aug. 20, 1864.
Louis Grieser	"	"	"	Promoted 1st Lieutenant..
Albert Heinecke	Lebanon........	"	"	Killed at Shiloh Apr. 6, '62.
John Schmidt	Summerfield ...	"	"	" "
Corporals.				
Louis Fisher	Belleville.......	July 28, 1861	July 28, 1861	Promoted 2d Lieutenant ..
Frank Zugenbuehler..	St. Clair co	"	"	Kil'd Ft. D'n'ls'n Feb. 15, 62
John Eichenberger ...	Lebanon........	"	"	Mustered out Aug. 20, 1864.
Lorenz Ackermann ...	Baden Baden...	"	"	Died of wounds, Apr. 15, '62
Augustus Wurmb.....	Belleville.......	"	"	Discharged Dec. 5, 1862 ....
Paul Martin	"	"	"	Mustered out Aug. 20, 1864.
Privates.				
Ackermann, George...	Belleville.......	July 28, 1861	July 28, 1861	Mustered out Aug. 20, 1864
Alde, Adolph	"	"	"	Died of wounds, May 4, '62.
Aman, Joseph	Summerfield ...	"	"	Mustered out Aug. 20, 1864.
Arnold, Mathias.......	O'Fallon........	"	"	Died of wounds, May 4, '62.
Baumann, Morand	French Village.	"	"	Disch. Sept. 23, 1862: w'nds
Bausham, Paul	Belleville.......	"	"	Mustered out Aug. 20, 1864.
Bauer, Jacob..........	Mascoutah......	"	"	" "
Bauer, Peter..........	"	"	"	Died of wounds, May 4, '62.
Betz, George..........	Belleville.......	"	"	....

Name and Rank.	Residence.	Date of rank or enlistment.	Date of muster.	Remarks.
Binkert, Martin	Belleville........	July 28, 1861	July 28, 1861	Wounded and missing. Feb. 15, 1862.
Crapp, Joseph.........	''	''	''	Kil'd at Corinth Oct. 4, '62.
Dittmar, Edward	Mascoutah	''	''	Killed at Shiloh Apr. 6, '62.
Danner, Albert.........		''	''	
Entz, Frederic	Belleville........	July 25, 1861	''	Disch. Jan. 28, '63; disabil.
Fath, Michael	Mascoutah	July 28, 1861	''	Died of wounds May 1, '62.
Gantner, Joseph	Highland	''	''	
Gannermann, Henry..	Belleville........	''	''	Killed at Fort Donelson Feb. 15, 1862................
Gribbling, John.......	''	''	''	
Jansen, Gerhard	''	''	''	Mustered out Aug. 20, 1864.
Koch, Christian.......	Lebanon........	''	''	Killed at Fort Donelson Feb. 15, 1862...............
Krieger, John	Belleville........	''	''	Disch. July 21, '62; wounds
Lauth, Charles.......	''	''	''	Mustered out Aug. 20, 1864.
Leopold, Augustus....		''	''	Died of wounds received at Shiloh ....
Lobe, Charles	''	''	''	Mustered out Aug. 20, 1864.
Maul, Conrad..........	Summerfield ...	''	''	Killed at Shiloh Apr. 6, '62.
Menne, Frederic	Mascoutah	''	''	Mustered out Aug. 20, 1862.
Menne, Jaynaz		''	''	Deserted ....
Mesh, John.............	Belleville........	''	''	Killed at Shiloh Apr. 6, '62.
Messerschmidt, Louis	Lebanon........	''	''	Died of wounds Mar. 19, '62
Newmann, Albert.....	''	''	''	Killed at Fort Donelson Feb. 15, 1862...............
Nalltner, Joseph......	Summerfield....	''	''	
Otto, Frank	Lebanon	''	''	Mustered out Aug. 20, 1864.
Pfister, Sebastian	Belleville........	''	''	Died of wounds Apr. 11, '62
Raffel, John	O'Fallon........	''	''	Disch. Sept. 30, '62; wounds
Reppel, Peter	''	''	''	Disch. Mar. 13, '62; wounds
Rudel, Fred George...	Centreville.....	''	''	Mustered out Aug. 20, 1864.
Salz, George	Mascoutah	''	''	'' ''
Schwab, John	Highland	''	''	
Schleffier, Frank.....	Lebanon	''	''	Missing at Shiloh Apr. 6, '62
Schellinger, Simon ...	''	''	''	Deserted ....
Schmidt, Henry.......	Summerfield ...	''	''	Died Oct. 26, 1862 ....
Schneider, Henry.....	Belleville........	''	''	
Schulz, Joseph........	Lebanon	''	''	Mustered out Aug. 20, 1864.
Schwarcopf, Anton ...		''	''	
Sensel, Frederic	Belleville........	''	''	'' ''
Spiess, Jacob..........	''	''	''	'' ''
Sulzer, Jacob..........		''	''	Killed at Corinth Oct. 3, '62
Sutter, Benedict......	Lebanon	''	''	
Taubert, Zacharias ...	Athens.........	''	''	Mustered out Aug. 20, 1864.
Werner, Daniel	Centreville.....	''	''	
Wienstrath, Anton....	Mascoutah	''	''	'' ''
Wisshack, Ferdinand.	Lebanon	''	''	'' ''
Zech, Michael.........	Belleville........	''	''	Killed at Fort Donelson Feb. 15, 1862...............
Recruits—Musicians.				
Hermann Wetter......	Mascoutah	Aug. 8, 1861	Aug. 31, 1861	Trans. to non. com. staff..
Henry Hill	St. Louis	Aug. 7, 1861	Aug. 7, 1861	Trans. from Co. A..........
Privates.				
Adam, Christopher ...	Summerfield ...	Jan. 14, 1864	Mar. 26, 1864	See Co. D, as consolidated
Alexander, William B		Aug. 1, 1862	Nov. 5, 1862	'' ''
Berger, John..........	Summerfield ...	Aug. 8, 1861	Aug. 31, 1861	Mustered out Aug. 20, 1864.
Blank, Gustav........	Lebanon	''	''	'' ''
Burkhardt, David	Belleville........	''	''	'' ''
Bitterwolf, John	Mascoutah	Aug. 15, 1861	''	
Crain, Francis........		Aug. 1, 1862	Nov. 5, 1862	See Co. D, as consolidated
Dachnert, Charles	Belleville........	Aug. 8, 1861	Aug. 31, 1861	Mustered out Aug. 20, 1864.
Dettweiler, John......	Summerfield ...	''	''	Killed at Fort Donelson Feb. 15, 1892...............
Darrow, Joseph		Aug. 1, 1862	Nov. 5, 1862	See Co. D, as consolidated
Eirkuss, Christian....	Belleville........	Aug. 4, 1861	Aug. 31, 1861	Mustered out Aug. 20, 1864.
Eirkuss, Jacob........		Aug. 8, 1861	''	Killed at Fort Donelson Feb. 15, 1862...............
Fisher, Philip	Lebanon	Aug. 10, 1861	''	Mustered out Aug. 20, 1864.
Geist, Paul	Belleville........	Aug. 8, 1861	''	
Gerig, Arnold	Summerfield ...	''	''	Deserted ....
Grin, Charles..........	Mascoutah	''	''	Mustered out Aug. 20, 1864.
Haas, Michael.........	Belleville........	''	''	'' ''
Harttman, Charles....		''	''	
Hellmuth, Conrad	Lebanon	''	''	Deserted May 13, 1862 ......
Herwig, Henry........	Belleville........	''	''	Killed at Fort Donelson Feb. 15, 1862...............
Hoffman, Edward.....	Mascoutah	''	''	Mustered out Aug. 20, 1864.
Hofmeister, John P...	Highland	Aug. 7, 1861	''	

Name and Rank.	Residence.	Date of rank or enlistment.	Date of muster.	Remarks.
Hays, Henry		Aug. 15, 1862	Nov. 5, 1862	See Co. D, as consolidated
Howerton, William P.		Aug. 1, 1862	"	"
Jenne, George	O'Fallon	Aug. 10, 1861	Aug. 31, 1861	
Jones, William		Aug. 1, 1862	Nov. 5, 1862	See Co. D, as consolidated
Kadel, Peter	Lebanon	Aug. 10, 1861	Aug. 31, 1861	Mustered out Aug. 20, 1864
Kadel, Valentine	"	Aug. 8, 1861	"	Sent to Inv.detach.May 6'63
Kinder, John	Belleville		"	Mustered out Aug. 20, 1864.
Kremer, Henry	Lebanon	Aug. 31, 1862	Oct. 31, 1862	See Co. D, as consolidated
Lindeman, Fred. Wm.	Belleville	Aug. 4, 1861	Aug. 31, 1861	Mustered out Aug. 20, 1864.
Linne, Louis		Aug. 8, 1861		
Luster, James		Aug. 15, 1862	Nov. 5, 1862	See Co. D, as consolidated
Leckinger, August		Jan. 15, 1864	Feb. 8, 1864	
Meyer, Nicholas	Belleville	Aug. 8, 1861	Aug. 31, 1861	Mustered out Aug. 20, 1864
Moser, Herman	Lebanon		"	"
McAnally, Isaac		Aug. 15, 1862	Nov. 5, 1862	See Co. D, as consolidated
Mennes, William S		Aug. 1, 1862	"	"
Obefell, Joseph	Lebanon	Aug. 8, 1861	Aug. 31, 1861	Disch. June 14, '62; wounds
O'Hare, John	Belleville	Aug. 26, 1862	Oct. 31, 1862	Died March 17, 1864.
Oemigen, Fred. Wm.	"	Aug. 30, 1862	"	See Co. D, as consolidated
Pohn, Simon	"	Aug. 8, 1861	Aug. 31, 1861	Mustered out Aug. 20, 1864
Rust, John	"			
Raney, Thomas R		Aug. 1, 1862	Nov. 5, 1862	See Co. D, as consolidated
Rodgers, William				
Schlatt, William	Belleville	Aug. 8, 1861	Aug. 31, 1861	Mustered out Aug. 20, 1864
Spiess, Phillip	"			Died M'y 3, '62; w'ds, Shiloh
Suemnicht, Herman	"		"	Disch. June 25, '62; wounds
Smith, Rolly		Aug. 15, 1862	Nov. 5, 1862	See Co. D, as consolidated
Seiler, John	Belleville	Jan. 16, 1864	Feb. 8, 1864	" "
Sutter, Benedict	Summerfield	Jan. 14, 1864		" "
Sanders, Isaac		Aug. 15, 1862	Nov. 5, 1862	" "
Schmid, James J		Aug. 1, 1861	"	" "
Smith, Thomas B			"	" "
Spring, Moses			"	" "
Smith, G. H			"	" "
Thomas, Joseph			"	" "
Thomas, Joshua			"	" "
Vantres, Grierson			"	" "
Weber, Henry	Mascoutah	Aug. 8, 1861	Aug. 31, 1861	Killed at Shiloh Ap. 6, 1862.
Wickerman, Christian	Belleville			Mustered out Aug. 20, 1864
Wright, Charles	"	Aug. 26, 1862	Oct. 31, 1862	See Co. D, as consolidated
Will, Michael	"	Jan. 14, 1864	Feb. 8, 1864	" "
Walker, George		Aug. 1, 1862	Nov. 5, 1862	" "
Walker, Seiles			"	" "
William, Alexander				
Under Cooks.				
Townsend, Dick		Dec. 18, 1863	Jan. 24, 1864	See Co. D, as consolidated
Carr, David		"	"	" "
Dixon, Berry		"	"	" "
Drake, Jake		"	"	" "

COMPANY C.

Name and Rank.	Residence.	Date of rank or enlistment.	Date of muster.	Remarks.
Captain.				
Diedrich F. Tiedeman	O'Fallon Stati'n	July 26, 1861	July 28, 1861	Prom. Lieut. Col. 2d Ala. A. D. about Dec. 26, 1863.
First Lieutenants.				
Oscar Rollman	Peoria	July 26, 1861	July 28, 1861	Trans. to I. C. Nov. 17, 1863
George Bender	Belleville	Nov. 17, 1863	Nov. 14, 1863	Mustered out Aug. 20, 1864
Second Lieutenant.				
Charles Schÿve	Mascoutah	July 26, 1861	July 28, 1861	Resigned Aug. 7, 1863
Eugene A. Hanke	Summerfield	Aug. 7, 1863	Mar. 6, 1864	Mustered out Aug. 20, 1864
Sergeants				
Charles Hahle	Peoria	July 26, 1861	July 28, 1861	Killed at Shiloh Apr. 6, 1862
Eugene A. Hanke	Summerfield	"	"	Veteran. Pro. 2d Lieut.
John M. Salzman	Alton	"	"	Trans'd to Co. H June 11, '62
George Bender	Belleville	Aug. 21, 1861	Aug. 28, 1861	Promoted 1st Lieutenant.
William Langenberg	"	Aug. 10, 1861	"	Mustered out Aug. 20, 1864

Name and Rank.	Residence.	Date of rank or enlistment.	Date of muster.	Remarks.
Corpornls.				
Charles King..........	Cairo............	Aug. 1,1861	Aug. 28,1861	Mustered out Aug. 20, 1864
Joseph Schweitzer....	Lebanon	July 26,1861	July 28,1861	"
Charles Ehrlick.......	Mascoutah......	Aug. 10,1861	Aug. 28,1861	....
Henry Kiesel..........	Smithtown	July 26,1861	July 28,1861	....
Frederic Staal.........	Belleville	Aug. 15,1861	Aug. 28,1861	Discharged August 19,1862
George M. Luther.....	Lebanon	Aug. 9,1861	"	Killed at Shiloh Apr. 6,1862
Musicians.				
Frank Baumer	Lebanon	July 26,1861	July 28,1861	Mustered out Aug. 20, 1864
George Harris.........	Jonesboro	Sept. 18,1861	Sept. 18,1861	Transferred to Co. F ......
Edward Stephen......	Bridgeport	Aug. 17,1861	Aug. 28,1861	Mustered out Aug. 20, 1864
Privates.				
Aderhals, Godfrey	Bridgeport	Aug. 18,1861	Aug. 28,1861	Died Nov. 18,1861..........
Arndt, Henry..........	Mascoutah......	Aug. 7,1861	"	Died of wounds Mar. 2,'62.
Avainus. Adelbert	Chicago.........	July 26,1861	July 28,1861	Died of wounds June 20,'62
Baumann, Leonard....	Cairo............	Aug. 9,1861	Aug. 28,1861	Disch. Apr. 4,'62; disabil..
Becker, Anthony	Mascoutah......	Aug. 15,1861		Disch. Aug. 15,'62; wounds
Behm, Henry	Georgetown	Aug. 18,1861	"	
Bence, Andrew	Fayetteville	"	"	Disch. Aug. 2,'62; arm off.
Boersig, Laurence.....	Summerfield ...	"	"	Killed, Donelson, Feb.15,'62
Bruening, William	Bridgeport	"	"	Died October 1, 1861......
Bub, Michael	Mascoutah......	Aug. 7,1861	"	Mustered out Aug. 20, 1864
Clementz, Phillip......	....			
Den, Adam.............	Cairo...........	July 26,1861	July 28,1861	Deserted February 28, 1862
Eilts, Menson.........	Fayetteville....	Aug. 18,1861	Aug. 28,1861	Mustered out Aug. 20, 1864
Engel, Jacob...........	Olney	July 26,1861	July 28,1861	Missing in action Feb.15,'62
Erb, Joseph...........	Belleville	Aug. 18,1861	Aug. 28, 1861	See Co. F, as consolidated.
Erbar, George	Bridgeport	"	"	Mustered out Aug. 20, 1864
Erbe, Phillip..........	Fayetteville ...	"	Aug. 31,1861	Disch. July 24, 1862, at St. Louis, Mo., acc't shot.....
Erbe, Conrad	"	"	"	Disch. June 23,'62; disabil.
Fisher, Michael N	Jonesboro	Sept. 27,1861	Sept. 27,1861	Transferred to Co. F ......
Fichter, George	Belleville	Aug. 15,1861	Aug. 28,1861	Disch. July 21,'62; wounds
Fray, John A	Bridgeport	Aug. 18,1861		
Friedrich, Charles	Cairo............	Aug. 29,1861	Aug. 29,1861	Disch. Aug. 23,'62; wounds
Guebe, William.........	Fayetteville	Aug. 18,1861	Aug. 28,1861	Disch. Aug. 15,'62; wounds
Graham, Louis	Carbondale ...	Sept. 27,1861	Sept. 27,1861	Transferred to Co. G......
Grauss, John	Cairo.........	Aug. 12,1861	Aug. 28,1861	
Haberkorn, Jacob	Mascoutah......	Aug. 7,1861	"	Disch. Aug. 15,'62; wounds
Hartmann, John.......	Belleville	Aug. 8,1861	"	Mustered out Aug. 20, 1864
Haeser, William.......	Fayetteville	Aug. 18,1861	"	Disch. June 18,'64; disabil.
Helfrich, Frank	"	"	"	Disch. Nov. 21,'62; wounds
Herbig, William.......	Bridgeport	"	"	Mustered out Aug. 20, 1864
Herpin, Jacob	Belleville	"	"	
Hillmann, Henry......	Fayetteville	Aug. 7,1861	"	Killed, Donelson, Feb.15, 62
Hugenburg, Frederick	Bridgeport	Aug. 18,1861	"	Died Oct. 12,1862; wounds.
Jacob, Christian	"	"	"	Mustered out Aug. 20, 1864
Keith, Christian	Summerfield ...	Aug. 7,1861	"	....
Klein, Christopher....	Mascoutah......	"	"	
Klingenberg, William.	Bridgeport	Aug. 18,1861	"	Killed at Shiloh Apr. 6,'62.
Knothe, Ottomar	Cairo............	July 26,1861	July 28,1861	
Lamburtus, Phillip ...	Fayetteville	Aug. 20,1861	Aug. 28,1861	Mustered out Aug. 20, 1864
Lamprecht, John......	Lebanon	Aug. 18,1861	"	Killed at Shiloh Apr. 6,'62.
Lehr, George	Bridgeport	"	"	" "
Lehr, Michael	Fayetteville	"	"	
Lippert, Frederic......	Bridgeport	"	"	" "
Maedel, Christian	Smithtown	"	"	....
Moses, Frank	Mascoutah......	Aug. 9,1861	"	
Mueller, Christian	Belleville	Aug. 7,1861	"	Died April 10,1862..........
Mueller, John.........	Bridgeport	Aug. 15,1861	"	
Miller, William.......	"	Aug. 7,1861	"	Deserted since Aug. 18, '62
Nadler, Andreas.......	"	Aug. 18,1861	"	
Oberts, John...........	Jonesboro	Sept. 27,1861	Sept. 27,1861	Trans. to Co. K Dec. 19, '61
Pietz, John	Mascoutah......	Aug. 18,1861	Aug. 28,1861	
Raehm, Thomas........	Olney	July 26,1861	July 28,1861	Died of disease Jan. 25,'64
Randall, Stephen......	Bridgeport	Aug. 18,1861	Aug. 28,1861	Died August 6,1862..........
Randall. Jacob.........	"	"	"	
Rauch, Thomas........	Peoria	July 30,1861	July 30,1861	Disch. Apr. 14,'62; disabil.
Rehfuss, Ludwig......	Fayetteville	Aug. 18,1861	Aug. 28,1861	Mustered out Aug. 20, 1864
Resch, Adam	Mascoutah......	Aug. 15,1861	"	Disch. Oct. 2,'62; wounds.
Richter, Henry	Bridgeport.....	Aug. 18,1861	"	Killed at Shiloh Apr. 6,'62.
Riedell, John	Smithtown	Aug. 28,1861	"	
Roehrwiem, William..	Bridgeport	Aug. 18,1861	"	Mustered out Aug. 20, 1864
Seibert, Anthony......	Fayetteville ...	"	"	
Summons, Adam	Carbondale	Sept. 27,1861	Sept. 27,1861	Deserted Aug. 18, 1862 .....
Sepafermeyer, Frank..	Fayetteville	Aug. 18,1861	Aug. 28,1861	Mustered out Aug. 20, 1864
Schenck, Charles......	Bridgeport	"	"	

Name and Rank.	Residence.	Date of rank of enlistment.	Date of muster.	Remarks.
Schenck, Christian....	Lebanon........	Aug. 10, 1861	Aug. 28, 1861	Killed at Shiloh Apr. 6, '62.
Schemph, Henry......	Mascoutah	Aug. 20, 1861	"	Mustered out Aug. 20, 1864.
Scheve, Frederic......	....	Aug. 17, 1861	"	.....
Schneider. Christian..	Fayetteville. ...	July 26, 1861	July 28, 1861	Died May 10, 1862.........
Schneider, Peter......	"	Aug. 18, 1861	Aug. 28, 1861	Mustered out Aug.20, 1864.
Schmitt, Henry........	Summerfield ...	Aug. 20, 1861	"	Died Nov. 2, 1862..........
Schouller. Nicholas...	Trenton	Aug. 15, 1861	"	Mustered out Aug. 20, 1864.
Spohnie, John.........	Bridgeport	Aug. 18, 1861		....
Stone, William........	Jonesboro	Sept. 27, 1861	Sept. 27, 1861	Died Dec. 7, 1861..........
Storch, William.......	Cairo........	July 28, 1861	July 28, 1861	Killed at Shiloh Apr 6, '62.
Striegel, William......	Trenton	Aug. 14, 1861	Aug. 28, 1861	Mustered out Aug. 20, 1864.
Tongeman, John......	Bridgeport	Aug. 18, 1861	"	Killed at Corinth Oct. 3, '62.
Theobald, Jacob	Shiloh	Aug. 7, 1861	"	Mustered out Aug. 20, 1864.
Uehli, Henry..........	Mascoutah	Aug. 10, 1861	"	....
Veidt, Conrad.........	....	Aug. 18, 1861	"	Died Feb. 13, 1862..........
Vogt, William........	Trenton	Aug. 15, 1861	"	Disch. Aug. 15.'62; wounds
Weber, Alvis...........	Olney...........	July 26, 1861	July 28, 1861	Mustered out Aug. 20, 1864.
Weis, Peter...........	Cairo...........	Aug. 6, 1861	Aug. 28, 1861	"
Wichard, Augustus...	Mascoutah	Aug. 18, 1861	"	Killed at Shiloh Apr. 6, '62.
Heifrick, John A......	Fayetteville	"	"	Mustered out Aug. 20, 1862.
Recruits.				
Abney, Paul..........		Aug. 1, 1862	Nov. 4, 1862	See Co. F, as consolidated.
Amand, William......	Lebanon........	Dec. 16, 1862	Feb. 28, 1863	See Co. D, as consolidated.
Alleson, William......		Aug. 1, 1862	Nov. 5, 1862	Died Dec. 16, 1864 on Stm'r Nor. Light................
Birdwell, John H......		Aug. 20, 1862	"	See Co. F, as consolidated.
Bauer, George	Belleville.......	Jan. 15, 1864	June 8, 1864	See Co. D, as consolidated.
Becker, Ferdinand....		Apr. 8, 1864	....	"
Carter, Sylvester......		Aug. 1, 1862	Nov. 4, 1862	See Co. F, as consolidated.
Clayton, George.......				
Dauritz, W. G.........		Aug. 11, 1862	Nov. 5, 1862	See Co. C. as consolidated.
Eaton, William		Aug. 1, 1862	Nov. 4, 1862	See Co. F, as consolidated.
Evans, James..........		Aug. 15, 1862	Nov. 5, 1862	See Co. D, as consolidated.
Flannigan, Richard...		Aug. 1, 1862	Nov. 4, 1862	See Co. F. as consolidated.
Forbs, David........		"	"	" "
Forbs, Madison M....		"	"	" "
Geiger, George........	Lebanon........	Aug. 16, 1862	Oct. 2, 1862	See Co. C, as consolidated.
Gill, Hezekiah C......		Aug. 1, 1862	Nov. 5, 1862	See Co. F, as consolidated.
Ha l, William		Aug. 15, 1862	"	" "
Hazlewood, John......		Aug. 1, 1862	Nov. 4, 1862	" "
Hewlett, Martin R....			"	" "
Howell, Jasper.......		Aug. 15, 1862	"	" "
Hall, Joseph		Aug. 1, 1862	"	" "
Hunter, Joseph........			Nov. 5, 1862	See Co. D, as consolidated,
Jackson, Nathan......		Aug. 15, 1862	"	" "
Kramp, Frederick....		Oct. 2, 1862	Feb. 28, 1863	See Co. F, as consolidated.
Kasing, William......	Lebanon........	Jan. 9, 1863		" "
Kellar, Mathias........	Centreville	Feb. 8, 1864	Feb. 18, 1864	See Co. D, as consolidated.
Moak, Abraham.......	Bridge's Cor's.	Aug. 15, 1862	Nov. 5, 1862	See Co. C, as consolidated.
Manning, Henry.......		Aug. 1, 1861	Nov. 4, 1862	See Co. F, as consolidated.
McCabe, John.........		"	"	" "
Morris, William F....		"	"	" "
Newhouse, Augustus.	Alton	Feb. 3, 1864	Mar. 26, 1864	" "
Pitcock, Newton......		Aug. 15, 1862	Nov. 4, 1862	See Co. C, as consolidated.
Peterman, Benjamin..		Aug. 1, 1862	"	See Co. F, as consolidated.
Peterman, George....		"	"	" "
Peterman, William G.		"	"	" "
Potter, Isaiah.........		Aug. 15, 1862	"	" "
Potter, William.......			"	" "
Rumsey, George H....		Aug. 1, 1862	"	" "
Riley, Gully..........		Aug. 15, 1862	Nov. 5, 1862	See Co. D, as consolidated.
Reed, Nicholas........		Aug. 19, 1861	Aug. 19, 1861	" "
Schilli, Fridolin......	Lebanon........	Aug. 27, 1862	Aug. 27, 1862	" "
Sweet, Thomas.......		Aug. 15, 1862	Nov. 5, 1862	See Co. C, as consolidated.
Smith, George H......		Aug. 1, 1862	"	See Co. D, as consolidated.
Sanders, George R....		Aug. 15, 1862	"	" "
Sanders, Jacob.......		"	"	" "
Shadewing, David....				
Talbert, William......		Aug. 1, 1862	"	See Co. C, as consolidated.
Turnage, Rheuben....		Aug. 15, 1862	"	See Co. F, as consolidated.
Thalbert, Thomas		Aug. 1, 1862	"	See Co. D, as consolidated.
Vatter, George........	Mascoutah	Aug. 31, 1862	Aug. 31, 1862	Died, Andersonville pris., July 13. '64; grave 3271..
Watson, Joseph.......		Aug. 1, 1862	Nov. 4, 1862	See Co. F, as consolidated.
Additional Recruits.				
Cantrell, Thomas.....		....	....	Disch. Feb. 4, '64; disabil..
Dougherty, John L....				Disch. Dec. 15, '63; disabil..
Jadowance, A. D.....				Trans. from 128th Ill. Inf..
McGuire, Dempsey....				" "

Name and Rank.	Residence.	Date of rank or enlistment.	Date of muster.	Remarks.
Pembleton, William..				Deserted June 15, 1864......
Spring, Samuel H....				Died Feb. 21, 1864.........
Stone, Calvin.........				Trans. Inv. C'rps Feb. 15, '64
Tatford, W. C.........				Trans. from 128th Ill. Inf..
Under Cooks.				
Grixby, Burk..........		Dec. 18, 1863	Jan. 24, 1864	See Co. F, as consolidated
Murry, Martin.........		" "	" "	" " " "
Taylor, Jim...........		" "	" "	" " " "
Townsend, Joe		" "	" "	" " " "

COMPANY D.

Name and Rank.	Residence.	Date of rank or enlistment.	Date of muster.	Remarks.
Captains.				
Rudolphus Beckier...	Belleville.......	July 26, 1861	July 26, 1861	Resigned Dec. 3, 1862......
Edward Krebs	" "	Dec. 3, 1862	Sept. 16, 1863	Mustered out Aug. 20, 1864.
First Lieutenants.				
Edward Krebs	Belleville.......	Aug. 10, 1861	Aug. 31, 1861	Promoted.................
Henry Webber........	" "	Dec. 3, 1862	Sept. 16, 1863	Mustered out Aug. 20, 1864.
Second Lieutenants.				
William Bohlen......	Belleville.......	July 27, 1861	July 27, 1861	Resigned Jan. 30, 1862......
Frederick E. Scheel..	" "	Jan. 30, 1862		Resigned Apr. 24, 1863......
Wm. Mochlenbrock...	Red Bud........	Apr. 24, 1863	Mar. 6, 1864	Mustered out Aug. 14, 1861?
First Sergeant.				
Henry Webber........	Belleville.......	Aug. 10, 1861	Aug. 31, 1861	Promoted 1st Lieutenant..
Sergeants.				
Adolphus Cornelius..	Red Bud........	Aug. 10, 1861	Aug. 31, 1861	Died Nov. 19, 1861..........
Gottfried Guckes......	Centreville.....	Aug. 10, 1861	" "	Re-enlisted as Veteran....
Francis Baumen	Mud Creek	Aug. 10, 1861	" "	....
Wm. Mochlenbrock...	Red Bud........	Aug. 14, 1861	" "	Promoted 2d Lieutenant..
Corporals.				
Henry Goessel	Centreville.....	Aug. 15, 1861	Aug. 31, 1861	Died Apr. 18, '62; wounds..
Phillip Sauer..........	Red Bud........	Aug. 14, 1861	" "	Died May 2, '62; wounds..
Anton Wolf...........	" "	Aug. 10, 1861	" "	Mustered out Aug. 20, 1864.
Louis Truttman.......	" "	" "	" "	Died Oct. 5, '62; wounds...
Amos Smith...........	" "	" "	" "	Mustered out Aug. 20, 1864.
William Heuer........	Centreville.....	Aug. 14, 1861	" "	
Christian Rahn	" "	Aug. 15, 1861	" "	Killed at Shiloh Apr. 6, '62.
Adam Reitz............	Red Bud........	Aug. 14, 1861	" "	Died May 18, '62; wounds..
Musicians.				
Fred Brandenberger..	Red Bud........	Aug. 10, 1861	Aug. 31, 1861	Mustered out Aug. 20, 1864.
Peter Schneider.......	Fayetteville	Aug. 18, 1861	" "	" "
Privates.				
Alberter, Charles	Centreville.....	Aug. 15, 1861	Aug. 31, 1861	Mustered out Aug. 20, 1864.
Auffinger, Martin.....	" "	" "	" "	Died Oct. 1, 1862 ....
Bange, Hermann......	" "	" "	" "	Disch. Aug. 15, '62; wounds
Baquet, Isadore.......	Belleville.......	Aug. 10, 1861	" "	Disch. June 21, '62; wounds
Baeversen, William...	Red Bud........	" "	" "	
Baer, John............	Belleville.......	Mar. 4, 1862	Mar. 31, 1862	Disch. Aug. 27, '62; wounds
Baumgartner, Fred...	Mascoutah	Aug. 26, 1862	Aug. 31, 1862	See Co. F, as consolidated.
Becker, Jacob	Belleville.......	Aug. 10, 1861	Aug. 31, 1861	Killed at Shiloh Apr. 6, '62.
Bense, William.......	Red Bud........	" "	" "	Died May 11, 1862 ....
Berthold, Jacob	Fayetteville	Aug. 18, 1861	" "	Died Oct. 30, '62; wounds..
Bergamein, Balthisar.	Red Bud........	Aug. 10, 1861	" "	Died Mar. 4, 1862..........
Bertram, Henry.......	" "	" "	" "	Re-enlisted as Veteran....
Bitterwolf, John	St. Clair co. ...	Aug. 17, 1861	" "	Transferred to Co. B......
Boester, Frederick....	Fayetteville	Aug. 15, 1861	" "	Disch. Aug. 15, '62; wounds
Borcherding, Henry..	Red Bud........	Aug. 10, 1861	" "	Died Nov. 5, 1862..........
Buesemayer, Henry..	Centreville.....	Aug. 15, 1861	" "	Disch. Apr. 4, '62; disabil..
Caspari, Henry........	Belleville.......	Aug. 14, 1861	" "	Re-enlisted as Veteran....
Daesch, George........	Centreville.....	Aug. 15, 1861	" "	
Daerr, John	O'Fallon........	Aug. 18, 1861	" "	Mustered out Aug. 20, 1864.
Eisenhauser, Joseph.	Centreville.....	Aug. 15, 1861	" "	....
Euler, Jacob..........		Aug. 14, 1861	" "	Re-enlisted as Veteran....

Name and Rank.	Residence.	Date of rank or enlistment.	Date of muster.	Remarks.
Erb, Jacob.............	Fayetteville....	Aug. 15, 1861	Aug. 31, 1861	Mustered out Aug. 20, 1864.
Freund, John..........	Red Bud........	Aug. 10, 1861	" "	Re-enlisted as Veteran....
Fritz, John...........	Centreville	Aug. 18, 1861	" "	Disch. Aug. 19,'62: wounds
Funck, Francis.......	" "	Aug. 15, 1861	" "	
Fuchs, Charles........	" "	....	" "	Mustered out Aug. 20, 1864.
Garthoeffner, Anton..	Red Bud....	Aug. 10, 1861	" "	Re-enlisted as Veteran....
Goehring, Robert	....		" "	Mustered out Aug 20, 1864.
Gsell, Conrad.........	Centreville	Aug. 15, 1861	" "	Killed at Shiloh Apr. 6,'62.
Hauser, John.........	" "	....	" "	Re-enlisted as Veteran....
Havermann, Freder'k.	Red Bud....	Aug. 10, 1861	" "	
Heidman, John C......	Centreville	Aug. 15, 1861	" "	Disch. Dec. 6,'62; wounds.
Hesser, John	Red Bud........	Aug. 10, 1861	" "	Mustered out Aug. 20, 1864.
Hohrein, John........	O'Fallon.......	Aug. 18, 1861	" "	See Co. F, as consolidated
Hirtz, Theodore.......	Red Bud........	Aug. 14, 1861	" "	Mustered out Aug. 20, 1864.
Huber, Charles........	Centreville.....	Aug. 15, 1861	" "	
Hurst, Henry..........	Fayetteville....	Aug. 18, 1861	" "	Mustered out Aug. 20, 1864.
Jaeckel, Joseph	Red Bud........	Aug. 15, 1861	" "	" " " "
Kahn, Moses	Belleville.......	Aug. 10, 1861	" "	" " " "
Kleber, Louis.........	Centreville.....	Aug. 15, 1861	" "	" " " "
Kopp, Joseph.........	Red Bud........	Aug. 10, 1861	" "	
Koenigsmark, Joseph.	Centreville	Aug. 15, 1861	" "	
Lambe, Christian	" "	....	Aug. 18, 1861	" "	Re-enlisted as Veteran....
Lauth, Frederick.....	" "	....	Aug. 15, 1861	" "	....
Lieser, William	" "	....	" "	" "	Mustered out Aug. 20, 1864.
Litschge, John	" "	....	" "	" "	Killed at Shiloh Apr. 6,'62.
Loebig, Adam.........			" "	" "	See Co. F, as consolidated
Ludwig, Balthisar	Red Bud.......	Aug. 26, 1862	Aug. 31, 1862	
Lauth, Jacob	Centreville	Aug. 18, 1861	Aug. 31, 1861	
Metzker, George	" "	....	Aug. 15, 1861	" "	
Meyer, Henry..........	Mud Creek		" "	Died June 28, 1862.........
Melcher, Frederick....	Fayetteville	Aug. 18, 1861	" "	Mustered out Aug. 20, 1864.
Mittelbuescher, Wm..				
Moeninger, Charles...	Centreville.....	Aug. 15, 1861	" "	Disch. Sept. 30,'62; arm off
Moor, William.........	St. Louis, Mo...	Aug. 18, 1861	" "	Re-enlisted as Veteran....
Muth, Peter...........	Centreville	Aug. 15, 1861	" "	Deserted Sept. 2, 1862 ......
Olinger, John			" "	
Offerding, Philip......	Red Bud........	Aug. 10, 1861	" "	Mustered out Aug. 20, 1864.
Reitz, George W.......		Aug. 14, 1861	" "	
Riether, Charles	Belleville.......	Aug. 10, 1861	" "	See Co. F, as consolidated
Riess, Jacob...........	Centreville.....	Aug. 15, 1861	" "	Killed at Shiloh Apr. 6,'62.
Roth Raffy, Charles...	Athens	Sept. 8, 1861	Sept, 30, 1861	Disch. Oct. 13,'62; wounds.
Schellenberg, Albert..	Fayetteville	Aug. 15, 1861	Aug. 31, 1861	Missing in action Apr. 6, '62
Scheide, John	Mascoutah	Aug. 17, 1861	" "	Re-enlisted as Veteran....
Schulze, Frederick....	Edwardsville ..	Aug. 18, 1861	" "	Killed at Shiloh Apr. 6,'62.
Schulze, Henry........	" "		" "	See Co. F, as consolidated
Schmutz, Herman	Centreville	Aug. 15, 1861	" "	
Stocker, Oswald......	Mud Creek		" "	Disch. Dec. 6,'62; wounds.
Schueszler, George ...	Belleville.......	Aug. 23, 1861	" "	Discharged July 21, 1862...
Schneider, Louis......	Red Bud........	Aug. 15, 1861	" "	Mustered out Aug. 20, 1864.
Smith, John		Aug. 25, 1862	Aug. 31, 1862	
Stallbories, Henry ...	Mascoutah......	Aug. 23, 1862		
Seybold, Samuel	St. Clair co....	Nov. 1, 1861	Nov. 30, 1861	Transferred to Co. I........
Theiss, Mathias.......	Belleville.......	Aug. 8, 1861	Aug. 31, 1861	Mustered out Aug. 20, 1864.
Teuting, Christian....	Red Bud........	Aug. 14, 1861	" "	Killed at Corinth Oct. 4,'62
Vogel, Bernhard......	Mud Creek	Aug. 10, 1861	" "	Re-enlisted as Veteran....
Vogelpohl, William...	Fayetteville	Aug. 14, 1861	" "	Died May 18, 1862...........
Voss, Henry		Aug. 18, 1861	" "	Died April 25, 1862.........
Weiss, John	Centreville	Aug. 15, 1861	" "	Re-enlisted as Veteran....
Weber, William.......	Red Bud........	Aug. 25, 1862	Aug. 31, 1862	See Co. F, as consolidated
Wehling, Charles	" "	....			
Zweibarth, Henry....		Aug. 10, 1861	Aug. 31, 1861	Re-enlisted as Veteran....
Veterans.				
Bartram, Henry.......	Belleville.......	Mar. 26, 1864	Mar. 26, 1864	See Co. F, as consolidated
Caspari, Henry.......	" "	......	" "	" "	
Daesch, George.......			" "	" "	See Co. D, as consolidated
Euler, Jacob..........	Chicago		" "	" "	See Co. F, as consolidated
Freund, John.........	Belleville.......		" "	" "	
Guckes, Gottfried....			" "	" "	
Garthoeffner, Anton..	Chicago		" "	" "	" " " "
Hauser, John.........	Belleville.......		" "	" "	" " " "
Lambe, Christ........	" "	......	" "	" "	" " " "
Lauth, Frederick.....	" "	......	" "	" "	" " " "
Moor, William........	" "	......	" "	" "	" " " "
Scheide, John	" "	......	" "	" "	
Vogel, Bernhard	" "	......	" "	" "	See Co. D, as consolidated
Weiss, John...........	" "	......	" "	" "	See Co. F, as consolidated
Zweibarth, Henry.....	" "	......	" "	" "	

Name and Rank.	Residence.	Date of rank or enlistment.	Date of muster.	Remarks.
Recruits.				
Baldre, Richard......		Aug. 1, 1862	Nov. 4, 1862	See Co. F, as consolidated
Bauer, George.........		Jan. 15, 1864	Feb. 3, 1864	Name from monthly ret'rn
Becker, F.............		Apr. 8, 1864		"
Beck, Joseph	Carbondale.....	Sept. 15, 1861	Sept. 30, 1861	
Curlee, James W......	"	....		Disch. May 1,'62; wounds.
Deason, William M ...		Aug. 1, 1862	Nov. 4, 1862	See Co. F, as consolidated
Deason, James A......		"	"	"
Dunn, Henry..........		"	"	"
Doering, Charles......	Belleville.......	Nov. 4, 1861	Nov. 30, 1861	Died Sept. 13, 1862
Enoch, Leonard........		Aug. 15, 1862	Nov. 4, 1862	See Co. F, as consolidated
Enoch, John..........		Aug. 1, 1862		
Edwards, M. C........		July 28, 1861	July 28, 1861	Deserted Feb. 14, 1864......
Glenn, James........		Aug. 1, 1862	Nov. 4, 1862	See Co. F, as consolidated
Grissum, Thomas.....		Sept. 15, 1861	Sept. 30, 1861	
Gore, James..........	Carbondale.....			
Greathouse, James....	"	Aug. 1, 1862	Nov. 4, 1862	See Co. A, as consolidated
Hefflin, James				See Co. F, as consolidated
Henry, John..........		Sept. 15, 1861	Sept. 30, 1861	"
Hall, James..........	Carbondale.....	Aug. 1, 1862	Nov. 4, 1862	
Jordan, William H....		Feb. 7, 1864	Mar. 26, 1864	See Co. F, as consolidated
Knight, Thomas A	Anna...........	Aug. 15, 1861	Sept. 30, 1861	
Kaelberer, William ...	Carbondale.....	Aug. 1, 1862	Nov. 4, 1862	
Lovell, William		Sept. 8, 1861	Sept. 30, 1861	See Co. F, as consolidated
Miller, Charles W.....	O'Fallon........	Aug. 1, 1862	Nov. 4, 1862	"
McCabe, James........		"	"	"
Morris, Robert		"	"	"
Neighbors, John C....		"	"	"
Oden, John W........		"	"	"
Rice, Jeremiah M.....		Jan. 4, 1863	Feb. 1, 1863	"
Schlother, Jacob	Lebanon........	Aug. 23, 1862	Aug. 31, 1862	"
Stalbories, Henry.....	"	Aug. 1, 1862	Nov. 4, 1862	"
Stevens, Thomas......		"	"	"
Stevens, William.....		"	"	"
Thurston, James M...		"	"	"
Underwood, James....	Carbondale.....	Sept. 8, 1861	Sept. 30, 1861	See Co. F, as consolidated
Williamson, Cornelius		Aug. 1, 1862	Nov. 5, 1862	
Under Cooks.				
Dreak, Sam...........		Dec. 18, 1863	Jan. 24, 1864	See Co. F, as consolidated
Simpson, Jesse........		"	"	"
Scott, James........		"	"	"
Townsend, Abraham..		"	"	"

COMPANY E.

Name and Rank.	Residence.	Date of rank or enlistment	Date of muster.	Remarks.
Captain.				
Alexander G. Hawes..	Belleville.......	July 26, 1861	July 28, 1861	Mustered out Aug. 20, 1864.
First Lieutenants.				
William D. Craig......	Aledo	Aug. 6, 1861	Aug. 9, 1861	Promoted Asst. Surgeon..
Roswell B. Patterson.	Belleville.......	June 8. 1862	Oct. 18, 1862	Mustered out Aug. 20, 1864.
Second Lieutenants.				
Roswell B. Patterson.	Belleville.......	July 26, 1861	July 28, 1861	Promoted...................
Charles B. Fleming...	Keithsburg.....	July 8, 1862	Not muste'd	Canceled ....
Lewis C. Bornman....	Belleville.......	June 8, 1862	Dec. 8, 1862	Mustered out Aug. 20, 1864.
First Sergeant.				
Lewis L. Troy.........	Belleville.......	July 26, 1861	July 28, 1861	Re-enlisted as Veteran....
Sergeants.				
August's T.Waterbury	Aledo	Aug. 6, 1861	Aug. 9, 1861	Died, February 2, 1862......
Lewis C. Bornman....	Belleville.......	Aug. 10, 1861	Aug. 10. 1861	Pro. to Second Lieutenant
Henry R. Challenor...	"	July 26, 1861	July 28, 1861	Mustered out Aug. 20, 1864.
Thomas F. M'Clintock	Aledo	Aug. 6, 1861	Aug. 9, 1861	Re-enlisted as Veteran....
Corporals.				
Silas Bunker	Lebanon........	Aug. 10, 1861	Aug. 10. 1861	Killed at Shiloh Apr. 6,'62.
Charles B Fleming....	Keithsburg.....	Aug. 6, 1861	Aug. 9, 1861	Re-enlisted as Veteran....
Frederick Dilg	Mascoutah......	July 26, 1861	July 28, 1861	" "

Name and Rank.	Residence.	Date of rank or enlistment.	Date of muster.	Remarks.
John A. Gilmore	Aledo	Aug. 6, 1861	Aug. 9, 1861	Mustered out Aug. 20, 1864.
Phillip Anderson	Belleville	Aug. 5, 1861	Aug. 5, 1861	" "
James G. Carnahan	Aledo	Aug. 6, 1861	Aug. 9, 1861	
William G. Triplett	Freeburg	Aug. 5, 1861	Aug. 5, 1861	Re-enlisted as Veteran....
Joseph R. Cox	Oxford	Aug. 6, 1861	Aug. 9, 1861	" ....
Musicians.				
Samuel Williams	Belleville	July 28, 1861	July 28, 1861	Mustered out Aug. 20, 1864.
George W. Rose	"	Aug. 10, 1661	Aug. 10, 1861	Re-enlisted as Veteran....
Wagoner.				
William Minor	Sunbeam	Aug. 6, 1861	Aug. 9, 1861	Deserted. Enlisted afterwards, Co. G, 149th Ill....
Privates.				
Anson, John	Belleville	Aug. 10, 1861	Aug. 10, 1861	Killed at Shiloh, Apr. 6, '62.
Atkinson, Cassius C	Lebanon	Aug. 15, 1861	Aug. 15, 1861	Kil'dFt.Don'ls'n Feb.15, '62:
Beaty, John	Millersburg	Aug. 6, 1861	Aug. 9, 1861	
Blake, James M	Mascoutah	Aug. 10, 1861	Aug. 10, 1861	Disch. Nov. 3, '62; wounds.
Boyer, William	Sunbeam	Aug. 6, 1861	Aug. 9, 1861	Re-enlisted as Veteran....
Bragg, John A. J	Lebanon	Aug. 14, 1861	Aug. 14, 1861	Mustered out Aug. 20, 1864.
Bromley, Matthew	Mascoutah	Aug. 5, 1861	Aug. 5, 1861	Died May 12, '62; wounds..
Bruner, George	Monmouth	Aug. 6, 1861	Aug. 9, 1861	
Burnett, Robert	Belleville	July 26, 1861	July 28, 1861	Mustered out Aug. 20, 1864.
Case, Henry H	Lebanon	Aug. 14, 1861	Aug. 14, 1861	Died Sept. 15, 1861
Campbell, George H	"			
Chapman, William	Cairo	"	"	Deserted Aug. 11, 1862
Cady, John C	Mascoutah	"	"	Killed at Shiloh Apr. 6, '62.
Cool, Russell W	Aledo	Aug. 6, 1861	Aug. 9, 1861	Disch. June 18, '62; wounds
Dilley, Aaron S	"	"	"	Mustered out Aug. 20, 1864.
Dryden, Charles	Keithsburg			
Durham, David M	Centralia	Aug. 14, 1861	Aug. 14, 1861	Died Mar. 2, 1862; wounds.
Dyer, James	Cairo	Aug. 10, 1861	Aug. 10, 1861	Killed at Fort Donelson, Feb. 15, 1862
Evans, William	Keithsburg	Aug. 6, 1861	Aug. 9, 1861	Mustered out Aug. 20, 1864.
Farley, Michael	Amboy	July 31, 1861	July 31, 1861	
Fletcher, John	Freeburg	Aug. 21, 1861	Aug. 21, 1861	Discharged Jan. 8, 1863 ....
Frothingham, Den. C.	Sunbeam	Aug. 6, 1861	Aug. 9, 1861	Re-enlisted as Veteran....
Fulmar, John	Belleville	Aug. 7, 1861	Aug. 7, 1861	
Furlong, Michael	Mascoutah	Aug. 8, 1861	Aug. 8, 1861	Mustered out Aug. 20, 1864.
Gilmore, James B	Sunbeam	Aug. 6, 1861	Aug. 9, 1861	Re-enlisted as Veteran....
Graham, Elisha	"			
Guy, William M	Lebanon	Aug. 17, 1861	Aug. 17, 1861	Mustered out Aug. 20, 1864.
Guy, George W	"			Died May 3, 1862
Gwinn, James	Athens	July 26, 1861	July 28, 1861	Died Nov. 25, 1861
Hagar, Simon	Belleville			
Harryman, John	Elkhorn	Aug. 5, 1861	Aug. 5, 1861	
Haverfield, James	Millersburg	Aug. 6, 1861	Aug. 9, 1861	Died April 8, 1862
Hampton, John G	Centralia	Aug. 15, 1861	Aug. 15, 1861	
Hubbard, Daniel	Millersburg	Aug. 6, 1861	Aug. 9, 1861	Mustered out Aug. 29, 1864.
Hoy, John W	Sunbeam	"	"	Re-enlisted as Veteran....
Hughes, Edwin	Keithsburg	"	"	
Jackson, Obediah	Mascoutah	Aug. 2, 1861	Aug. 2, 1861	Died Dec. 18, 1861
Johnson, William J	Paris	Aug. 6, 1861	Aug. 9, 1861	
Jackson, Martin W	Freeburg	Aug. 5, 1861	Aug. 5, 1861	Re-enlisted as Veteran....
Jones, Joseph B	Aledo	Aug. 6, 1861	Aug. 9, 1861	Died May 9, 1862; wounds.
Kelly, William P	Arlington	"	"	Missing Oct. 4, 1852
Kimberlin, John	Mascoutah	Aug. 10, 1861	Aug. 10, 1861	Disch. Oct. 13, '62; wounds.
Lee, George F	Aledo	Aug. 6, 1861	Aug. 9, 1861	Mustered out Aug. 20, 1864.
Livingston, John H	Monmouth	"	"	Discharged Apr. 23, 1862
Lyons, John	O'Fallon	Aug. 7, 1861	Aug. 7, 1861	Re-enlisted as Veteran....
Martin, Calvin	New Boston	Aug. 6, 1861	Aug. 9, 1861	Died May 19, 1862
Maddox, Michael	Mascoutah	Aug. 20, 1861	Aug. 20, 1861	Mustered out Aug. 20, 1864.
Malone, James	Centreville	Aug. 5, 1861	Aug. 5, 1861	Discharged June 10, 1863
Meyer, George	Belleville	July 26, 1861	July 28, 1861	
Miller, James	Aledo	Aug. 6, 1861	Aug. 9, 1861	Re-enlisted as Veteran....
Mock, Jesse	Pope Creek	"	"	Killed at Shiloh Apr. 6, '62.
Mock, William	"	"	"	Mustered out Aug. 20, 1864.
Moorehead, John	Aledo	"	"	See Co. E, as consolidated
Moore, Frank M	"	"	"	Killed at Shiloh Apr. 6, '62.
Murphy, Francis J	Nilwood	July 28, 1861	July 28, 1861	Mustered out Aug. 20, 1864.
McKenzie, James	Belleville	"	"	Killed at Shiloh Apr. 6, '62.
Nevin, William D	Ohio Grove	Aug. 6, 1861	Aug. 9, 1861	
O'Neill, Edward	Belleville	Aug. 10, 1861	Aug. 10, 1861	Mustered out Aug. 20, 1864.
Prendegrast, John	O'Fallon	Aug. 8, 1861	Aug. 8, 1861	Disch. Jan. 18, '65; disabil..
Primley, William F	Sunbeam	Aug. 6, 1861	Aug. 9, 1861	Re-enlisted as Veteran....
Phillips, Daniel	Olney	Aug. 14, 1861	Aug. 14, 1861	Mustered out Aug. 20, 1864.
Riley, William H. H	Aledo	Aug. 6, 1861	Aug. 9, 1861	Re-enlisted as Veteran....
Selby, Samuel	Keithsburg	"	"	Mustered out Aug. 20, 1864.
Sheldon, George N	Berlin	"	"	Disch. July 19, '62; disabil.
Smith, William H. H.	Sunbeam	"	"	Re enlisted as Veteran....

Name and Rank.	Residence.	Date of rank or enlistment.	Date of muster.	Remarks.
Smith, Samuel M	Ohio Grove.....	Aug. 6, 1861	Aug. 9, 1861	Disch. Feb. 24, '62; disabil.
Shoemaker, John N...	Oxford	'' ''	'' ''	Died Apr. 17, '62; wounds.
Stulkahl, Thomas......	New Boston....	'' ''	'' ''	Mustered out Aug. 20, 1864
Snyder, George.......	Aledo...........	'' ''	'' ''	....
Shroyer, James	Keithsburg.....	'' ''	'' ''	Re-enlisted as Veteran....
Stuart, James	O'Fallon........	July 26, 1861	July 28, 1861	'' ''
Stevens, Jack L.......	Belleville.......			.....
Taylor, Ira	Mascoutah	Aug. 2, 1861	Aug. 2, 1861	Re-enlisted as Veteran....
Till, John..............	O'Fallon........	Aug. 14, 1861	Aug. 14, 1861	Mustered out Aug. 20, 1864,
Tillotson, Frank	Cairo	July 26, 1861	July 28, 1861	Re-enlisted as Veteran....
Thornsburg, Charles..	Belleville.......	Aug. 10, 1861	Aug. 10, 1861	Disch. Oct. 4, 1861; disabil.
Tyler, Ephraim J	Aledo...........	Aug. 6, 1861	Aug. 9, 1861	Mustered out Aug. 20, 1863
Ward, James..........	O'Fallon........	Aug. 2, 1861	Aug. 2, 1861	Re-enlisted as Veteran....
White, Jacob	Aledo	Aug. 6, 1861	Aug. 9, 1861	'' ''
Williams, James F ...	'' ''			.....
Wordin, Charles C....	Keithsburg....	'' ''	'' ''	Mustered out Aug. 20, 1864
Veterans.				
Boyer, William........	Aledo	Mar. 25, 1864	Mar. 25, 1864	See Co. E, as consolidated
Cox, Joseph R.........	'' ''	'' ''	'' ''	'' ''
Dilg, Frederick	Mascoutah	'' ''	'' ''	See Co. B, as consolidated
Dodson, Abisha.......	Keithsburg.....	'' ''	'' ''	See Co. E, as consolidated
Frothingham, Den. C.	Chicago	'' ''	'' ''	'' ''
Fleming, Charles B...	Keithsburg.....	Mar. 31, 1864	Mar. 31, 1864	See Co. A, as consolidated
Graham, Elisha P....	Chicago	Mar. 25, 1864	Mar. 25, 1864	See Co. E, as consolidated
Gilmore, George	Boston..........	Mar. 31, 1864	Mar. 31, 1864	'' ''
Gilmore, James B.....				'' ''
Fulmer, John..........	Belleville.......	Jan. 4, 1864	Jan. 4, 1864	'' ''
Hughes, Edwin	Chicago			'' ''
Jackson, Martin W....	Belleville.......	Mar. 25, 1864	Mar. 25, 1864	'' ''
Lyons, John...........	Chicago	'' ''	'' ''	'' ''
McClintock, Thos. F..	Aledo	'' ''	'' ''	'' ''
Miller, James.........	Chicago	'' ''	'' ''	'' ''
Primley, William F...	....	'' ''	'' ''	'' ''
Reilly, William H. H.	Aledo	'' ''	'' ''	'' ''
Rose, George W	Chicago	'' ''	'' ''	'' ''
Shroyer, James	'' ''	'' ''	'' ''	'' ''
Smith, William H. H.	....	'' ''	'' ''	'' ''
Stewart, James........	Belleville.......	'' ''	'' ''	'' ''
Taylor, Ira	....	'' ''	'' ''	'' ''
Tillotson, Frank M....	Chicago	'' ''	'' ''	'' ''
Triplett, William G...	Belleville.......	'' ''	'' ''	'' ''
Troy, Lewis L........	....	Mar. 31, 1864	Mar. 31, 1864	See Co. D, as consolidated
White, Jacob M	Aledo	Mar. 25, 1864	Mar. 25, 1864	See Co. E, as consolidated
Ward, James	Belleville.......	Jan. 4, 1864	Jan. 4, 1864	'' ''
Recruits.				
Bickers, John	....	Aug. 1, 1862	Nov. 4, 1862	See Co. C, as consolidated
Bickers, M. F	....	Aug. 15, 1862	'' ''	'' ''
Cox, Augustus B......	Aledo		Aug. 15, 1862	See Co. E, as consolidated
Carter, W. B	....	Aug. 1, 1862	Nov. 4, 1862	See Co. C, as consolidated
Crane, Seburn V......	....	Aug. 15, 1862		'' ''
Dodson, Abisha.......	Keithsburg.....	Oct. 6, 1861	Oct. 6, 1861	Re-enlisted as Veteran....
Dunn, John R..........	....	Aug. 15, 1862	Nov. 4, 1862	See Co. E, as consolidated
Feater, Antony........	....			'' ''
Gilmore, George	New Boston....	Oct. 6, 1861	Oct. 6, 1861	Re-enlisted as Veteran....
Hoy, John	Aledo	Jan. 28, 1864	Mar. 25, 1864	See Co. E, as consolidated
Hill, William J........	....	Aug. 1, 1862	Nov. 4, 1862	See Co. C, as consolidated
Hunter, Charles T	....	Aug. 20, 1862	Nov. 5, 1862	See Co. F, as consolidated
Kilpatrick, George W.	Aledo	Jan. 28, 1864	Mar. 25, 1864	See Co. E, as consolidated
Kirk, John.............	....	Aug. 15, 1862	Nov. 4, 1862	See Co. A, as consolidated
Matthews, William ...	Fayetteville	Sept. 25, 1861	Sept. 25, 1861	Died March 19, 1862.........
Miller, Eugene........	Belleville.......	May 1, 1864	May 1, 1864	See Co. E, as consolidated
Mock, Abraham.......	....		May 11, 1864	'' ''
Mifflin, John..........	....	Aug. 1, 1862	Nov. 4, 1862	See Co. C, as consolidated
Phoemister, Silas G ..	....		Aug. 4, 1862	See Co. A, as consolidated
Poteete, George W....	....	'' ''	Nov. 4, 1862	See Co. C, as consolidated
Reed, Alfred	Lebanon........	Oct. 20, 1862	Oct. 20, 1862	....
Robertson, Samuel ...	....	Aug. 1, 1862	Nov. 4, 1862	See Co. C, as consolidated
Roberts, E. B	....	Aug. 15, 1862	'' ''	Name taken from monthly return ....
Swyer, Francis........	Belleville......	Sept. 20, 1862	Sept. 20, 1862	See Co. E, as consolidated
Vestal, Neal..........	Aledo	Dec. 18, 1861	Dec. 18, 1861	'' ''
Woods, Thomas W....	Belleville.......	Feb. 18, 1864	Mar. 26, 1864	'' ''
Walker, John..........	....	Apr. 12, 1862	Nov. 4, 1862	See Co. A, as consolidated
Yurgens, John	Red Bud........	Oct. 21, 1862	Oct. 21, 1862	....
Abney, Francis M.....	....	Aug. 1, 1861	Nov. 4, 1862	See Co. F, as consolidated

Name and Rank.	Residence.	Date of rank or enlistment.	Date of muster.	Remarks.
Under Cooks.				
Mason, Israel..........	....	Dec. 1,1863	Jan. 24,1864	See Co. E, as consolidated
Daris, Peter..........	....		" "	" "
Williams, George.....	....	Jan. 24,1864	" "	" " " "
Simmons, William....	....	Aug. 1,1863	" "	" " " "

COMPANY F.

Name and Rank.	Residence.	Date of rank or enlistment.	Date of muster.	Remarks.
Captains.				
Loren Webb...........	Mascoutah	July 26,1861	July 28,1861	Resigned July 10, 1862.....
William Britt.........	" "	July 10,1862	....	Killed, Corinth Oct. 3,1862.
George W. Williford..	Hillsboro.......	Oct. 3,1862	Sept. 3,1863	Mustered out Aug. 20,1864.
First Lieutenants.				
William Britt.........	Mascoutah	July 28,1861	July 28,1861	Promoted ....
George W. Williford..	Hillsboro.......	July 10,1862	Oct. 18,1862	" " ....
Second Lieutenants.				
George W. Williford..	Hillsboro.......	July 26,1861	July 28,1861	Promoted......................
William C. Hawley ...	Mascoutah	July 10,1862	July 11,1862	Prom. Major 2d Ala. A. D. Jan. 9, 1864................
First Sergeant.				
Charles T. Saltmarsh.	Mascoutah	July 25,1861	July 28,1861	Mustered out Aug. 20,1864.
Sergeants.				
Fred E. Scheel........	Belleville.......	July 28,1861	July 28,1861	Transferred to Co D.......
William Hawley	Mascoutah	" "	" "	Promoted 2d Lieut.........
Joseph C. Gates.......	Collinsville	July 26,1861	" "	
Thomas C. Kidd	Springfield	" "	" "	See Co. E, as consolidated
Corporals.				
Andrew Webster......	Mascoutah	July 26,1861	July 28,1861	Killed at Shiloh Apr. 6,1862
John W. Hadley.......	Collinsville	" "	" "	Died Nov. 18,1861..........
H. H. Klock..........	Alhambra	July 25,1861	" "	Promoted Adjutant........
Robert Crump........	Springfield	July 26,1861	" "	Died Aug. 6,1861 ....
A. J. White	Mascoutah	July 25,1861	" "	....
R. J. Simpkins	Springfield	July 26,1861	" "	....
James Niece	Oconee	" "	" "	Killed, accident, Aug. 10,'61
James A. Fike........	Mascoutah	July 25,1861	" "	Mustered out Aug. 20,1864.
Musicians.				
Percy C. Coffee	Mascoutah	July 26,1861	July 28,1861	....
William McGuire	Paducah, Ky...	Aug. 8,1861	Aug. 31,1861	Mustered out Aug. 20,1864.
Privates.				
Ashton, David N......	Edwardsville ..	July 26,1861	July 21,1861	Killed at Fort Donelson Feb. 15, 1862................
Bridges	Lebanon.........	July 25,1861	" "	Disch. July 21,'62; disabil.
Banes, Marques.......	" "	" "	" "	Disch. Aug. 15,'62; disabil.
Ballow, Marellis	Paducah, Ky...	July 26,1861	" "	Mustered out Sept. 2,1864.
Borrow, John S	Mascoutah	" "	" "	Mustered out Aug. 20,1864.
Birgin, Frederick.....	" "	Aug. 7,1861	Aug. 31,1861	Disch. Apr. 24,'62; disabil.
Baily, Albert	Marine.........	Aug. 14,1861	" "	Died Nov. 1, 1861...........
Brown, James S.......	" "	July 26,1861	July 28,1861	Disch. June 25,'62; disabil.
Barnett, Thomas......	Alton	Aug. 13,1861	Aug. 31,1861	Mustered out Aug. 20, 1864.
Born, John P..........	Edwardsville ..	Aug. 20,1861	" "	....
Bence, Lewis..........	Fayetteville ...	July 24,1861	" "	M.O.Sept.1'64,Jon'sb'ro,Ga
Bassett, Harlow	Alton	Aug. 22,1861	" "	....
Buschmiller,Christian	Fayetteville	Aug. 15,1861	" "	Mustered out Aug. 20,1864.
Burnes, Alexander....	Mascoutah	July 25,1861	July 28,1861	Disch. Apr. 28,'62; disabil.
Crocker, William C...	" "	" "	" "	Disch. Dec. 24,'61; disabil.
Collins, John	Alton	July 30,1861	Aug. 31,1861	Mustered out Aug. 20,1864.
Cox, Thomas W	Lebanon........	" "	" "	Killed, Shiloh, Apr. 6, 1862.
Charlick, John E...	Marine..........	July 26,1861	July 28,1861	....
Chenoweth, John B...	Alton	Aug. 28,1861	Aug. 31,1861	Died June 6, 1862; wounds.
Campbell, Michael....	Rock Island....	July 30,1861	" "	....
Cory, Elnathan.......	Aurora..........	Aug. 8,1861	" "	....
Duncan, James F	Marine..........	July 25,1861	July 28,1861	Died May 1, 1862; wounds.
Dye, John W ..	Mascoutah	Aug. 12,1861	Aug. 31,1861	Disch. May 5,'62; wounds.
Ellison, Thomas	Marine..........	July 24,1861	July 28,1861	....
Foushee,.John O	Paducah, Ky...	Sept. 15,1861	Oct. 31,1861	Killed, Corinth, Oct. 4,1862
Garrott, Joseph H	Mascoutah	July 26,1861	July 28,1861	Mustered out Aug. 20,1864.
Glenn, James..........	" "	July 24,1861	" "	" "

Name and Rank.	Residence.	Date of rank or enlistment.	Date of muster.	Remarks.
Gmelin, Henry........	Fayetteville	Aug. 15, 1861	Aug. 31, 1861	See Co. E, as consolidated
Getty, James..........	Monmouth	Aug. 30, 1861	"	Disch. July 9,' 62; wounds.
Hill, Charles	Mascoutah	Aug. 24, 1861	July 28, 1861	Killed, Shiloh, Apr. 6, 1862.
Hancock, Benjamin F	Harrisburg.....	Aug. 7, 1861	Aug. 31, 1861	Disch. July 19, '62; disabil.
Hadley, James N. W..	Collinsville	Aug. 13, 1861	"	Pro. 1st Lt. 1st Tenn. Art.. Aug. 13, 1863............
Hickman, James M...	Fayetteville	July 20, 1861	July 28, 1861	Mustered out Aug. 20, 1864.
Hess, James (or Carl)	"	Aug. 12, 1861	Aug. 31, 1861	Died Oct. 17, 1861 ....
Heimberger, R'd'lph W	Mascoutah	Aug. 15, 1861	"	Mustered out Aug. 20, 1864.
Hughes, James........	Alton	Aug. 11, 1861	"	Died Jan. 13, 1862..........
Jorgeon. John........	Fayetteville	Aug. 15, 1861	"	Mustered out Aug. 20, 1864.
Lynch, Nathan.......	Marine..........	July 24, 1861	July 28, 1861	"
Lauchly, John H......	"	Aug. 14, 1861	Aug. 31, 1861	Promoted Lt. 2d Ala. C.T., Feb. 11, 1864............
Miller, Joseph L	Paducah, Ky....	July 24, 1861	July 28, 1861	Re-enlisted as Veteran....
Mills, John W	Alton	Aug. 8, 1861	Aug. 31, 1861	Mustered out Aug. 20, 1864.
Merritt, William	Paducah, Ky....	Aug. 13, 1861	"	Disch. June 11, '62; disabil.
Murry, William	Rock Island....	Aug. 31, 1861	"	....
McAllister, Matthew..	"	July 16, 1861	July 28, 1861	Died Sept. 15, '61; wounds.
McCulloch, Duncan...	Chicago	Aug. 14, 1861	Aug. 31, 1861	Killed, Shiloh, Apr. 6, 1862.
McCully, John.........	Pilot Knob, Mo.	Aug. 12, 1861	"	Disch. Apr. 5, '62; disabil..
McCarter, John W	Rock Island....	July 27, 1861	July 28, 1861	....
McShafer, James......	"	July 30, 1861	Aug. 31, 1861	Mustered out Aug. 20, 1864.
McGinnes, John.......	Joliet	"	"	Re-enlisted as Veteran....
Neal, Henry H.........	Jamestown	July 26, 1861	July 28, 1861	Mustered out Aug. 20, 1864.
Potthart, Francis	Mascoutah	"	"	Killed at Shiloh Apr. 6, '62.
Rowland, Constant C.	"	Aug. 7, 1861	Aug. 31, 1861	Killed at Fort Donelson Feb. 15, 1862............
Rank, John............	Fayetteville	Aug. 15, 1861	"	See Co. E, as consolidated.
Rodgers, James.......	Rock Island....	July 27, 1861	July 28, 1861	Mustered out Aug. 20, 1864.
Stoulfouth, John......	Mascoutah	Aug. 14, 1861	Aug. 31, 1861	"
Schmiersaul, Henry..	Fayetteville	Aug. 16, 1861	"	Disch. June 11, '62; disabil.
Snouffer, John G......	Mound City	Aug. 10, 1861	"	Killed at Shiloh Apr. 6, '62.
Scott, Richard C......	Carbondale.....	Aug. 16, 1861	"	Disch. Apr. 17, '62; disabil.
Tichnor, John M, C...	Olney..........	July 26, 1861	July 28, 1861	Pro. 1st S'g't 2d Ala. Col'd Troops, Feb. 11, 1864.....
Teear, Joshua G.......	Alton	Aug. 12, 1861	Aug. 31, 1861	Killed at Shiloh Apr. 6, '62.
Wagner, Francis X ...	Fayetteville	July 15, 1861	July 28, 1861	Trans to non-com'd staff, as Sergeant Major.......
Wallace, Thomas L...	Paducah, Ky....	July 26, 1861	"	Mustered out Aug. 20, 1864.
Winters, Napoleon B.	Mascoutah	"	"	"
Wiggand, Frederick..	Fayetteville	Aug. 15, 1861	Aug. 31, 1861	Killed at White House Oct. 3, 1862.............
Gmelin, Andrew.......	"	Aug. 13, 1861	"	Mustered out Aug. 20, 1864.
Veterans.				
Hicks, Jones (or Jas.L	Carbondale.....	Jan. 4, 1864	Jan. 4, 1864	See Co. E, as consolidated
Miller, Joseph L......	Paducah, Ky....	"	"	"
McGinnes, John.......	Rock Island....	"	"	" "
Recruits.				
Anderson, Thornbery.	....	Aug. 15, 1861	Nov. 4, 1862	See Co. E, as consolidated
Anderson, William G.	....	"	"	" "
Allabaugh, Robert R.	....	"	"	" "
Ayers, Joseph........	....	"	"	" "
Allen, Byron H.......	....	Oct. 1, 1862	Dec. —, 1862	" "
Anderson, Henry C...	....	Aug. 15, 1861	Nov. 4, 1862	See Co. A, as consolidated
Bevel, William H	Jonesboro	Sept. 21, 1862	Oct. 31, 1861	See Co. E, as consolidated
Bayles, David S.......	....	Aug. 15, 1862	Nov. 4, 1862	
Bynham, William Y .	....	"	"	Mustered out July 18, 1865.
Burnes, Thomas G....	....	"	"	
Burks, Alpheus.......	....	"	"	See Co. A, as consolidated
Bogardus, L. C.......	....	"	"	
Campbell, George W..	Blairsville......	Sept. 22, 1861	Oct. 31, 1861	Disch. Aug. 11, '62; disabil.
Curtner, Daniel.......	....	Aug. 15, 1862	Nov. 4, 1862	See Co. E, as consolidated
Carmichael, Geo. W .	....	"	"	" "
Dillard, William	....	"	"	" "
Dixon, John..........	....	"	"	" "
Dunning, Joy.........	....	....	....	Disch. June 30, '64; disabil.
Eltis, William M......	Union co	Sept. 15, 1861	Oct. 31, 1861	Disch. May 14, '62; disabil.
Edmonson, Thomas A	....	Aug. 20, 1862	Nov. 4, 1862	See Co. A, as consolidated
Evaland, William H..	....	Aug. 15, 1862		See Co. A, as consolidated
Foster, Toliver........	Carbondale.....	Sept. 18, 1861	Oct. 31, 1861	Killed at Shiloh Apr. 6, '62.
Foster, Joel...........	"	"	"	
Furlow, William	Blairsville......	Sept. 22, 1861	"	Disch. Apr. 24, '62; disabil.
Fisher, Michael F.....	Jonesboro	Sept. 14, 1861	"	See Co. E, as consolidated
Fox, Calvin E	....	Aug. 15, 1862	Nov. 4, 1862	" "
Frazier, William	....	"	"	" "
Ferrell, Wyatt C	....	Aug. 20, 1862	"	" "
Forby, William........	Carbondale.....	Sept. 15, 1861	Oct. 31, 1861	Disch. Apr. 24, '62; disabil.

Name and Rank.	Residence.	Date of rank or enlistment.	Date of muster.	Remarks.
Farro, James N........	....	Aug. 15, 1862	Nov. 4, 1862	See Co. A, as consolidated
Forby, William........	....	Aug. 25, 1863	Aug. 25, 1863	See Co. E, as consolidated
Greathouse, James M.	Murphysboro ..	Sept. 15, 1861	Oct. 31, 1861	Disch. Apr 5, '62; disabil.
Goodman, Henry......	....	Aug. 15, 1862	Nov. 4, 1862	See Co. E, as consolidated
Hobbs, James	Paducah, Ky ...	Sept. 25, 1861	Oct. 31, 1861	W'nded Apr. 6,'62, Pittsb'rg
Herald, James W	Carbondale....	Sept. 15, 1861	"	Deserted June 2. 1862......
Hickes, James	"	Oct. 15, 1861	"	Re-enlisted as Veteran....
Houston, Samuel W...	South Pass....	Sept. 22, 1861	"	Disch. May 14, 62; disabil.
Haines, George C	Jonesboro	Sept. 18, 1861	"	
Hickes, John A........	Union co........			Died Dec. 18, 1861..........
Hickman, Hugh A.....	Fayetteville....	Feb. 5, 1864	Mar. 25, 1864	See Co. E, as consolidated
Hewlett, Altenmount..	....	Aug. 15, 1862	Nov. 4, 1862	
Hewlett, Lemuel	....	"	"	" "
Hall, Willis	....	"	"	" "
Hall, Ryssell	....	"	"	
Howerton, John P.....	....	"	"	Mustered out July 20. 1865.
Hale, Marion	....	"	"	See Co. A, as consolidated
Johnson, Lemuel......	....	"	"	See Co. E, as consolidated
Jones, James T........	....	"	"	
Koontz, Jacob........	Paducah, Ky ...	Sept. 10, 1861	Oct. 31, 1861	Killed at Shiloh Apr. 6,'62.
Keys, John	....	Aug. 1, 1862	Nov. 4, 1862	See Co. C, as consolidated
Knight, Warren	....	Aug. 15, 1862	"	See Co. A, as consolidated
Knight, Isaac.........	....			
McLeish, George......	Carbondale.....	Sept. 22, 1861	Oct. 31, 1861	Killed at Shiloh Apr. 6,'62.
Martin, Samuel J. B..	....	Aug. 15, 1862	Nov. 4, 1862	See Co. E, as consolidated
Miller, William T......	Paducah, Ky ...	Sept. 15, 1861	Sept. 18, 1861	
Moore, Robert........	....	Sept. 18, 1861	Oct. 31, 1861	Died July 17, 1864 ....
Norton, John W.......	Union co........			Died Nov. 28, 1861 ....
Pemberton, Joshua ...	....	Aug. 15, 1862	Nov. 4, 1862	See Co. E, as consolidated
Rease, William P.....	....			
Rayhill, Mathew	....			Disch. Oct. 25, '61; disabil.
Singleton, Eli T.......	Carbondale.....	Sept. 4, 1861	Oct. 31, 1861	Died May 11, 1862; wounds.
Singleton, William F..	"	Sept. 18, 1861		Disch. June 16,'62; disabil.
Struble, D. M. C......	....		Sept. 18, 1861	See Co. E, as consolidated
Smith, Milton	....	Aug. 20, 1862	Nov. 4, 1862	" "
Spinkes, James J......	....	Aug. 15, 1862		" "
Stevens, William J....	....	"	"	
Stevens, F. M.........	....	"	"	See Co. C, as consolidated
Smith, Wilford.......	....	"	"	See Co. A, as consolidated
Stephens, Milton.....	....	"	"	" "
Sanders, Silas........	....	"	"	
Sanders, L. L.........	....			Disch. Feb. 3, 1864; disabil.
Tope, William	Carbondale.....	Sept. 22, 1861	Oct. 31, 1861	
Talday, William......	....	Aug. 15, 1862	Nov. 4, 1862	See Co. E, as consolidated
Stilley, Davis A......	....			See Co. A, as consolidated
Warren, George W....	Carbondale.....	Sept. 15, 1861	Oct. 31, 1861	See Co. E, as consolidated
Wilhelm, Marshall....	....	Aug. 15, 1862	Nov. 4, 1862	" "
Wollard, John R......	....			
Under Cooks.				
Anderson, Loyal	....	Dec. 18, 1863	Jan. 24, 1864	See Co. E, as consolidated
Hewley, Sam	....	Jan. 23, 1864	"	" "
Talda, Jack...........	....	Dec. 18, 1863	"	" "
Talda, Hartwell.......	....	"	"	" "

COMPANY G.

Name and Rank.	Enrolled at.	Date of rank or enlistment.	Date of muster.	Remarks.
Captains.				
Eager M. Lowe........	Pulaski	July 26, 1861	July 27, 1861	M. O. for pro. 1st Alabama
Isaac Clements........	Carbondale.....	May 24, 1863	Oct. 22, 1863	Mustered out Aug. 20, 1864.
First Lieutenants.				
John S. Tutton........	Carbondale.....	July 27, 1861	July 27, 1861	Resigned Sept. 13, 1862 ....
Isaac Clements........	"	Sept. 13, 1862	Aug. 12, 1863	Promoted ....
Nimrod G. Perrine.....	Bainbridge.....	May 24, 1863	Oct. 23, 1863	Mustered out Aug. 20, 1864.
Second Lieutenants.				
Isaac Clements........	Carbondale.....	July 27, 1861	July 27, 1861	Mustered out Aug. 20, 1864.
Nimrod G. Perrine....	Bainbridge.....	Sept. 13, 1862	Aug. 27, 1863	Promoted ....
Benjamin T. Brown...	"	May 24, 1863	Mar. 25, 1864	Mustered out Aug. 20, 1864.
First Sergeant.				
Nimrod G. Perrine....	Bainbridge.....	July 27, 1861	July 27, 1861	Promoted 2d Lieut.........

Name and Rank.	Residence.	Date of rank or enlistment.	Date of muster.	Remarks.
Sergeants.				
James M. Hampton...	Williamson co..	July 27,1861	July 27,1861	Died March 4,1862..........
William Hampton				Mustered out Aug. 20,1864.
John B. Russell.......	Fredonia........	..	..	Died May 13,'62; wounds ..
Benjamin K. Mulkey .	Williamson co..	..	..	Mustered out Aug. 20,1864.
Corporals.				
John Worthen.........	Jackson co......	July 27,1861	July 27,1861	Died Dec. 28, 1864..........
Napoleon B Hampton	Williamson co..			Died April 15,1862..........
Benjamin Jacobs......	Jackson co.....	..	..	Killed at Fort Donelson, Feb. 15,1862............
John Collier..........	..	..		Deserted Oct. 30, 1862......
Granville M. Wise	Johnson co	Aug. 18,1861	Aug. 18,1861	Mustered out Aug. 20,1864.
William B. Dubois....				Disch. May 20,'62; wounds.
Edward B. Rhodes....	East Bainbri'ge	Aug. 1,1861	Aug. 1,1861	Disch. Aug. 15,'62; wounds
John E. Glenn.........	Jackson co.....	July 27,1861	July 27,1861	....
Musicians.				
John McCann..........	New York	July 27,1861	July 27,1861	Re-enlisted as Veteran....
Franklin Winchester .	Jackson co......	..	..	....
Privates.				
Addison, Joel..........	Jackson co......	July 27,1861	July 27,1861	Mustered out Aug. 20,1864.
Addison, William	Jefferson co			
Applegate, Louis R ...	Williamson co..	Aug. 18,1861	Aug. 18,1861	....
Akin, Columbus, C....	Jackson co......	July 27,1861	July 27,1861	Mustered out Aug. 20,1864.
Armpriest, Oliver P ..	Henry co......	Aug. 1,1861	Aug. 1,1861	Died Oct. 29,1861 ....
Brown, Henry.........	Jackson co......	July 27,1861	July 27,1861	Re-enlisted as Veteran....
Brown, John W	..			
Brown, Nathaniel G ..	..	..	..	.. ....
Brown, William L	..		..	.. Disch. Oct. 13,'62; wounds.
Brown, Francis A.....	..	Aug. 18,1861	Aug. 18,1861	Died Nov. 4,1861..........
Beggs, James A.......	Johnson co	Aug. 21,1861	Aug. 21,1861	Died Jan. 1,1862 ....
Beggs, David..........	....	Aug. 18,1861	Aug. 18,1861	
Beggs, John...........	Union co........			Mustered out Aug. 20,1864.
Bradbury, John S......	Jackson co......	July 27,1861	July 27,1861	Disch. July 13,'62; disabil.
Bascom, Alpheus	Alexander co...	..	..	Killed at Shiloh Apr. 6,'62.
Bascom, William H...	..			Disch. Apr. 4,1862; disabil.
Cox, Russell R	Jackson co.....	..	..	Re-enlisted as Veteran....
Cureton, James	Johnson co	Aug. 18,1861	Aug. 18,1861	Disch. Aug. 15,'62; disabil.
Carlker, Dariel A	..			Killed accid'ly Feb. 10,'62.
Cox, Jesse	Williamson co..	Aug. 27,1861	Aug. 27,1861	Died March 18,1864........
Cox, John.............	..			Disch. Sept. 5,'61; disabil.
Derossett, John W....	Jackson co.....	July 27,1861	July 27,1861	Re-enlisted as Veteran....
Edwards, Allen	Johnson co	Aug. 18,1861	Aug. 18,1861	Died July 4,1862.........
Garrett, Elijah	Jackson co......	July 27,1861	July 27,1861	Re-enlisted as Veteran....
Gore, Joseph P........	Johnson co	Aug. 18,1861	Aug. 18,1861	.. ..
Gore, William		..	..	Mustered out Aug. 20,1864.
Hampton, Jonathan...	Williamson co..	July 27,1861	July 27,1861	
Hampton, Wade.......	..	..	..	Mustered out Aug. 20,1864.
Hall, John W..........	Jackson co......			
Harris, Henry W.....	.. ..	Aug. 18,1861	Aug. 18,1861	
Hunter, William	.. ..	Aug. 23,1861	Aug. 24,1861	Died Nov. 26,1861 ....
Hagler, William J	.. ..			Re-enlisted as Veteran....
Hartsell, Simon P.....	Johnson co	July 27,1861	July 27,1861	
Jones, William........	..			Died April 28,1862........
Jones, David W	Jackson co......	Aug. 1,1861	Aug. 1,1861	Killed at Shiloh Apr. 6,'62.
Jones, Jesse E	Union co........	Aug. 18,1861	Aug. 18,1861	Died Dec. 31,1861.
Lipe, Hamilton........	Jackson co......	July 27,1861	July 27,1861	Died Nov. 5,1861.
Lipe, Jackson	......			See Co. A, as consolidated
Lasswell. Thomas R..	Franklin co.....	..	..	Re-enlisted as Veteran....
Leary, Patrick	Paris...........	..	..	Mustered out Aug. 20,1864.
Lefler, George F	Johnson co	..	..	Died Oct. 30,1861.
McCord, John	Jackson co......	..	..	Killed while prisoner Oct. 5,1862..........
McKinney, James H..	Williamson co..	..	..	Disch. Mar. 31,'62; disabil.
McKinney, John H....	..	Aug. 4,1861	Aug. 4,1861	Died May 6,1862..........
McCord, William F ...	Johnson co	Aug. 18,1861	Aug. 18,1861	Died Oct. 31,1861 ....
Marshall, Robert......	Jackson co......	July 27,1861	July 27,1861	Mustered out Aug. 20,1864.
Mason, James E.......	Saline co.......			
Miller, Charles W.....	Williamson co..	Aug. 11,1861	Aug. 11,1861	Mustered out Aug. 20,1864.
Morgan, Irwin M......	Johnson co	Aug. 18,1861	Aug. 18,1861	
Martin, William J.....	Pope co.........			Disch. Mar. 3,'62; disabil.
Olney, Thomas J......	Williamson co..	July 27,1861	July 27,1861	Killed at Shiloh Apr. 6,'62.
Pipkins, Wiley H	Johnson co	Aug. 18,1861	Aug. 18,1861	Died Mar. 31,1862.........
Paregien, James A....	Jackson co......	July 27,1861	July 27,1861	
Peterson, Monroe	Williamson co..			Disch. Apr. 4,'6?; disabil..
Pyron, Anderson......	Jackson co......	..	..	Re-enlisted as Veteran....
Quinlan, John F.......	Alexander co...	..	..	Mustered out Aug. 20,1864.
Ross, Robert	Carbondale	..	..	Died Nov. 17,1861.........

Name and Rank.	Residence.	Date of rank or enlistment.	Date of muster.	Remarks.
Ryan, Daniel	Washington co.	Aug. 18, 1861	Aug. 18, 1861	Disch. May 28, '62; wounds
Richardson, David J..	Johnson co	" "	" "	Disch. Oct. 5, '61; disabil..
Stotlar, Bennett H	Williamson co..	Aug. 11, 1861	Aug. 11, 1861	Mustered out Aug. 20, 1864
Stotlar, Thomas	"			....
Stotlar, John A........	"	Aug. 27, 1861	Aug. 27, 1861	....
Slavins, Daniel F.....	Johnson co	Aug. 18, 1861	Aug. 18, 1861	Mustered out Aug. 20, 1864
Scott, Richard C......	New York	Aug. 10, 1861	Aug. 10, 1861	Transferred to Co. F .....
Smith, Joseph M	Pulaski co......	Aug. 27, 1861	Aug. 27, 1861	
Stripling, Amos B.....	Johnson co	Sept. 1, 1861	Sept. 1, 1861	Deserted Aug. 18, 1862 ....
Stripling, John J	Union co........	" "	" "	Disch. July 22,'62; wounds
Tyler, Daniel	Johnson co	Aug. 18, 1861	Aug. 18, 1861	Died Nov. 4, 1861 ....
Tutton, Amasim'nd'rB	Carbondale....	Aug. 4, 1861	Aug. 4, 1861	Disch. July 15, '62; wounds
Taylor, James F......	Webster	Aug. 28, 1861	Aug. 28, 1861	Re-enlisted as Veteran....
Tuffnell, William......	Williamson co..			Died Jan. 15, 1862 ....
Tippy, John J	"	Aug. 4, 1861	Aug. 4, 1861	Mustered out Aug. 20, 1864
Watley, Joseph H	Marion co.......	July 27, 1861	July 27, 1861	" "
White, John J	Williamson co..	Aug. 11, 1861	Aug. 11, 1861	Died Apr. 25, '62; wounds .
White, Simeon F	Johnson co	Aug. 18, 1861	Aug. 18, 1861	Re-enlisted as Veteran....
Willhelm, James	" "			Killed at Fort Donelson Feb. 15, 1862 ....
Wilson, James H	Union co......	" "	" "	Disch. Oct. 5, '61; disabil.
Worthen, Richard J...	Jackson co	" "	" "	Mustered out Aug. 20, 1864
White, Warren S	Williamson co..	" "	" "	Re-enlisted as Veteran....
Willheim, Jacob	Johnson co	Aug. 27, 1861	Aug. 27, 1861	Died Nov. 14, 1862.........
Wise, Louis, Jr	" "			Mustered out Aug. 20, 1864
Wise, Granville M., Jr.	" "	Aug. 18, 1861	Aug. 18, 1861	Died Oct. 28, 1861..........
Welch, Stephen	Jackson co	Sept. 1, 1861	Sept. 1, 1861	Died Nov. 11, 1861..........
Veterans.				
Brown, N. G	Carbondale	Jan. 4, 1864	Jan. 4, 1864	See Co. A, as consolidated
Brown, Henry M	" "	" "	" "	
Brown, John W.......	" "	" "	" "	Killed at Sugar Valley, Ga. May 10, 1864 ....
Cureton, James........	Dongola	" "	" "	See Co. A, as consolidated
Dixon, William H	Anna............	Mar. 23, 1864	Mar. 23, 1864	
Edward, Allen........	Dongola	Jan. 4, 1864	Jan. 4, 1864	" "
Gore, William B	" "	" "	" "	" "
Gore, Josish P	" "	" "	" "	" "
Gore, James B	Cobden	" "	" "	" "
Heglar, William......	Carbondale	" "	" "	" "
Hampton, Jonathan...	" "	" "	" "	" "
Loyd, James A	Nickolsville	Mar. 23, 1864	Mar. 23, 1864	" "
Lasswell, Thomas R ..	Cairo...........			" "
McCann, John	Carbondale	Mar. 27, 1864	Mar. 27, 1864	" "
Pyron, Anderson......	"	Jan. 4, 1864	Jan. 4, 1864	" "
Perdew, Eugene.......	Keokuk, Ia.....	Mar. 23, 1864	Mar. 23, 1864	" "
Taylor, James F	Cairo...........			" "
Winchester, E. P......	Carbondale	Jan. 4, 1864	Jan. 4, 1864	" "
White, Simeon F	Cairo...........	Mar. 23, 1864	Mar. 23, 1864	" "
White, Warren S	DeSoto	Mar. 27, 1864	Mar. 27, 1864	" "
Recruits.				
Ausley, David N	" "	Feb. 24, 1864	Feb. 24, 1864	See Co. A, as consolidated
Bradley, William R ...	Union co.......	Sept. 11, 1861	Sept. 11, 1861	Disch. July 22; '62; wounds
Brown, James M	Jackson co......	Sept. 15, 1861	Sept. 15, 1861	See Co. A, as consolidated
Brown, Benjamin F...	" "			Promoted 2d Lieutenant ..
Babbitt, Charles W...	" "	Sept. 30, 1861	Sept. 30, 1861	
Bartley, Alfred	Williamson co..	July 10, 1862	July 10, 1862	Died Oct. 7. 1862; wounds.
Bradbury, John S	Carbondale	Mar. 23, 1864	Apr. 9. 1864	Killed at Sugar Valley, Ga., May 10, 1864.
Biggs, William	....			Deserted June 5, 1864 ......
Casey, Moses	....	Aug. 7, 1862	Nov. 4, 1862	See Co. A, as consolidated
Camden, William N...	....	Aug. 15, 1862	" "	" "
Camden, George W...	....		" "	" "
Craig, William	....	Oct. 1, 1862	" "	" "
Cannon, James L......	....	Aug. 15, 1862	" "	" "
Cantrell, Richard.....	....	" "	" "	" "
Chamness, T. M	....	" "	" "	" "
Chenoworth, William .	....	" "	" "	" "
Dungy, Timothy H....	....	" "	" "	See Co. C, as consolidated
Dunn, William D.....	....	" "	" "	See Co. E, as consolidated
Dixon, Thomas	....	Mar. 23, 1864	Mar. 23, 1864	See Co. A, as consolidated
Dye, David	....	Aug. 16, 1862	Nov. 4, 1862	" "
Davis, William H	....	Aug. 15, 1862	" "	" "
Donelson, William M .	....	Aug. 16, 1862	" "	" "
Dial, Burris..........	....			Disch. July 8, '64; disabil .
Etherton, Albert	....	Aug. 26, 1862	Aug. 26, 1862	See Co. A, as consolidated
Gore, James B	Union co.......	Sept. 15, 1861	Sept. 15, 1861	Re-enlisted as Veteran....
Graham, Caleb	Jackson co......	" "	" "	
Goshnell, Oliver......	Carbondale	Jan. 18, 1861	Jan. 18, 1864	See Co. A, as consolidated

Name and Rank.	Residence.	Date of rank or enrollment.	Date of muster.	Remarks.
Goshnell, James.......	Carbondale.....	Jan. 18, 1864	Jan. 18, 1864	See Co. A, as consolidated
Gamble, William A....	....	Aug. 25, 1862	Nov. 4, 1862	" "
Gamble, William D....				" "
Hall, James P..........	Jackson co	Sept. 15, 1861	Sept. 15, 1861	" "
Hammon, William B..	....	Aug. 15, 1862	Nov. 4, 1862	" "
Harris, William H....	....	Aug. 18, 1861	Aug. 18, 1861	" "
Irby, Henderson.......	....	Aug. 16, 1862	Nov. 4, 1862	" "
Joplin, Howell T	....	Aug. 19, 1862	"	" "
Keeler, Thomas H.....	....	Aug. 18, 1862	"	" "
Lee, Albert	....	Aug. 27, 1862	"	" "
Loyd, James A	....	....	Aug. 10, 1861	Re-enlisted as Veteran....
Maloney, Thomas	....	Oct. 1, 1862	Nov. 4, 1862	See Co. A, as consolidated
McNeil, George M.....	....	Aug. 18, 1862	Dec. 10, 1862	" "
Newton, James D.....	....	"	"	" "
Newcomb, Aaron......	....			" "
Odom, Thomas	....	Aug. 12, 1862	Nov. 4, 1862	" "
Odom, Wiley	....			" "
Pleasant, Thomas J ...	Jackson co	Sept. 4, 1861	Sept. 4, 1861	Disch. July 22, '62; wounds
Phemister, Andrew J.	....	Aug. 18, 1862	Nov. 4, 1862	See Co. A, as consolidated
Roach, Davis	....	Aug. 12, 1862	"	" "
Riggs, William	....	Aug. 18, 1862	"	" "
Spillers, Perrine	....	Aug. 15, 1862	"	See Co. C, as consolidated
Sperry, William H	....	Aug. 18, 1862	"	See Co. A, as consolidated
Sutherland, Thomps'n	....	Aug. 1, 1862	"	" "
Stone, William	....	Oct. 1, 1862	"	" "
Stanton, Charles	....	Oct. 4, 1862	"	" "
Sanders, W. M........	....	....	....	Died Apr. 24, 1864..........
Tyler, John A.........	....	Aug. 12, 1862	Nov. 4, 1862	See Co. A, as consolidated
Thornton, Robert.....	....	Aug. 26, 1862	"	" "
Upchurch, Joseph C..	....			" "
Walker, James	Jackson co	Oct. 14, 1861	Oct. 14, 1861	Killed at Shiloh Apr. 6, '62.
Walker, Emsley.......	Perry co........	Oct. 31, 1861	Oct. 31, 1861	Killed, Donelson, Feb. 15, '62
Wilson, John W	Jackson co	May 20, 1862	May 20, 1862	See Co. A, as consolidated
Wise, Robert H	....	Aug. 4, 1862	Nov. 4, 1862	" "
Waggoner, C. M......	....	Aug. 15, 1862	"	" "
Whittington, F. M.....	....	"	"	" "
Under Cooks.				
Mathews, Michael.....	....	Jan. 4, 1864	Jan. 4, 1864	See Co. A, as consolidated
Rice, Daniel	....	"	"	" "
Lee, General..........	....	"	"	" "

COMPANY H.

Name and Rank.	Residence.	Date of rank or enrollment.	Date of muster.	Remarks.
Captain.				
William F. Armstrong	Hillsboro	July 26, 1861	July 28, 1861	Mustered out Aug. 20, 1864.
First Lieutenant.				
Cyrus H. Gilmore.....	Hillsboro	July 28, 1861	July 28, 1861	Mustered out Aug. 20, 1864.
Second Lieutenants.				
Alfred Cowgill	Hillsboro	July 26, 1861	July 28, 1861	Trans. to Inv. C.. Nov. 1, '63
James M. Arthens	"	Nov. 1, 1863	Apr. 27, 1864	Mustered out Aug. 20, 1864.
First Sergeant.				
Francis D. Hubbell....	Hillsboro	July 28, 1861	....	Killed at Shiloh Apr. 6, '62.
Sergeants				
Daniel Pentzer........	Hillsboro	July 28, 1861	....	Disch. Dec. 2, '62; wounds.
Jacob Miller..........	"	"	....	Re-enlisted as Veteran....
Sidney B. Phillips	"	Aug. 2, 1861	....	Died June 8, '62; leg amp..
James M. Arthurs	"	July 28, 1861	July 28, 1861	Promoted 2d Lieutenant ..
Corporals.				
Zacheus C. Wilson....	Hillsboro	Aug. 17, 1861	....	Prom. Capt. 2d Ala. C. T. Jan. 26, 1864.............
Nicholas Keeler.......	Litchfield.......	July 28, 1861	....	Mustered out Aug. 20, 1864.
Alonzo F. McEwen....	Hillsboro	Aug. 15, 1861	Aug. 15, 1861	
Paul Roberts	Montgomery co.	July 28, 1861	....	Died May, 1862 ....
Henry Miller	Hillsboro	"	....	Died July 8, 1862...........
James W. Osborn.....	Montgomery co.	"	July 28, 1861	Mustered out Aug. 20, 1864.
Joseph W. Warren....	"	"	"	" "

Name and Rank.	Residence.	Date of rank or enlistment.	Date of muster.	Remarks.
Musicians.				
Warren Y. Jenkins...	Hillsboro	July 28,1861	July 28,1861	Mustered out Aug. 20,1864.
James F. Witherspoon	"	Aug. 8,1861		Disch. Apr. 28,'62; disabil,
Privates.				
Arnold, Gabriel W....	Williamson co..	Sept. 15,1861		Deserted Mar. 14,1862......
Ackerman. A. L........	Hillsboro	July 28,1861		Died Jan. 24, 1861.........
Arney, John G........	"			Died Aug. 25, '62; wounds.
Adams, Eli William..	Montgomery co.	Aug. 13,1861		See Co. C, as consolidated.
Balderman, William..	Hillsboro	July 28,1861		Re-enlisted as Veteran....
Brady, James	Montgomery co.	"	July 28,1861	Mustered out Aug. 20,1864
Boone, W. S	Hillsboro	Aug. 15,1861		Re-enlisted as Veteran....
Bahno, Dennis..........	"	"		Mustered out Aug. 20,1864.
Bannon, William......	"	Aug. 30,1861		
Bartlett, John W......	Irving............	Aug. 17,1861	Aug. 17,1861	Mustered out Aug. 20,1864.
Brienbrier, Charles...	Hillsboro	Aug. 13,1861		
Blatier, Conrad	Montgomery co.	Aug. 24,1861		Re-enlisted as Veteran....
Bennett, Nelson.......	"	Sept. 4,1861		Died Dec. 12,1861.........
Darriker, Daniel J....	"	July 28,1861		Disch. July 22,'62; disabil.
Cheeney, W. T........	Christian co....	"		
Cottingham, Wm. A...	Montgomery co.	"		Died Nov. 21,1862; wounds.
Craig, George W......	"	"	July 28,1861	Mustered out Aug. 20,1864.
Crandall, A. A..........	"	Sept. 20,1861		
Clotfelter. James A...	"	Sept. 24,1861		See Co. C, as consolidated.
Danford, Joseph	DuQuoin	July 28,1861		Re-enlisted as Veteran....
Dort, Ira L............	Butler	"		Died July 21,1862.........
Davis, Richard........	Irving	"		Mustered out Aug. 20,1864.
Davis, James M.......	"	Aug. 17,1861		Re-enlisted as Veteran....
Dempsey, Michael....	Montgomery co.	July 28,1861	July 28,1861	Mustered out Aug. 20,1864.
Droesch, John	Hillsboro	Aug. 30,1861		Re-enlisted as Veteran....
Duvalt, George W....	Union co........	Sept. 1,1861		Disch. Apr. 5,'62; disabil..
Dry, George H........	Montgomery co.	Mar. 31,1862	Mar. 31,1862	See Co. C, as consolidated.
Ebert. J. H	Christian co....	July 28,1861		Disch. Apr. 28,'62; disabil.
Fry, Thomas..........	Hillsboro	Aug. 8,1861		
Finlay, Robert........	Montgomery co.	Aug. 17,1861	Aug. 17,1861	Mustered out Aug. 20,1864.
Gaisinger, Samuel....	Union co........	Sept. 1,1861		Killed at Corinth Oct.3,'62.
Gaw, Erasmus........	"	Sept. 22,1861		Disch. Dec. 3,'62; wounds.
Haller, W. R..........	Montgomery co.	July 28,1861		Killed at Shiloh Apr. 6,'62.
Haller, Israel..........	"	"	July 28,1861	Mustered out Aug. 20,1864.
Haller, V. C..........	"	Aug. 23,1862		
Hoober, Frank	Bond co........	July 28,1862		See Co. C, as consolidated,
Hendimann, Charles..	Litchfield......	Aug. 17,1861		Disch. Oct. 20, '62; disabil.
Holly, John...........	Alexander co...	July 27,1861		Re-enlisted as Veteran....
Illsley, William H....	Montgomery co.	July 28,1861		Mustered out Aug. 20,1864.
Jones, Merlin.........	St. Clair co.....	Aug. 15,1861	Aug. 15,1861	"
Kelp, William.........	Hillsboro	Aug. 8,1861		"
Livingood, John B....	"	Aug. 24,1861		Killed at Corinth Oct. 4,'62.
Lee, Henry M.........	Montgomery co.	Aug. 30,1861		Re-enlisted as Veteran....
Lamb, John G........	Alexander co...	Sept. 1,1861		"
Moore, John F........	Hillsboro	July 28,1861		"
Monyhan, Patrick	Montgomery co.	"	July 28,1861	Mustered out Aug. 20,1864.
Mapes, Wesley ....:..	Hillsboro	"		Died April 4, 1864........
Mason, Lafayette.....	Irving	"		Died June 22, '62; wounds.
Manchester, William..	Hillsboro	"		Discharged for disability.
McGullion, J. S........	Pana...........	"		Died July 13, '62; wounds.
Myers, Daniel.........	Irving	Aug. 17,1861		Disch. Feb. 22,'62; disabil.
Myers, Moses.........	"	"		Died Mar. 27, 1862........
Myers, Aaron	"	Sept. 3,1861		Disch. June 7, '62; disabil.
Magner, David N.....	Montgomery co.	Aug. 27,1861		
McLean, Alvin A......	"	Sept. 24,1861		See Co. C, as consolidated.
Nail. Edward.........	"	July 28,1861		
Newcomb, Charles H.	"	Aug. 17,1861	Aug. 17,1861	Mustered out Aug. 20,1864.
Nichodemus, M. H....	"	Aug. 23,1861		See Co.C, as consolidated.
Preston, Martin.......	"	July 28,1861		Re-enlisted as Veteran....
Pleasant, Thomas F...	Jackson co......	Sept. 4,1861		Transferred to Co. G......
Qualls, George........	Montgomery co.	July 28,1861		Re-enlisted as Veteran....
Ricket, William F....	"	"		Deserted June 6, 1862.....
Reckhart, William....	Hillsboro	"	July 28,1861	Mustered out Aug. 20,1864.
Reese, Leroy..........	Mound City....	Aug. 31,1861		
Ralph, George........	Tower Hill.....	Sept. 3,1861		Disch. Oct. 8,'62; wounds.
Stoddard, W. F........	Hillsboro	July 28,1861		
Sibley, George W.....	Pana...........	"		Disch. June 27,'62; disabil.
Swinderman. Sebast'n	Montgomery co.	"		Killed at Corinth Oct. 4,'62
Stickle, F. M..........	"	"		See Co. C, as consolidated.
Sharrock, James.......	Tower Hill.....	Aug. 13,1861		Died Jan. 12,1861.........
Sharrock, John	"	Sept. 3,1861		Disch. July 31,62; disabil..
Sharrock, D. L........	"	"		See Co.C, as consolidated.
Simmons, D. A. D......	"	Aug. 13,1861		Disch. Dec. 12,'63; disabil.
Sanders, Lewis........	Montgomery co.	Aug. 17,1861	Aug. 17,1861	Mustered out Aug. 20,1864.
Suits, Gideon..........	"	July 28,1861	July 28,1861	" "

Name and Rank.	Residence.	Date of rank or enlistment.	Date of muster.	Remarks.
Schuceler, George	Montgomery co.	July 24, 1861	....	Transferred to Co. D......
Southworth, E. B......	Litchfield.......	Aug. 30, 1861	....	Died July 7, 1862 ....
Saltzman, John	Alton	Aug. 2, 1861	....	Re-enlisted as Veteran....
Smith, Isaac..........	Jackson co	Sept. 15, 1861	....	Disch. June 27, '62; disabil.
Taulbee, Joseph E....	Irving	July 28, 1861	....	Re-enlisted as Veteran....
Timmins, Cromwell...	Nokomis	''	....	Disch. Apr. 18, '62; disabil.
Turner, M. H..........	Hillsboro.	Aug. 30, 1861	....	Killed at Nancy Cr'ek, Ga., July 17, 1864..............
Whalen, Patrick	''	July 28, 1861	....	Disch. Aug. 26, '62; wounds
White, W. M..........	''	Aug. 8, 1861	....	Disch. Dec. 22, '62; disabil.
White, Daniel C......	''	July 28, 1861	....	Killed at Shiloh, Apr. 6, '62
Wiegart, George	Litchfield	Aug. 8, 1861	....	Re-enlisted as Veteran....
Wood, James..........	Alexander co...	Sept. 1, 1861	....	Died Nov. 13, 1861..........
Wright, Thomas	''	Sept. 4, 1861	....	Killed at Shiloh, Apr. 6, '62
Wilson, W. R..........	Jackson co......	Sept. 15, 1861	....	Deserted June 6, 1862 ......
Veterans.				
Boone, William S	Hillsboro	Mar. 23, 1864	Mar. 23, 1864	See Co. C, as consolidated
Blatter, Conrad	''	''	''	
Boldeman, William ...	''	''	''	See Co. D, as consolidated
Droesch, John........	''	Jan. 4, 1864	Jan. 24, 1864	See Co. C, as consolidated
Davis, James M........	''			'' ''
Danford, Joseph	Keokuk, Iowa..			'' ''
Holly, John.............	Cairo..........	Mar. 23, 1864	Mar. 23, 1864	'' ''
Lamb, John G.........	Irving	Jan. 4, 1864	Jan. 24, 1864	'' ''
Lee, Henry M..........	Hillsboro			'' ''
Miller, Jacob..........	''	Mar. 23, 1864	Mar. 23, 1864	'' ''
Moore, John F........	''			'' ''
Preston, Martin	''	Jan. 4, 1864	Jan. 24, 1864	'' ''
Qualls, George W	''	Mar. 23, 1864	Mar. 23, 1864	'' ''
Salzman, John	Bloomington ...			See Co. D, as consolidated
Taulbee, Joseph E....	Irving	Jan. 4, 1864	Jan. 24, 1864	See Co. C, as consolidated
Wiegert, George	Litchfield	Mar. 23, 1864	Mar. 23, 1864	'' ''
Recruits.				
Adams, W. C		Aug. 1, 1862	Aug. 15, 1862	See Co. C, as consolidated
Arnold, William D....		....	....	Killed at Sugar Valley, Ga., May 9, 1864............
Boutwell, O. W........	Hillsboro	Aug. 23, 1862	Aug. 25, 1862	See Co. B, as consolidated
Boutwell, George H...	''	Dec. 29, 1863	Dec. 29, 1863	See Co. C, as consolidated
Bishop, William B....	Litchfield	Feb. 2, 1864	Mar. 26, 1864	'' ''
Berry, William........	Hillsboro	Apr. 22, 1864	Apr. 22, 1864	
Chamness, George B..		Aug. 15, 1862	Nov. 4, 1862	See Co. A, as consolidated
Chitty, J. H.............		''	Aug. 15, 1862	See Co. C, as consolidated
Chitty, Oliver W......		''	''	'' ''
Chadoin, Thomas B...		''	''	'' ''
Dorris, William R		Aug. 1, 1862	Aug. 1, 1862	'' ''
Dorris, Wesley W......				'' ''
Duncan, John W......		Aug. 15, 1862	Aug. 15, 1862	'' ''
Everett, George W		Aug. 1, 1862	Nov. 4, 1862	'' ''
Everett, John C......				'' ''
Erek, William..........	Union co	Aug. 31, 1861	....	'' ''
Fry, Simeon		Aug. 15, 1862	Aug. 15, 1862	'' ''
Fletcher, Calvin......				'' ''
Gower, Jefferson......		Aug. 1, 1862		'' ''
Glass, Thomas		''	''	'' ''
Gregory, William......				'' ''
Hatfield, John..........	Montgomery co.	Aug. 15, 1861	....	Deserted Jan. 21, 1863, Benton Bks, Mo..............
Hickman, W. B	Litchfield	Feb. 11, 1864	June 16, 1864	See Co. C, as consolidated
Hicks, Samuel		Aug. 1, 1862	Aug. 15, 1862	'' ''
Herron, Ephraim		Aug. 10, 1862	Sept. 5, 1862	'' ''
Jorden, Blewford.....		Aug. 1, 1862	Aug. 15, 1862	'' ''
Jenkins, S. M..........	Hillsboro	Feb. 2, 1864	Apr. 19, 1864	'' ''
Jackson, Harvey......		Aug. 1, 1862	Aug. 15, 1862	'' ''
Moynahan, Philip.....	Montgomery co.	Nov. 17, 1862	Nov. 17, 1862	'' ''
McAnelly, R. Martin..		Aug. 1, 1862	Aug. 15, 1862	'' ''
Moraine, Harvey......		Mar. 1, 1864	Apr. 19, 1864	'' ''
Neal, W. H		....	....	Disch. Feb. 15, '64; disabil.
Phelts, Benjamin		Aug. 15, 1862	Aug. 15, 1862	See Co. C, as consolidated
Powell, John		Aug. 14, 1862	''	'' ''
Richardson, Samuel...		''	''	'' ''
Short, George A.......	Montgomery co.	Aug. 23, 1862	''	'' ''
Shelton, Joseph A	''	''	''	'' ''
Stacey, James H	Marion..........	Feb. 13, 1864	Feb. 13, 1864	'' ''
Stephens, Columbus J		Aug. 14, 1862	Aug. 16, 1862	'' ''
Stephens, David		Aug. 15, 1862	Aug. 15, 1862	'' ''
Stroud, J. C..........		Aug. 14, 1892	Aug. 20, 1862	'' ''
Stroud, J. P..........		''	''	'' ''
Turner, James V......	Hillsboro	Sept. 4, 1861	....	Disch. Feb. 22, '62; disabil.

Name and Rank.	Residence.	Date of rank or enlistment.	Date of muster.	Remarks.
Turnage, Henry........	....	Aug. 15, 1862	Aug. 15, 1862	See Co. C, as consolidated
Turnage, Phillip	....			
Webber, John A.......	Hillsboro	Sept. 24, 1861	Sept. 24, 1861	" "
Winters, William H...	....	Aug. 15, 1862	Aug. 15, 1862	" "
Under Cooks.				
Bailey, Charles........	....	Dec. 18, 1863	Jan. 24, 1864	See Co. C, as consolidated
Grigsby, Martin	....	" "	" "	Deserted May 27, 1864......
Kimbal, Jasper........	....	" "	" "	See Co. C, as consolidated
White, Thomas........	....	" "	" "	

COMPANY I.

Name and Rank.	Residence.	Date of rank or enlistment.	Date of muster.	Remarks.
Captains.				
Joseph G. Robinson ..	Edwardsville ..	July 26, 1861	Aug. 31, 1861	Trans. to Invalid Corps, Nov. 16, 1863 ....
Samuel T. Hughes....	" " ..	Aug. 25, 1863	Dec. 31, 1863	Pro. Lieut. Col.; trans. as consolidated ....
First Lieutenants.				
William H. Purviance	Troy	July 31, 1861	Aug. 31, 1861	Discharged Aug. 16, 1862...
Samuel T. Hughes....	Edwardsville ..	Aug. 16, 1862	Sept. 18, 1862	Promoted...................
William Padon........	Troy	Aug. 25, 1863	Jan. 1, 1864	Pro. Capt. Co. A.; trans. as consolidated ....
Second Lieutenants.				
Samuel T. Hughes....	Edwardsville ..	July 31, 1861	Aug. 31, 1861	Promoted...................
William Padon	Troy	Aug. 16, 1862	Sept. 18, 1862	" "
George Woodbury	" "	Aug. 25, 1863	Mar. 6, 1864	Pro. Capt. Co. B.; trans. as consolidated ....
First Sergeant.				
William Padon.........	Troy	July 31, 1861	Aug. 31, 1861	Promoted 2d Lieutenant ..
Sergeants.				
George Woodbury	Troy	July 31, 1861	Aug. 31, 1861	
William W. Jarvis....	" "	" "	" "	Mustered out Aug. 20, 1864
William H. Dunagan,	Wanda..........	July 12, 1861	" "	" "
James W. Crosby,.....	Omph Ghent ...	July 27, 1861	" "	" " " "
Corporals.				
George Stice,.........	Troy	July 31, 1861	Aug. 31, 1861	See Co. B, as consolidated
Monroe A. Cornman..	" "			
Robert R. Swain......	" "	Aug. 19, 1861	" "	See Co. B, as consolidated
John G. Irwin.........	Edwardsville ..	" "	" "	Mustered out Aug. 20, 1864.
Thomas Pete ,........	" "	July 31, 1861	" "	" "
Alfred T. Stanton.....	Marine..........	" "	" "	" "
Ferdina'd A. Cornman	Troy	Aug. 19, 1861	" "	Killed at Moalton, Ala., March 21, 1864.............
James B. Thomas.....	" "	July 31, 1861	" "	Mustered out Aug. 20, 1864.
Privates.				
Abbott, Nathaniel.....	Carlyle	Aug. 9, 1861	Aug. 31, 1861	....
Burgess, Eben H......	Edwardsville ..	July 31, 1861	" "	Mustered out Aug. 20, 1864.
Baird, John............	Collinsville	" "	" "	
Baird, William	" "	" "	" "	Mustered out Aug. 20, 1864.
Breyfogle, Daniel G ..	Marine..........	" "	" "	" "
Barber, Norman C ...	Troy	" "	" "	....
Ballard, James G......	Wanda..........	" "	" "	
Bass, John............	Troy	Aug. 12, 1861	" "	Killed at Shiloh, Apr. 6, '62.
Behrendtz, Charles F.	Edwardsville ..	" "	" "	Mustered out Aug. 20, 1864.
Burches, Zachariah...	" "	" "	" "	Died Apr. 3, 1862; wounds..
Barden, Aaron C......	Brighton	Aug. 19, 1861	" "	Mustered out Aug. 20, 1864.
Berry, Isaiah..........	Carlyle	Aug. 9, 1861	" "	Died Apr. 26, 1862; wounds
Boes, Anthony	Troy	Aug. 28, 1861	" "	Kill'd in an affray July 4, 64
Cowell, Charles	Omph Ghent...	July 27, 1861	" "	Mustered out Aug. 20, 1866.
Crews, Josephus......	Edwardsville ..	Aug. 12, 1861	" "	....
Collins, James G......	Six Mile	" "	" "	Disch. Apr. 4, '62; disabil..
Clark, George W	Edwardsville ..	" "	" "	Mustered out Aug. 20, 1864.
Cupinall, George W...	Six Mile	" "	" "	See Co. D, as consolidated
Davidson. Samuel E..	Wanda..........	Aug. 9, 1861	" "	Mustered out Aug. 20, 1864.
Dayton, Charles E	Edwardsville ..	Aug. 12, 1861	" "	Disch. Aug. 10, '62; wounds
Davis, Emanuel.......	Carbondale.....	Sept. 17, 1861	Sept. 17, 1861	....
Davis, Charles	" "	" "	" "	Disc. Apr. 25, '62; disabil ..
Dunnagan, Joshua S..	Wanda..........	Aug. 12, 1861	Aug. 31, 1861	Died Oct. 29, 1861..........
Elliott, John..........	Preston.........	Sept. 10, 1861	Sept. 10, 1861	See Co. B, as consolidated

Name and Rank.	Residence.	Date of rank or enlistment.	Date of muster.	Remarks.
Fitzsimmons, Henry..	Vicksburg,Miss	July 27, 1861	Aug. 31, 1861	Mustered out Aug. 29, 1864.
Fisher, Theodore......	Carlyle	Aug. 9, 1861	"	....
Fuller, Heaston	Troy	Aug. 12, 1861	"	Disch. July 16,'62; wounds
Graham, John.	Collinsville	July 31, 1861	"	Died ....
Gillman, Thomas C...	Edwardsville ..	Aug. 19, 1861	"	Mustered out Aug. 20, 1864.
Gillespie, Joseph J....	"	Sept. 7, 1861	Sept. 9, 1861	Disch. June 4,'62; disabil..
Hawley, John	Troy	July 31, 1861	Aug. 31, 1861	Died March, 1862...........
Hays, Oliver	"	"	"	Re-enlisted as Veteran.....
Hammock, Andrew J.	....	"	"	Disch. Oct. 8, '62; disabil ..
Hanratty, James......	Edwardsville ..	Aug. 12, 1861	"	Disch. July 29,'62; wounds
Helms, William S.....	"	"	"	"
Harker, Hiram........	Troy............	"	"	Mustered out Aug. 20,1864.
Hauskins,Thomas L..	Edwardsville ..	Aug. 19, 1861	"	"
Holcomb, Mahlon D ..	Troy............	Sept. 3, 1861	Sept. 3, 1861	See Co. B, as consolidated
Irwin, Samuel.........	Edwardsville ..	Aug. 19, 1861	Aug. 31, 1861	Mustered out Aug. 20, 1864.
Jaka, John............	Troy	July 31, 1861	"	"
Jarvis, Sidney B	"	"	"	" "
Johnson, James N.....	"	"	"	Killed at Fort Donelson, Feb. 15, 1862.
Johnson. David	"	"	"	Mustered out Aug. 20,1864.
Kluge, Augustus......	"	"	"	Killed at Fort Donelson, Feb. 15, 1862.
Keegon, Edward R....	"	"	"	Died Apr. 15, '62; wounds..
Kyle, David	"	"	"	Mustered out Aug. 20, 1864.
Kinder, George W.....	Edwardsville ..	"	"	Killed at Fort Donelson, Feb. 15, 1862.
Lornyer, Charles......	" ..	"	"	Killed at Fort Donelson, Feb. 15, 1862.
Lent, George	Wanda..........	"	"	Disch. Oct. 14, '62; wounds
Lawson, George.......	Greenville......	Aug. 12, 1861	"	....
Lang, James	Troy	"	"	See Co. B, as consolidated
Lane, Dennis..........	Edwardsville ..	"	"	Killed at Fort Donelson, Feb. 15, 1862.
Lewis, James..........	" ..	"	"	Mustered out Aug. 20, 1864.
Lewis, Charles C....	" ..	"	"	"
Lawrence, John N....	" ..	Aug. 19, 1861	"	....
Livingston, Alonzo...	" ..	"	"	Killed at Fort Donelson, Feb. 15, 1862.
Mills, Albert..........	Troy	July 31, 1861	"	Died Apr. 27, '62; wounds..
McKinley, George S ..	"	"	"	Died Aug. 18, 1862 ....
McMahan, Hugh	....	"	"	Killed at Fort Donelson, Feb. 15, 1862.
McKinney, John K....	Omph Ghent...	"	"	Killed at Fort Donelson, Feb. 15, 1862.
Morehead, Samuel....	Edwardsville ..	Aug. 12, 1861	"	Disch. Oct. 14, '62; wounds
McDermott, Charles ..	" ..	"	"	Killed at Fort Donelson, Feb. 15, 1862.
Mitchell, James.......	" ..	Aug. 19, 1861	"	....
Moore, George W	Troy	Aug. 28, 1861	"	Died Feb. 15, '62; wounds..
Parker, William.......	"	July 31, 1861	"	Mustered out Aug. 20,1864.
Prentice, John E	"	Aug. 12, 1861	"	Disch. Nov. 4,'62; disabil..
Patton, Charles S	Venice	"	"	See Co. B, as consolidated
Pearl. Lawford........	Edwardsville...	Aug. 19, 1861	"	Disch. Jan. 1,'62; disabil..
Richards, Edward H..	Carlyle.........	"	"	....
Reid, Nicholas	Venice.....	"	"	"
Readman, Charles A.	Wanda..........	"	"	Mustered out Aug. 20,1864.
Reid, Samuel..........	Marine..........	Sept. 11, 1861	Sept. 11, 1861	See Co. B, as consolidated
Riggin, William H	Troy	Sept. 3, 1861	Sept. 3, 1861	"
Robertson, Thomas R.	Omph Ghent...	July 27, 1861	Aug. 31, 1861	Died Oct. 20, 1861.........
Swartz, Frederick	Troy	July 31, 1861	"	Killed at Shiloh Apr. 6,'62.
Sanders, Henry	Venice..........	Aug. 12, 1861	"	Mustered out Aug. 20, 1864.
Stevenson, Joseph P..	Troy	Aug. 19, 1861	"	Killed at Fort Donelson, Feb. 15, 1862.
Stallman, Frederick ..	Edwardsville ..	Aug. 12, 1861	"	Mustered out Aug. 20, 1864.
Stringer, Joseph E....	Wanda..........	Aug. 28, 1861	"	....
Smith, Jacob	Edwardsville...	Aug. 12, 1861	"	Died Nov. 7, 1861..........
Turner, James D... .	" ..	"	"	Mustered out Aug. 20,1864.
Vanhooser, John R....	"	July 31, 1861	"	....
Webster, Olander T...	Omph Ghent...	July 27, 1861	"	Died Dec. 15, 1861.........
Wilson, William T	Edwardsville...	July 31, 1861	"	Disch. Aug. 21,'62; wounds
Williams, David	Troy	"	"	Killed at Fort Donelson, Feb. 15, 1862.
Willis, George.........	"	Aug. 12, 1861	"	....
Willson, John	"	"	"	Kil'd, Dallas,Ga.,May 26.'64
Wormyer, Henry......	Wanda..........	Aug. 19, 1861	"	Mustered out Aug. 20, 1864.
Veteran, Hays, Oliver	Troy	Mar. 29, 1864	Mar. 29, 1864	Deserted July 7, 1864......

Name and Rank.	Residence	Date of rank or enlistment.	Date of muster.	Remarks.
Recruits.				
Bohanon, James M....	Edwardsville ..	Nov. 10,1863	Nov. 10,1863	See Co. B, as consolidated
Cornman, Horatio	Troy	Aug. 20,1862	Aug. 20,1862	'' ''
Cox, William T........	Edwardsville ..	Nov. 10,1863	Nov. 10,1863	'' ''
Fowler, James	Wanda..........	Dec. 22,1863	Dec. 22,1863	'' ''
Fortner, Robert......		Aug. 18,1862	Nov. 4,1862	'' ''
Furlough, James......		Aug. 15,1862	'' ''	'' ''
Hawkins, William T..				
Johnson, Sidney L....	Troy	Mar. 19,1862	Mar. 19,1862	
Jones, John	Springfield	Mar. 25,1864	Apr. 19,1864	Transferred to Co. K......
Jordan, Richard......				Died Mar. 22,'64; wounds .
Kluck, James W		May 20,1863	Oct. 31,1863	See Co. B, as consolidated
McRoy, John		Aug. 15,1862	Nov. 4,1862	'' ''
McRoy, William		'' ''	'' ''	'' ''
McClintock, John A...		'' ''	'' ''	'' ''
Moake, George W.....		'' ''	'' ''	'' ''
Moake, Andrew		'' ''	'' ''	'' ''
Moore, Samuel P......		'' ''	'' ''	'' ''
Martin, George W.....		'' ''	'' ''	'' ''
Ollis, George W......		'' ''	'' ''	'' ''
Odin, James..........		'' ''	'' ''	'' ''
Padon, James	Troy	Aug. 24,1862	Aug. 24,1862	'' ''
Padon, Judson	''	Aug. 29,1862		Died Jan. 24,1864 ....
Reese, Barnett B......		Aug. 15,1862	Nov. 4,1862	See Co. B, as consolidated
Seybold, Samuel	Troy	Nov. 1,1861	Nov. 1,1861	'' ''
Smith, Isaac		Aug. 15,1862	Nov. 4,1862	See Co. D, as consolidated
Smith, James.........				
Snowden, Vachall.....	Anna..........	Mar. 14,1864	Apr. 17,1864	See Co. B, as consolidated
Snell, Araldon.......		Aug. 15,1862	Nov. 4,1862	'' ''
Stilley, James B		'' ''	'' ''	'' ''
Shaw, James B.......				
Shaw, Sebastian		Aug. 15,1862	Nov. 4,1862	Transferred from 128th Ill
Woodard, George W..		'' ''	'' ''	See Co. B, as consolidated
Williams, James R....		Aug. 28,1862	Aug. 28,1862	'' ''
Sanders, FrederickW.	Troy	Aug. 20,1862	Aug. 20,1862	'' ''
Under Cooks.				
Odom, Archibald......		Aug. 1,1862	Nov. 5,1862	See Co. D, as consolidated
Townsend, Simeon....		Dec. 19,1863	Jan. 24,1864	See Co. B, as consolidated
Tyler, John..........		'' ''	'' ''	'' ''
Brown, Henry........		'' ''	'' ''	'' ''
Brown, Preston		'' ''	'' ''	'' ''

COMPANY K.

Name and Rank.	Residence.	Date of rank or enlistment.	Date of muster.	Remarks.
Captain.				
George B. Poor........	Cairo..........	July 26,1861	July 26,1861	Resigned Dec. 10,1861......
James C. McCleary ...	Ullin..........	Dec. 10,1861	....	Died of wounds July 9,1862
Gilbert G. Lowe.......	Carbondale.....	July 9,1862	Dec. 9,1862	Mustered out Aug. 20,1864.
First Lieutenants.				
John L. A. Reeves		....	....	Resigned Oct. 2,1861.......
James C. McCleary ...	Ullin..........	Oct. 2,1861	....	Promoted...............
Gilbert G. Lowe.......	Carbondale.....	Dec. 10,1861	June 2,1862	....
James Oates..........	Springfield	July 9,1862	July 9,1862	Mustered out Aug. 20,1864.
Second Lieutenants.				
James C. McCleary ...	Ullin..........	July 26,1861	July 26,1861	Promoted..................
Gilbert G. Lowe.......	Carbondale.....	Oct. 2,1861	Oct. 29,1861	''
James, Oates........	Springfield	Dec. 10,1861	Feb. 4,1862	'' ....
Benjamin L. Ulen.....	Ullin..........	July 9,1862	July 9,1862	Mustered out Aug. 20,1864.
First Sergeant.				
Andrew J. Snider.....	Murphysboro ..	Aug. 5,1861	Aug. 5,1861	Mustered out Aug. 20,1864.
Sergeants.				
John Barber..........	Cairo..........	Aug. 1,1861	Aug. 1,1861	Died Jan. 26,1864..........
Charles A. Spatee.....	Ullin..........	Aug. 5,1861	Aug. 5,1861	Pro. to Commissary Serg..
James Oates..........	Springfield	July 26,1861	Dec. 9,1861	Promoted 2d Lieutenant ..
Ferdinand Hinckley..	Belleville.......	Aug. 1,1861	Aug. 1,1861	Discharged Sept. 2,1862 ...

Name and Rank.	Residence.	Date of rank or enlistment.	Date of muster.	Remarks.
Corporals.				
Charles N. Brown.....	Auburn.........	July 26,1861	July 26,1861	Mustered out Aug. 20,1864.
George Lincoln........	Ullin............	Aug. 5,1861	Aug. 5,1861	Foot shot off and nine bullet wounds at Donelson. Taken prisoner and died March, 1862............
Robert G. McGill......	Ullin............	"	"	Mustered out Aug. 20,1864.
Walter Walsh	Auburn.........	July 26.1861	July 26,1861	Killed at Fort Donelson, Feb. 15,1862...........
George Meyers........	Springfield.....	"	"	Re-enlisted as Veteran....
Benjamin L. Ulen.....	Ullin....	Aug. 13,1861	Aug. 13,1861	Promoted 2d Lieutenant ..
James Troy...........	Springfield.....	July 26,1861	July 26,1861	Mustered out Aug. 20,1864.
John Richmond	Ullin............	"	"	Wounded at Shiloh. Died in prison, Sept. 17,1862, at Augusta, Ga.............
Privates.				
Alexander, William...	Pulaski	July 26,1861	July 26,1861	Died Aug. 17,1862 ....
Anderson, Reuben M..	Cobden	Sept. 30,1861	Sept. 30,1861	Killed at Fort Donelson, Feb. 15,1862.............
Boland, Edward......	....	July 26,1861	July 26,1861	Mustered out Aug. 20,1864.
Burk, John ....:...		"	"	
Broadie, James.......	Mound City	"	"	Disch. May 26,'62; wounds
Brown, George		Aug. 6,1861	Aug. 6,1861	Mustered out Aug. 20,1864.
Brewer, Isaac.........	Cairo...........	"	"	" "
Bass, Henry	Ullin............	Aug. 13,1861	Aug. 13,1861	" "
Burton, Andrew J.....	"	"	"	Killed at Fort Donelson, Feb. 15,1862.............
Barlow, Robert D.....	New Madrid, M.	Aug. 18,1861	Aug. 18,1861	Died May 6,1862............
Burton, George W., Sr.	Cobden	Sept. 30,1861	Sept. 30,1861	....
Burton, William T	"	Sept. 3,1861	Sept. 3,1861	Re-enlisted as Veteran....
Burton, George W., Jr.	....	"	"	See Co. B, as consolidated
Bowles, Charles W....	Jackson co	"	"	Re-enlisted as Veteran....
Corbin, Charles	Union City, Ky.	July 26,1861	July 26,1861	Died at Memphis, Tenn....
Cogdal, Henderson....	Pittsburg.......	"	"	Wounded at Shiloh. Died Apr. 13,1862............
Crockett, David	Mound City	"	"	Died May 5,1862...........
Creed, John L	Mound City Jun	"	"	Wounded at Shiloh. Died May 1,1862............
Creed, Colby..........	"	Aug. 6,1861	Aug. 6,1861	Died Apr. 5,1862...........
Cosebone, Henry......	Shawneetown ..	"	"	Mustered out Aug. 20,1864.
Condon, Joseph N.....	....	Aug 10,1861	Aug. 10,1861	Deserted Jan. 22, 1863.....
Clifford, John........	Ullin............	Aug. 13,1861	Aug. 13,1861	Mustered out Aug. 20,1864.
Cording, William A...	St. Louis, Mo...	Aug. 31,1861	Aug. 31,1861	Wounded at Shiloh. Died May 18,1862.............
Casebeer, Charles	Bryan, Ohio	Sept. 3,1861	Sept. 3,1861	Killed at Fort Donelson, Feb. 15,1862.............
Casey, Henry.........	Union co........	Sept. 18,1861	Sept. 18,1861	See Co. B, as consolidated
Dewire, Thomas......	Mound City Jun	July 26,1861	July 26,1861	Mustered out Aug. 20,1864.
Duran, Alfred	Quincy	Aug. 26,1861	Aug. 26,1861	
Daley, William	Union co.......	Aug. 13,1861	Aug. 13,1861	Mustered out Aug. 20,1864.
Emery, John..........	Johnson co.....	Sept. 3,1861	Sept. 3,1861	Killed at Fort Donelson, Feb. 15,1862.............
Fieny, John...........	Pulaski	July 26,1861	July 26,1861	Mustered out Aug. 20,1864.
Foster, William	Ullin............	Aug. 13,1861	Aug. 13,1861	Killed at Shiloh, Apr. 6,'62
Flagles, Francis......		"	"	Mustered out Aug. 20,1864.
Flowers, William	Lebanon........	July 26,1861	July 26,1561	Died Sept. 5,1861...........
Gibbson, John.........	Ullin............	"	"	
Gibbs, Levi		Aug. 16,1861	Aug. 16,1861	Mustered out Aug. 20,1864.
Gatewood, Seymour...	Charleston, Mo.	Aug. 13,1861	Aug. 13,1861	Disch. June 20,'62; wounds
Grills, James.........	Ullin............	July 26,1861	July 26,1861	Died Oct. 16,1861...........
Hazlewood, Joshua ...	Alexander co...	Aug. 13,1861	Aug. 13,1861	Killed at Fort Donelson, Feb. 15,1862.............
Hobbs, William	Springfield	July 26,1861	July 26,1861	Died Aug. 10,1862...........
Hall, Peter...........	Ashley..........	Aug. 5,1861	Aug. 5,1861	Disch. May 7,'64,Jeff. b'ks, Mo ; shot Oct. 8,1863.....
Harn, John	Bryan, Ohio	Sept. 3,1861	Sept. 3,1861	See Co. B, as consolidated
Hagler, William J.....	Jackson co	Sept. 18,1861	Sept. 18,1861	
Hagler, Thomas J.....	"	.....		Disch. June 2,'62; wounds.
Kridler, James L......	....	Aug. 5,1861	Aug. 5,1861	Killed at Shiloh, Apr. 6,'62
Kimbal, Albert W.....	Centralia	Sept. 3,1861	Sept. 3,1861	See Co. B, as consolidated
Kennedy, Jesse........	Cobden	Sept. 6,1861	Sept. 6,1861	
Lipe, William R	Jackson co	Sept. 18,1861	Sept. 18,1861	" "
Lipe, Aaron...........				
Maloy, John..........	Cairo	July 26,1861	July 26,1861	Disch. June 20,'62; wounds
Massey, Peter		Aug. 5,1861	Aug. 5,1861	Mustered out Aug. 20,1864.
Morgan, William	Okaw...........	Aug. 17,1861	Aug. 17,1861	" "
Mitchell, Alfred	Pulaski co......	Aug. 13,1861	Aug. 13,1861	" "
Miller, Samuel L	Columbus, Ky..	July 26,1861	July 26,1861	
McEwen, Henry P.....	Ligonier, Ind...	"	"	See Co. B, as consolidated
May, Zero.............	Mound City Jun	"	"	Wounded at Ft. Donelson; died May 13,1862.........

Name and Rank.	Enrolled at.	Date of rank or enlistment.	Date of muster.	Remarks.
Munn, Columbus......	Ullin............	Aug. 30,1861	Aug. 30,1861	Deserted Sept. 5,1862......
Mulinax, Lemuel J....	Union co........	Sept. 3,1861	Sept. 3,1861	Died July 13,1862...........
Martin, William........	Cairo			Deserted Sept. 15,1861.....
McCauley, Michael....	....	Aug. 1,1861	Aug. 1,1861	Deserted Sept. 4,1861......
Nicol,.John...........	....	July 26,1861	July 26,1861	Mustered out Aug. 20,1864.
Newcomb, David......	Mound City Jun	Aug. 23,1861	Aug. 23,1861	Killed, Fort Donelson, Feb. 15,1862..................
Obearts, John.........	Jackson co	Sept. 30,1861	Sept. 30,1861	See Co. B, as consolidated
Patterson, James......	Ullin............	Aug. 13,1861	Aug. 13.1861	Killed, Fort Donelson, Feb. 15,1862
Palmer, John C........	Coloma	''	''	Mustered out Aug. 20,1864.
Peeler, Henry M	Pulaski	Sept. 3,1861	Sept. 3,1861	Disch. Feb. 22, '62; disabil.
Parrish, William......	''	Aug. 31,1861	Aug. 31,1861	Deserted Sept. 2, 1861.....
Renfrew, Bartley......	Mound City Jun	Aug. 13,1861	Aug. 13.1861	Disch. Oct. 6, '62; disabi ...
Ramsey, Robert E....	....			
Sloan, George.........	Jacksonville ...	July 26,1861	July 26,1861	Killed at Shiloh Apr. 6, '62.
Sloan, Samuel W......	''	Aug. 10,1861	Aug. 10,1861	Mustered out Aug. 20,1864.
Sanders. Frank M.....	Mound City Jun	July 26,1861	July 26,1861	'' ''
Smith, Michael........	Pulaski co......	Aug. 12,1861	Aug. 12,1861	'' ''
Seevers, John	Mound City	Aug. 6,1861	Aug. 6,1861	'' ''
Stenger, Henry........	''	Aug. 16,1861	Aug. 16,1861	'' ''
Stripling, Jesse........	Mound City Jun	Aug. 13,1861	Aug. 13,1861	Died Feb. 15,1862...........
Sumners, John B.....	Ullin............	Aug. 22,1861	Aug. 22,1861	Mustered out Aug. 20,1864.
Stone, Jonathan.......	Union co........	Sept. 3,1861	Sept. 3,1861	Disch. Aug. 20, '62; wounds
Salyers, Andrew J....	Jackson co	Sept. 18,1861	Sept. 18,1861	See Co. B, as consolidated
Tomlinson, Charles...	Springfield.....	July 26,1861	July 26,1861	Wounded at Shiloh; died April 23,1862.............
Tollman, Richard.....	Pulaski	''	''	Disch. Nov. 1,1861; disabil.
Thompson, William....	Cairo	Aug. 5,1861	Aug. 5,1861	Died Feb. 17, '62; wounds..
Tomlinson, William....	Springfield.....	July 26,1861	July 26,1861	Deserted Aug. 12,1861.....
Ulen, Hamilton C....	Ullin............	Aug. 13,1861	Aug. 13,1861	Disch. Oct. 19, '62; wounds
Ulen, James...........	''	Aug. 22,1861	Aug. 22,1861	....
Ulen, Samuel.........	''	Aug. 13,1861	Aug. 13,1861	....
Vanbrazell, William..	Mound City Jun	Aug. 18,1861	Aug. 18,1861	....
Walton, Thomas......	''	Aug. 7,1861	Aug. 7,1861	Killed at Shiloh Apr. 6, '62.
Walsh, John...........	Auburn..........	Aug. 10,1861	Aug. 10,1861	See Co. B, as consolidated
Winstread, Frank M..	Ullin............	July 26,1864	July 26,1861	Mustered out Aug. 20,1864.
Williams, George	Missouri co., Mo			
Yeeley, George........	Mound City	Aug. 6,1861	Aug. 6,1861	Died Dec. 19,1861...........
Casey, Simeon P......	Union co........	Sept. 6,1861	Sept. 6,1861	Disch. June 20, '62; wounds
Veterans.				
Burton,ThomasW.,(or William T.)...........	Cairo	Jan. 4,1864	Jan. 24;1864	See Co. B, as consolidated
Boles, Charles W......	''	Jan. 4,1864		
Myers, George.........	Chicago	Mar. 27,1864	Mar. 27,1864	'' ''
Recruits.				
Abernathy, George W	....	Oct. 1,1863	Oct. 1,1863	See Co. B, as consolidated
Adams, James M......	....	Aug. 1,1862	Nov. 4,1862	'' ''
Barnett, Nathaniel E.	....	Aug. 4,1862	Aug. 4,1862	'' ''
Cavitt, William	....	Aug. 18,1862	Nov. 4,1862	'' ''
Davis, Emanuel........	Anna	Sept. 17,1861	Sept. 17,1861	'' ''
Emery, Moses.......	....	Mar. 18,1864	Apr. 19,1864	'' ''
Eubanks, William H..	....	Aug. 4,1862	Nov. 4,1862	'' ''
Goddard, John L......	....	Aug. 18,1862		'' ''
Gregory, John C	Anna	Mar. 18,1862	July 5,1864	'' ''
Grace, Henry..........	....	Aug. 18,1862	Nov. 4,1862	'' ''
Goodman, Jeff........	....	....	....	Died Feb. 15,1864..........
Gowan, James M......	....			Mustered out July 20,1865.
Hegler, Daniel	Anna	Mar. 9,1864	Apr. 19,1864	See Co. B, as consolidated
Hudgeons, John.......	....	Aug. 15,1862	Nov. 4,1862	'' ''
Hall, Joseph..........	....	Dec. 4,1862	Dec. 4,1862	'' ''
Jordon, Dr. F..........	....	Aug. 15,1862	Nov. 4,1862	'' ''
Jones, David	....			'' ''
Jackson, John.........	....	''	Aug. 15,1862	'' ''
Jones, John	Springfield.....	Mar. 24,1864	Apr. 19,1864	'' ''
Johnson, John R......	....			Died Nov. 30,1863.........
Kearney, John	....	Dec. 9,1862	Dec. 9,1862	See Co. B, as consolidated
Koonce, Thomas B....	....	Aug. 15,1862	Nov. 4,1862	'' ''
Knight, Ellis B........	....			'' ''
Lamar, Joseph P......	Anna	Jan. 26,1864	Mar. 26,1864	'' ''
Lines, William.........	....	Sept. 20,1862	Nov. 4,1862	'' ''
McInturff, Alfred B...	....	Oct. 20,1862	''	'' ''
Moaks, Jacob..........	....	Aug. 15,1862	''	'' ''
Osborn, Samuel.......	Anna	Mar. 18,1864	July 5,1864	'' ''
Owens, Moses.........	....	Aug. 15,1862	Nov. 4,1862	'' ''
Ollis, Daniel W	....	''	''	'' ''
Parks, John	....	''	''	'' ''

Name and Rank.	Residence.	Date of rank or enlistment.	Date of muster.	Remarks.
Pankey, Joseph	....	Aug. 15, 1862	Nov. 4, 1862	Deserted March 8, 1864.....
Rummage, John H	....	" "	" "	See Co. B, as consolidated
Ranney, Isham	....			
Rice, William R	....	Mar. 9, 1864	Apr. 19, 1864	" "
Scott, Benjamin F.....	South Pass.....	" "	" "	" "
Smith, Jonathan	....	" "	Aug. 18, 1862	" "
Warner, Asa H	....	....	....	" "
Under Cooks.				
Galloway, James	....	Dec. 18, 1863	Jan. 24, 1864	See Co. B, as consolidated
Fulton, Charles........		" "	" "	
Wilson, Dan			....	Deserted March 6, 1864.....
Drake, Henry..........	....	Dec. 18, 1863	Jan. 24, 1864	See Co. B, as consolidated
Smith, Aaron	....	Apr. 4, 1864	" "	" "

HISTORY OF NINTH INFANTRY.

On the 26th day of April, 1861, the Ninth Illinois Infantry Volunteers was mustered into the service at Springfield for the term of three months. It was one of the six regiments organized under the first call of the President, at the commencement of the war of the rebellion. Six companies—A, B, C, D, E and F—were from St. Clair county; G, I and K, from Madison, and H from Montgomery. The regiment was ordered to Cairo, where it was stationed, doing garrison duty until the close of the term of service, July 26th, 1861, when it was mustered out. During that time the garrison at Cairo was composed of the 8th, 9th, 10th and 12th Infantry. The brigade was composed of these regiments and the 7th and 11th Infantry, the latter being stationed at Bird's Point, Mo., and the 7th a part of the time at Cairo, and a part of the time at Mound City. The brigade was commanded by General Prentiss. During the three months' service the work of the soldier was made up of fatigue duty, building barracks, clearing off parade grounds, building fort defenses and the redan earthwork where the Ohio river is wedded to the Mississippi, and which guarded the confluence of those rivers from the possible advance of rebel gunboats. The monotonous work of this period was broken only by one incident, a march into the swamps of Missouri, back of Commerce, after Jeff. Thompson. The marching column was composed of battalions from the several regiments, including one from the Ninth.

At the expiration of the term of service of the regiments herein named there was no force to take their place as a garrison, which placed Cairo and the vast government stores almost at the mercy of the enemy, but this difficulty was happily overcome by volunteer response from the officers and men of the disbanded regiments to do garrison duty until their places could be filled by soldiers who had enlisted in the three years' service, which was from four to six days. Some two hundred and fifty of this volunteer garrison was composed of the Ninth Infantry, who proposed to re-enlist. In this way the enlistment for the three years' service began with the Ninth. On this mere skeleton of a regiment of officers and men recruiting began in earnest, and in less than thirty days it was again a full regiment. It was organized at Cairo with companies B, C, D and F from St. Clair county; A and I from Madison; H from Montgomery; G from Pulaski; K from Alexander, and E from St. Clair and Mercer.

On the night of September 5th, 1861, General Grant moved with the Ninth and Twelfth Infantry from Cairo to Paducah, taking possession of that city early on the morning of the 6th, thus defeating a similar movement on the part of the rebels only five or six hours. The ninth was ordered to move out and tear up railroad track and destroy a bridge which was about twelve miles out from Paducah. This being accomplished, the regiment returned to Paducah, where it was stationed until early in February, 1862. The brigade to which the Ninth belonged was directed to make a feint on Columbus, on the day of the battle at Belmont, which occurred November 7th, 1861. The regiment made several reconnoisances during the time it was stationed at Paducah, but the chief duty was the constant drill and picket duty with the steady demand for fatigue parties for the construction of fortifications, which prepared the soldier for duty in the field.

On October 15, 1861, about three hundred men of the Ninth moved up the Cumberland river on a steamboat, convoyed by the gunboat "Conestoga," and landed at night a few miles north of Eddyville, Kentucky, and marching out in the night, attacked at sunrise next morning about two hundred rebels at Saratoga, killing and wounding from ten to fifteen, and capturing about thirty-six prisoners. In this engagement, the only loss or casualties sustained by the Ninth was in having three wounded. Subsequently the detachment returned to Paducah.

On the 5th of February, 1862, all the regiments, save Company H, which was left as provost guard at Paducah, embarked on steamboats to a point five miles below Fort Henry, landing on the left bank of the Tennessee river, and moving with the column to attack Fort Heiman, opposite Fort Henry, whilst the latter place was attacked by the gunboats and First Division. The regiment composed a part of the Second Brigade, Second Division of the Army of the Tennessee in that movement, and was a part of the column that moved on Fort Donelson. The Second Brigade Second Division, commanded by Colonel John McArthur, was ordered to support the First Division, commanded by General McClernand, on the 13th, and on the night of the 14th was moved to the extreme right of the Union army; the position of the Ninth being the left of the Brigade; the Twelfth was on the right and the Fortieth and Forty-first in the center. The position of the Ninth placed them across the road over which the Confederate forces attempted to break out on the 15th. But eight companies were in position, Company H being left at Paducah and Company A detached as skirmishers to cover the front of a battery. When the battle of the 15th opened before Fort Donelson. the Second Brigade Second Division met the first attack of the enemy. About six hundred men of the eight companies of the Ninth reported for duty, and they sustained a loss of thirty-five killed, one hundred and sixty wounded and six prisoners.

On February 22d the regiment moved up the Cumberland to Fort Sevier, near Clarksville, and on the 27th marched to Nashville; thence from Nashville, March 1st, to Clarksville, and March 6th, embarked for Pittsburg Landing as a part of the Army of the Tennessee. The regiment was at Shiloh, and here again the Second Brigade Second Division was detached and ordered to the left of General Hurlbut, to fill the gap between the Brigade of Colonel Stuart and the left of General Hurlbut, which was wide enough to require more than a large division to fill. On this part of the line the regiment was engaged until driven back about two o'clock by the enemy, being unable to flank them because of the wide gap to the left. After procuring a new supply of ammunition, the regiment was again engaged until night on the first day of the battle. The regiment went into the field with 578 present for duty, and sustained a loss of sixty-one killed, three hundred wounded and five prisoners, and of those prisoners three were wounded, thus showing a loss of killed and wounded unparalleled by the history of any regiment during the war, which sufficiently attests its gallantry. The regiment took part in the advance on Corinth, and was on garrison duty there, except on occasional reconnoisances, until the second battle of Corinth. October 3d and 4th, 1862, at which time the Second Division was commanded by General Davis, and the Second Brigade by General R. J. Oglesby. In this battle the regiment sustained a loss of twenty killed, eighty-two wounded and fifty-seven prisoners.

On the 15th of March, 1863, General G. M. Dodge, commanding left wing Sixteenth Army Corps, which comprised the army then stationed at Corinth, ordered the Ninth to be mounted, and from that time until the expiration of its term of service it remained so, and to write a history of its marches, skirmishes and battles would require more space than that alloted to the history of a regiment in the Adjutant General's Report.

On the 14th of April, the Ninth moved with a cavalry brigade composed of the Tenth Missouri, a battalion of the Fifteenth Illinois and Seventh Kansas under command of Colonel Comyne on a scout in north Alabama, the purpose of which was to make a feint until the expedition of Colonel Streight, who was making a raid around Chattanooga, could pass the cavalry of the enemy. This feint caused the brigade to be engaged in several skirmishes, in one of which one company of the Ninth moving in an exposed position, under an order of the brigade commander, was captured. The loss of the regiment during this expedition was five wounded and fifty-nine prisoners. During this scout the regiment was engaged in five unimportant skirmishes, and was on the march eighteen days. From May 26th to May 31st, 1863, the regiment was engaged as part of the cavalry force on a raid from Corinth to Florence, Alabama, for the purpose of destroying certain factories there. In this raid the Ninth was engaged in several skirmishes. On June 3d, the regiment was ordered with camp equipage to be stationed at Pocahontas, Tenn. It was out on scout from the 8th of June to the 11th, in western Tennessee, and again from the 12th to the 22d, it was engaged in a raid through north Mississippi to Ripley, New Albany, Pontotoc and other points; was engaged during this raid in several sharp encounters with the enemy, particularly at Meed Creek Swamps. From the 8th of July to the 15th the regiment was on a continuous scout in west Tennessee, having several skirmishes and a sharp encounter at Jackson. From July 20th to August 3d it was on a raid through west Tennessee, without incidents of importance.

On the 3d of August the ranks of the regiment were increased by the assignment of 105 deserters, who were sent from Fort Pickering, at Memphis, where they had been held some time as prisoners. These deserters were from many different regiments, and on being assigned to duty made good soldiers. But two of the number again deserted. The fault of their original desertion was evidently not in the men alone, for they were trusted and fully retrieved their character.

On the 6th of August, by reason of an order issued by Major General Hurlbut, commanding the Sixteenth Army Corps, a detachment of the One Hundred and Twenty-eighth Infantry numbering 103 men was consolidated with the Ninth, which further added to the efficient strength of the regiment. These men were assigned to different companies and proved themselves brave men and true, and in many warm conflicts showed themselves good soldiers.

On the 12th of August, the Ninth formed a part of a column of cavalry concentrated at Oxford, Mississippi, and made a raid to Grenada, where was destroyed 60 locomotives, 450 cars, and a large supply of Confederate stores. The regiment returned to camp at Pocahontas, August 24th, having been engaged on a most arduous march and in several slight skirmishes. During the months of September and October the regiment was constantly moving in west Tennessee and north Mississippi, with occasional skirmishes, one at Salem, Mississippi, being a hot fight, and another at Wyatt, Mississippi, was a spirited encounter.

The killed and wounded from the time the regiment was mounted, March 15th, 1863, to October 30th, 1863, were as follows: At Jackson, Tenn., 1 killed and 5 wounded; at Cherokee, Alabama, 1 wounded; at Meed Creek Swamps, Mississippi, 2 killed and 10 wounded; at Salem, Mississippi, 4 killed and 14 wounded; at Wyatt, Mississippi, 1 killed and 3 wounded; at Florence, Alabama, 1 wounded; at Montezuma, Tennessee, 1 killed; at Athens, Alabama, 2 wounded; at Grenada, Mississippi, 1 wounded. Total, 9 killed, 37 wounded.

During the month of November, the regiment was constantly moving and scouting through North Mississippi, north Alabama and central Tennessee, going into camp at Athens, where it remained until February, when it went into camp at Decatur, Alabama. From the 1st of November, 1863, to the 1st of May, 1864, the regiment was almost constantly moving, and had frequent engagements, particularly at Moulton, Athens, Florence and Flint River, in each of which several men were killed and wounded.

Early in May, 1864, the regiment was ordered to take the wagon and ambulance trains of the Fifteenth and Sixteenth Army Corps from Huntsville, Alabama, to Chattanooga, Tennessee. When this was accomplished the regiment was ordered to move to the front, and it led the advance of the Army of the Tennessee in the movement to flank Dalton and Buzzards' Roost, Georgia. In getting possession of Snake Creek Gap, a hard, sharp fight ensued, in which several men were lost.

During the Atlanta campaign the regiment was engaged in scouting on the flanks of the army, and this duty was continued until the close of the term of service of the regiment in July, 1864.

Whilst at Decatur, Alabama, in April, 1864, about 40 of the men re-enlisted as veterans; those with the 105 termed deserters, and the 103 transferred from the One Hundred and Twenty eighth, together with a few recruits, altogether numbering about 150 men, were, by authority of the following order, consolidated:

Special Field Orders.

HEADQUARTERS DEPARTMENT NO. 74.
ARMY OF THE TENNESSEE, BEFORE ATLANTA, GEORGIA,
JULY 21st, 1864.

I.   The enlisted men of the Ninth Illinois Infantry whose term of service expires during the present month, with such officers of same as by reason of expiration of term desire to be mustered out of service, will forthwith proceed to Chattanooga, Tennessee, under charge of Colonel Mussy, for purpose of muster-out.

II.   The remaining men of the regiment will be consolidated into one or more companies of the legal maximum standard, under the command of Lieutenant Colonel Jesse J. Phillips, and the requisite number of other commissioned officers will be appointed and assigned on the recommendation of Major General G. M. Dodge, commanding left wing Sixteenth Army Corps.

III.   Major General G. M. Dodge will order an officer from the battalion thus organized to Nashville, Tennessee, to procure a sufficient number of Spencer rifles to arm the command.

By order of Major General James B. McPherson.

(Signed),   WILLIAM T. CLARK,
                                    Assistant Adjutant General.

Under which order the remaining men were consolidated into a battalion consisting of seven companies. This battalion moved with the army to Savannah; thence to North Carolina, where the Confederate forces surrendered, being constantly on the flank or in advance of the army.

The regiment was mustered out July 9th, 1865, at Louisville, Ky.

NINTH INFANTRY (CONSOLIDATED) REGIMENT.

THREE YEARS' SERVICE.

FIELD AND STAFF.

Name and Rank.	Residence.	Date of rank or enlistment.	Date of muster.	Remarks.
Colonel. Samuel T. Hughes....	Edwardsville...	July 9, 1865	Not must'ed	M. O. (as Lt.Col)July 9, '65
Lieutenant Colonels. Jesse J. Phillips	Hillsboro	Sept. 3, 1861	Nov. 14, 1861	Resigned Aug.31, '64. Prom. Bvt.Brig.Gen., Mar.13,'65.
Samuel T. Hughes....	Edwardsville ..	Aug. 31, 1864	Oct. 11, 1864	Promoted....................
Major. William Padon........	Troy	Oct. 29, 1864	Dec. 18, 1864	Mustered out July 9, 1865..
Adjutant. Lewis L. Troy	Belleville.......	Aug. 20, 1864	Oct. 11, 1864	Mustered out July 9, 1865..
Quartermaster. Samuel Cover	Vienna..........	Aug. 20, 1864	Sept. 11, 1864	Mustered out July 9, 1865..
Surgeon. David P. Bigger........	Henderson	Apr. 24, 1865	May 22, 1865	Mustered out July 9, 1865..

NON-COMMISSIONED STAFF.

Name and Rank.	Residence.	Date of rank or enlistment.	Date of muster.	Remarks.
Sergeant Majors. Francis K. Wagner ...	Fayetteville	....	....	Pro.Capt.Co.D,Oct.11, '64.
Joseph L. Miller	Paducah, Ky...	Jan. 4, 1864	Jan. 25, 1864	Mustered out July 9, 1865..
Q. M. Sergeant. Elisha P. Graham.....	Chicago	Mar. 24, 1864	Mar. 30, 1864	Mustered out July 9, 1865..
Com. Sergeants. Samuel Cover	....	....	....	Promoted Quartermaster.
Robert H. Wise	....	....	....	Mustered out July 9, 1865..
Hospital Stewards. George M. Gilmore....	Boston..........	Mar. 31, 1864	Mar. 31, 1864	Died Feb. 23, 1865..........
Francis M. Swyer.....	Belleville.......	Sept. 20, 1862	....	Mustered out May 22, 1865.
William F. Primley...	Chicago	Mar. 25, 1864	Mar. 28, 1864	Mustered out July 9, 1865..
Chief Bugler. John M. Saltzmann ...	Bloomington ...	Mar. 23, 1864	Mar. 28, 1864	Mustered out July 9, 1865..

129

COMPANY A.

Name and Rank.	Residence.	Date of rank or enlistment.	Date of muster.	Remarks.
Captains.				
William Padon........	Troy	Aug. 20, 1864	Oct. 11, 1864	Promoted Major ....
Henry M. Brown......	Carbondale.....	Oct. 29, 1864	Apr. 1, 1865	Mustered out July 9, 1865..
First Lieutenants.				
William Padon........	Troy	Aug. 25, 1863	Jan. 1, 1864	Promoted ....
Henry M. Brown......	Carbondale.....	Oct. 29, 1864	Oct. 11, 1864	''
Charles B. Fleming...	Keithsburg.....	Aug. 20, 1864	Apr. 1, 1865	Mustered out July 9, 1865..
Second Lieutenants.				
Charles B. Fleming...	Keithsburg.....	Aug. 20, 1864	Oct. 11, 1864	Promoted ....
Andrew J. Phemister.	....	July 4, 1865	Not must'd.	M. O. as Sergt. July 9, 1865
First Sergeant.				
Henry M. Brown......	Carbondale.....	Jan. 4, 1864	Jan. 25, 1864	Promoted 1st Lieutenant..
Sergeants.				
Charles B. Fleming...	Keithsburg.....	Mar. 31, 1861	Mar. 31, 1864	Promoted 2d Lieutenant ..
John McCann..........	Carbondale.....	Mar. 27, 1864	Mar. 27, 1864	Mustered out July 9, 1865..
Andrew J. Phemister.	Bainbridge.....	Aug. 15, 1862	Nov. 4, 1862	''
Warren S. White......	DeSoto	Mar. 28, 1864	Mar. 29, 1864	Disch. June 28, 1865; order General Hooker..........
Corporals.				
Josiah P. Gore	Dongola	Jan. 4, 1864	Jan. 4, 1864	Mustered out July 9, 1865..
Moses Casey...........	....	Aug. 1, 1862	Nov. 4, 1862	Mustered out June 22, 1865.
Robert H. Wise	''	Aug. 4, 1862	''	Prom. Commissary Serg..
Nathaniel G. Brown ..	Carbondale.....	Jan. 4, 1864	Jan. 4, 1864	M. O. July 9, 1865, as Serg..
William J. Haglar	''	''	''	Mustered out July 9, 1865..
Thomas Odom	....	Aug. 12, 1862	Nov. 4, 1862	''
Alpheus Burkes.......	....	Aug. 15, 1862	''	Disch. May 22, 1865; order General Gilmore.........
James Cureton........	Dongola	Jan. 4, 1864	Jan. 4, 1864	Mustered out July 9, 1865..
Veterans.				
Dixon, William........	Anna	Mar. 23, 1864	Mar. 23, 1864	Mustered out July 9, 1865..
Edwards, Allen........	Dongola	Jan. 4, 1864	Jan. 4, 1864	''
Gore, William R	''	''	''	'' ''
Gore, James B	Cobden	''	''	'' ''
Goshnell, Oliver	Carbondale.....	Jan. 18, 1864	Jan. 18, 1864	'' ''
Hampton, Jonathan ..	''	Jan. 4, 1864	Jan. 4, 1864	'' ''
Loyd, James A.........	Nicholsville....	Mar. 23, 1864	Mar. 23, 1864	'' ''
Laswell, Thomas R...	Cairo	''	''	'' ''
Perdue, Eugene.......	Keokuk, Ia.....	''	''	Absent on detached service at M.O. of organiz'n
Pyron, Anderson......	Carbondale.....	Jan. 4, 1864	Jan. 4, 1864	Mustered out July 13, 1865
Taylor, James F.......	Cairo	Mar. 23, 1864	Mar. 23, 1864	Mustered out July 9, 1865.
White, Simeon F......	''	''	''	'' ''
Winchester, Fr'klin P.	Carbondale.....	Jan. 4, 1864	Jan. 4, 1864	'' ''
Recruits.				
Ausley, David N	....	Feb. 24, 1864	Feb. 24, 1864	Mustered out July 9, 1865.
Anderson, Henry C...	....	Aug. 15, 1862	Nov. 4, 1862	'' ''
Brown, James M	Jackson	Sept. 15, 1861	Sept. 15, 1861	Mustered out Sept. 15, 1864
Bogardus, D. C........	....	Aug. 15, 1862	Nov. 4, 1862	Mustered out July 9, 1865.
Camden, William C...	....	''	''	'' ''
Camden, George W ...	....	''	''	'' ''
Craig, William	....	Oct. 1, 1862	''	'' ''
Cannon, James L	....	Aug. 15, 1862	''	'' ''
Cantrell, Richard	....	''	''	'' ''
Chamness, George B..	....	''	''	'' ''
Chamness, T. W	....	''	''	'' ''
Dixon, Thomas........	....	Aug. 18, 1862	''	'' ''
Dye, David	....	Aug. 16, 1862	''	Mustered out May 30, 1865..
Davis, William H.....	....	Aug. 15, 1862	''	Mustered out July 9, 1865.
Donelson, William M.	....	Aug. 6, 1862	''	'' ''
Evaland, William H ..	....	Aug. 15, 1862	''	'' ''
Farro, James N	....	''	''	'' ''
Gamble, William A ...	....	Aug. 25, 1864	''	'' ''
Gamble William D...	....	''	''	'' ''
Goshnell, James	Carbondale.....	Jan. 18, 1864	Jan. 18, 1864	'' ''
Hammon, William B..	....	Aug. 15, 1862	Nov. 4, 1862	Mustered out May 30, 1865..
Hale, Marion	....	''	''	Disch. May 9, '65; disabil..
Irby, Henderson	....	Aug. 16, 1862	''	Mustered out July 9, 1865 .
Joplin, Howell T......	....	Aug. 19, 1862	''	'' ''
Kirk, John.............	....	Aug. 15, 1862	''	'' ''
Knight, Warren.......	....	''	''	'' ''
Keeler, Thomas H....	....	Aug. 18, 1862	''	See 31st Ill. Infantry ......
Maloney, Thomas.....	....	Oct. 1, 1862	''	Mustered out July 9, 1865..

Name and Rank.	Residence.	Date of rank or enlistment.	Date of muster.	Remarks.
McNeal, George M	....	Aug. 18,1862	Dec. 10, 1862	Mustered out July 9, 1865..
Newton, James D......	....	"	"	" "
Newcomb, Aaron.......	....			" "
Phemister, Silas G....	....	Aug. 1,1862	Aug. 4, 1862	" "
Sperry, William H	....	Aug. 18,1862	Nov. 4, 1862	" "
Sutherland, Th'mps'n.	....	Aug. 1,1862	"	Mustered out May 30, 1865.
Stone, William	....	Oct. 1,1862	"	Mustered out July 9, 1865..
Stanton, Charles	....	Oct. 4,1862	"	" "
Smith, Wiliford	....	Aug. 15,1862	"	Trans. to Co. B,Dec. 28,'64.
Stilley, David A......	....		"	Mustered out July 9, 1865..
Stephens, Milton	....	"	"	" "
Sanders, Silas	....	"	"	
Riggs, William	....	Aug. 18,1862	"	Supposed to be dead, since December, 1863...........
Roach, David	....	Aug. 11,1862	"	Mustered out July 9, 1865..
Tyler, John A........	....	Aug. 12,1862	"	" "
Thornton, Robert.....	....	Aug. 26,1862	"	" "
Upchurch, Joseph C ..	....	"	"	" "
Waggoner, C. M	....	Aug. 15,1862	"	" "
Whittington, F. M.....	....		"	Disch. Mar. 9,1865; wounds
Wilson, John W	Jackson co	May 29,1862	May 30, 1862	Mustered out May 27, 1865.
Walker, John..........	....	Aug. 12,1862	Nov. 4, 1862	Mustered out July 9,1865..
Greathouse, James P..	Carbondale.....	Sept. 15,1861	Sept. 15,1861	" "
Stilley, William	....	Aug. 1,1862	Nov. 4, 1862	" "
Prisoners of War.				
Chenoworth, William	....	Aug. 15,1862	Nov. 4, 1862	Died, Anders'nville pris'n, July 12, 1864; gr. 3295.....
Etherton, Albert	....	Aug. 26,1862	Aug. 26, 1862	Died, Marietta,Ga., July 22, 1864.......................
Harris, William H	....	Aug. 18,1862	Aug. 18, 1862	Died, Anders'nville pris'n. Oct. 7, 1864; gr. 10447.....
Hall, James P	Jackson co	Sept. 15,1861	Sept. 15,1861	Died, Anders'nville pris'n. Aug. 29, 1864; gr. 7194 ....
Lee, Albert	....	Aug. 27,1862	Nov. 4, 1862	Died, Marietta,Ga., July 17, 1864.....................
Lipe, Jackson..........	Jackson co	July 27,1861	July 27,1861	M.O.Sept.18, 1864. Return'd prisoner of war..........
Knight, Isaac	....	Aug. 15,1862	Nov. 4, 1862	Died, Anders'nville pris'n, Aug. 6, 1864; gr. 4908 .....
Odom, Wiley	....	Aug. 12,1862	Nov. 12,1862	Died, Anders'nville pris'n, July 19, 1864; gr. 3609.....
Under Cooks & Teamsters of A. D.				
Daniel Rice...........	....	Jan. 4, 1864	Jan. 4, 1864	Mustered out July9, 1865..
General Lee	....			" "
John Tyler	....	Dec. 18,1863	Dec. 24,1863	" "
Michael Mathews	....	Jan. 4, 1864	Jan. 4, 1864	Absent, sick. in hospital, at muster-out of regiment .

COMPANY B.

Rame and Rank.	Residence.	Date of rank or enlistment.	Date of muster.	Remarks.
Captains.				
George Woodbury	Troy	Aug. 20,1864	Oct. 11,1864	Killed March 15, 1865.......
Frederick Dilg	Mascoutah	July 4, 1865	Not must'rd	M. O. as 1st Lt. July 9, 1865
First Lieutenants.				
Frederick Dilg	Mascoutah	Aug. 20,1864	Oct. 18,1864	Promoted.................
George W. Woodward.	....	July 4, 1865	Not must'rd	M. O. as 2d Lt. July 9, 1865.
Second Lieutenants.				
Samuel Seybold	Troy	Aug. 20,1864	Not must'rd	Canceled ....
George W. Woodward.	....		Feb. 28,1865	Promoted.................
James W. Crosby	Caseyville......	July 4, 1865	Not must'rd	M. O. as Sergt. July 9, 1865
First Sergeant.				
George W. Woodward.	....	Aug. 15,1862	Nov. 4, 1862	Promoted 2d Lieutenant ..
Sergeants.				
Frederick Dilg	Mascoutah	Mar. 25,1864	Mar. 25,1864	Promoted 1st Lieutenant..
Frederick W. Zanders	Troy	Aug. 20,1862	Aug. 20,1862	Discharged May 28, 1865 ...
Horatio N. Cornman..	"			
Samuel Seybold.......	"	Nov. 1,1861	Nov. 1,1861	Mustered out Nov. 2,1864..

Name and Rank.	Residence.	Date of rank or en- listment.	Date of muster.	Remarks.
Corporals.				
John H. Rummage...	....	Aug. 15, 1862	Nov. 4, 1862	Mustered out July 9. 1865..
John L. Goddard.....	....	Aug. 18, 1862	" "	Mustered out June 30, 1865.
William T. Burton ...	Cairo............	Jan. 4, 1864	Jan. 24, 1864	Killed, Orangeburg, S. C., Feb. 11, 1865.............
Asa H. Warner........	....	Aug. 15. 1862	Aug. 18, 1862	Disch. order War Dep't, May 28, 1865.......
Singleton Woolsey....	....	" "	Nov. 4, 1862	Mustered out July 9, 1865..
Burnett B. Reece......	....	" "	" "	" "
William T. Hawkins..	....	" "	" "	" "
Veterans.				
Boles, Charles W.....	Cairo............	Jan. 4, 1864	Jan. 21, 1864	Mustered out July 9, 1865..
Meyers. George........	Chicago..........	Mar. 27, 1864	Mar. 27, 1864	" "
Recruits.				
Abernathy, George W.	....	Oct. 1, 1863	Oct. 1, 1863	Mustered out July 9, 1865..
Bohannon, James M..	Edwardsville ..	Nov. 10, 1863	Nov. 10, 1863	" "
Cox, William T........	" "	" "	" "	" "
Emery, Moses........	Anna............	Mar. 18, 1864	Apr. 19, 1864	" "
Fowler, James	Wanda..........	Dec. 22, 1863	Dec. 22, 1863	" "
Gregory, John C......	Anna	Mar. 18, 1864	July 5, 1864	" "
Hegler, Daniel........	" "	Mar. 9, 1864	Apr. 19, 1864	" "
Jones, John............	Springfield	Mar. 24, 1864		" "
Lamar, Joseph........	Anna............	Jan. 26, 1864	Mar. 26, 1864	" "
Osborn, Samuel.......	" "	Mar. 18, 1864	July 5, 1864	" "
Scott, Benjamin F....	South Pass.....	Mar. 9, 1864	Apr. 19, 1864	" "
Snowdon, Vachale....	Anna............	Mar. 14, 1864		" "
Non-Veterans.				
Adams, James M.......	....	Aug. 1, 1862	Nov. 4, 1862	Mustered out May 30, 1865.
Burton, George W....	Cobden	Sept. 3, 1861	Sept. 3, 1861	Mustered out Sept. 11, 1864.
Burnett, Nathaniel E.	....	Aug. 4, 1862	Aug. 4, 1862	Disch. order War Dep't, May 28, 1865.............
Boutwell, Oliver W....	Hillsboro	Aug. 23, 1862	Aug. 25, 1862	Disch. order War Dep't, May 28, 1865.............
Casey, Henry........	Union co........	Sept. 13, 1861	Sept. 13, 1861	Mustered out Oct. 1, 1864..
Cavitt. William.......	....	Aug. 18, 1862	Nov. 4, 1862	Mustered out July 9, 1865..
E .banks,, William H..	....	Aug. 4, 1862	Nov. 4, 1862	" "
Elliott, John	Preston	Sept. 10, 1861	Sept. 10, 1861	Mustered out Sept. 11. 1864
Fortner. Robert.......	....	Aug. 18, 1862	Nov. 4, 1862	Mustered out July 9, 1865..
Furlough, James......	....	Aug. 15, 1862	" "	" "
Grace, Henry..........	....	Aug. 18, 1862		Mustered out June 5, 1865..
Hegler, William J.....	Jackson co.....	Sept. 18, 1861	Sept. 18, 1861	Mustered out Sept. 29, 1864
Harn, John	Bryan, Ohio....	Sept. 3, 1861	Sept. 3, 1861	Mustered out Sept. 11. 1864
Hudgeons, John.......	....	Aug. 15, 1862	Nov. 4, 1862	Mustered out July 9, 1865..
Hall. Joseph..........	....	Dec. 4, 1862	Dec. 4, 1862	" "
Holcomb, Mahlon D...	Troy	Sept. 3, 1861	Sept. 3, 1861	Mustered out Sept. 11, 1864
Jordan, Doctor F......	....	Aug. 15, 1862	Nov. 4, 1862	Absent. sick, at muster- out of organization......
Jones, David	....	" "	" "	Died, Jan. 24, 1865..........
Jackson, John..........	....	" "	Aug. 15, 1862	Disch. May 28, 1865, order War Dep't.............
Kimball, Alf. W.......	Centralia	Sept. 3, 1861	Sept. 3, 1861	Mustered out Sept. 11, 1864
Kearney, John.........	....	Dec. 9, 1862	Dec. 9, 1862	Mustered out July 9, 1865..
Kenneday, Jesse.......	Cobden	Sept. 6, 1861	Sept. 6, 1861	Mustered out Sept 11, 1864.
Kluck, James W.......	....	May 20, 1863	Oct. 31, 1863	Died Sept. 6, 1864..........
Koonce, Thos. W or B.	....	Aug. 18, 1862	Nov. 4, 1862	Mustered out June 9, 1865.
Knight, Ellis E........	....	Aug. 15, 1862		M. O. July 9, '65, as Corp'l.
Lines, William........	....	Sept.....,1862	" "	Absent on detached duty at M. O. of organization.
Lipe, William R.......	Jackson co.....	Sept. 18, 1861	Sept. 18, 1861	Mustered out Sept. 18, 1864
McEwan, Henry P....	Ligonier, Ind..	Sept. 2, 1861	Sept. 2, 1861	Mustered out Sept. 28. 1864
McInturff, Alfred B...	....	Oct. 20, 1862	Nov. 4, 1862	Absent, sick, at muster- out of organization......
McRoy, John	....	Aug. 15, 1862	" "	Mustered out July 9, 1865..
McRoy, William.......	....	" "	" "	" "
McClintock, John A...	....	" "	" "	" "
Moake, Jacob.........	....	" "	" "	" "
Moake, George W.....	....	" "	" "	" "
Moake, Andrew J.....	....	" "	" "	" "
Moore, Samuel P......	....	" "	" "	" "
Martin, George W.....	....	" "	" "	" "
Owens, Moses........	....	" "	" "	" "
Obarts, John.........	Jackson co.....	Sept. 30, 1861	Sept. 30, 1861	Discharged; term expired.
Ollis, George W.......	....	Aug. 15, 1862	Nov. 4, 1862	Killed, Rome, Ga., Oct. 24, '64
Ollis, Daniel W.......	....	" "	" "	Disch. June 30, '65: disabil.
Odin, James..........	....	" "	" "	M. O. July 9, '65, as Corp'l..
Parks, John..........	....	" "	" "	Absent. sick, at muster- out of organization......

Name and Rank.	Residence.	Date of rank or enlistment.	Date of muster.	Remarks.
Ranney, Isham		Aug. 15, 1862	Nov. 4, 1862	Mustered out July 9, 1865..
Rice, William R.				
Reid, Samuel	Marine	Sept. 11, 1861	Sept. 11, 1861	Mustered out Sept. 11, 1864
Riggin, William H	Troy	Sept. 3.1861	Sept. 3, 1861	" "
Swain, Robert R	"	Aug. 19, 1861	Aug. 19, 1861	Mustered out Dec. 18, 1864.
Salyer, Andrew J.	Jackson co.	Sept. 18, 1861	Sept. 18, 1861	Mustered out Sept. 18, 1864
Smith, Jonathan		Aug. 15, 1862	Nov. 4, 1861	Mustered out July 9, 1865..
Snell, Araldon				
Silley, James B.		"	"	Transferred to Co. D
Shaw, James B.		"	"	
Williams, James R.		"	"	Mustered out July 9, 1865..
Recruits subsequent to Re-organization.				
Barnett, Jesse	Troy precinct.	Feb, 2, 1865	Feb. 2, 1865	Mustered out July 9, 1865..
Brody, Peter	"	Jan. 31, 1865	Jan. 31, 1865	" "
Crosby, James W.	Caseyville	Feb. 17, 1865	Feb. 17, 1865	M.O. July 9,'65, as 1st Serg.
Cowell, Charles	"	"	"	Mustered out July 9, 1865..
Cussy, Roger W.	Troy precinct.	Feb. 2, 1865	Feb. 2, 1865	" "
Donohoo, William T.	"	Jan. 30, 1865	Jan. 30, 1865	" "
Darrow, Joseph		Aug. 1, 1862	Nov. 4, 1862	" "
Gully, Riley		Aug. 15, 1862	"	Mustered out June 27, 1865.
Duffy, James	Minonk.	Jan. 11, 1865	Jan. 11, 1865	Mustered out July 9, 1865..
Duffy, Charles	"	"	"	
Henry, August	Troy precinct.	Jan. 31, 1865	Jan. 31, 1865	" "
Holmes, James	Bethalto	Jan. 30, 1865	Jan. 30, 1865	Mustered out June 29, 1865.
Hunter, Joseph		Aug. 15, 1862	Nov. 4, 1862	Absent, sick, at muster-out of organization
Moore, Thomas	Metamora	Jan. 14, 1865	Jan. 14, 1865	Absent, on detached duty, at M. O. of organization.
Morran, Martin	Troy precinct.	Jan. 31, 1865	Jan. 31, 1865	Mustered out July 9, 1865..
Morris, John	Troy	Jan. 30, 1865	Jan. 30, 1865	" "
Newhouse, Henry A.		Jan. 1, 1864	Jan. 1, 1864	Absent, sick, at muster-out of organization
Olderson, William	Bethalto	Jan. 30, 1865	Jan. 30, 1865	Mustered out July 9, 1865..
Padon, Henry	Troy	"	"	" "
Riggin, Jackson	"	"	"	Mustered out July 3, 1865..
Ryan, Dennis	Minonk.	Jan. 11, 1865	Jan. 11, 1865	Mustered out July 9. 1865..
Shaw, Sebastian		Aug. 15, 1862	Nov. 4, 1862	" "
Smith, Wiliford W.	"			Disch. June 27,'65; disabil.
Troy, James	Minonk.	Jan. 11, 1865	Jan. 11, 1865	Mustered out July 9, 1865..
Tompkins, Richard	Bethalto	Jan. 30, 1865	Jan. 30, 1865	" "
Trull, James		Aug. 15, 1862	Nov. 4, 1862	Absent, sick, at muster-out of organization
Vingard, Philip J.	Troy precinct.	Feb. 2, 1865	Feb. 2, 1865	Mustered out July 9, 1865..
Vanhooser, John R.	"	"	"	
Vohringer, George	Troy	Jan. 30, 1865	Jan. 30, 1865	" "
Whitney, Charles B.	Troy precinct.	Jan. 31, 1865	Jan. 31, 1865	" "
Zanders, Edward	Troy	Jan. 30, 1865	Jan. 30, 1865	" "
Miller, Samuel L.		July 26, 1861	July 26, 1861	Discharged; term expired
Prisoners of War.				
Cupinall, George W.	Six Mile	Aug. 12, 1862	Aug. 12, 1861	Mustered out Sept. 3, 1864.
Davis, Emanuel		Sept. 17, 1861	Sept. 17, 1861	Missing in action at Mud Creek, Miss., June 20 '63.
Lang, James	Troy	Aug. 12, 1861	Aug. 12, 1861	Mustered out Feb. 11, 1865.
Padon, James	"	Aug. 20, 1862	Aug. 20, 1862	Missing in act'n at Athens, Ala., Jan. 26, 1864
Patton, Charles	Venice	Aug. 12, 1861	Aug. 12, 1861	Missing in action at Mud Creek, Miss., June 20,'63.
Stice, George W.	Troy	July 31, 1861	July 31, 1861	M. O. Feb. 2,'65, as Corp'l.
Walsh, John	Auburn.	Aug. 10, 1861	Aug. 10, 1861	Mustered out June 4, 1865..
Under Cooks and Teamsters.				
Brown, Henry		Dec. 18, 1863	Jan. 24, 1864	Mustered out July 9, 1865..
Brown, Preston		"	"	" "
Drake, Henry		"	"	" "
Fulton, Charley		"	"	" "
Galloway, James				
Smith, Aaron		Apr. 4, 1864		Transferred to Co. D
Tyler, John		Dec. 18, 1863	Jan. 24, 1864	Transferred to Co. A
Townsend, Simeon		"	"	Transferred to Co. D

Name and Rank.	Residence.	Date of rank or enlistment.	Date of muster.	Remarks.
Captains.				
Samuel T. Hughes.....	Edwardsville ..	Jan. 1,1864	Jan. 1,1864	Promoted..................
Frederick Benkeman.	....	Aug. 20,1864	Not must'r'd	Canceled..................
Jacob Miller...........	Hillsboro	" "	Mar. 28,1865	Mustered out July 9, 1865.
First Lieutenant.				
Ambrose J. Shelton...	Montgomery co.	Aug. 20,1864	Oct. 11,1864	Mustered out July 9, 1865.
Second Lieutenants.				
George Short..........	Montgomery co.	Aug. 20,1864	Oct. 11,1864	Killed in battle Nov. 23,'64
John Droesch..........	Hillsboro	July 4,1865	Not must'r'd	M. O. (as Serg't) July 9,'65
First Sergeant.				
George A. Short.......	Montgomery co.	Aug. 23,1862	Aug. 23,1862	Promoted 2d Lieutenant ..
Sergeants.				
Jacob Miller...........	Hillsboro	Mar. 23,1864	Mar. 28,1864	Promoted Captain.........
John Webber...........	" "	Sept. 24,1861	Sept. 24,1861	Mustered out Sept. 24, 1864
A. J. Shelton	Montgomery co.	Aug. 23,1862	Aug. 23,1862	Promoted 1st Lieutenant..
George Everett........	....	Aug. 1,1862	Aug. 15,1862	Mustered out July 9, 1865.
Corporals.				
Henry M. Lee	Hillsboro	Jan. 4,1864	Jan. 24,1864	Disch. Mar. 31,'65, per S.O. 71, H'dq'rt's Army Tenn.
Joseph Danford.......	Keokuk. Iowa..	" "	" "	Mustered out June 24, 1865.
John Droesch	Hillsboro	Mar. 23,1864	Mar. 23,1864	Mustered out July 9, 1865.
Martin Preston.......	" "	Jan. 4,1864	Jan. 24,1864	" "
R. M. McAnnelly.....	....	Aug. 1,1862	Aug. 15,1862	" "
Bluford Jordan........	....			
J. A. Clotfelter........	Montgomery co.	Sept. 24,1861	Sept. 24,1861	Mustered out Sept. 24, 1864
John Everett..........	....	Aug. 1,1862	Aug. 15,1862	Mustered out July 9, 1865.
Privates.				
Boone. William S......	Hillsboro	Mar. 23,1864	Mar. 23,1864	Mustered out July 9, 1865.
Blattier, Conrad......	" "			
Davis, James M		Jan. 4,1864	Jan. 24,1864	Deserted Dec. 7, 1864.......
Holly, John..........	Cairo	Mar. 23,1864	Mar. 23,1864	Died Mar. 19, 1865 ....
Lamb, John G	Irving	Jan. 4,1864	Jan. 24,1864	Mustered out June 24,1865.
Moore, John F........	Hillsboro	Mar. 23,1864	Mar. 23,1864	Mustered out July 9, 1865.
Qualls, George W	" "			" "
Taulbee, Joseph E	Irving	Jan. 4,1864	Jan. 24,1864	" "
Weigart, George	Litchfield......	Mar. 23,1864	Mar. 23,1864	Mustered out June 15, 1865.
Boutwell, George H...	Hillsboro	Dec. 29,1863	Dec. 29,1863	Mustered out July 9, 1865.
Bishop, William B ...	Litchfield......	Feb. 2,1864	Mar. 26,1864	" "
Berry, William.......	Hillsboro	Apr. 22,1864	Apr. 22,1864	" "
Hickman, W. B........	Litchfield......	Feb. 11,1864	Feb. 11,1864	" "
Jenkins, S. M..........	Hillsboro	Feb. 2,1864	Apr. 19,1864	Taken prisoner May 9,'64, at Snake Gap, Ga. No discharge furnished.....
Morain, Harvey......	....	Mar. 1,1864	" "	Mustered out July 9, 1865.
Stacy, James A........	Marion..........	Feb. 13,1864	Feb. 13,1864	Taken prisoner Nov. 23,'64, near Milledgeville, Ga. No discharge furnished.
Adams, William E....	....	Aug. 13,1862	Jan. 13,1863	Mustered out June 24 1865
Adams, W. C	....	Aug. 1,1862	Aug. 15,1862	Disch. Apr. 22,'65; disabil.
Bickers, John	....	" "	Nov. 4,1862	Mustered out June 29, 1865
Bickers, M. F.........	....			Died Mar. 1,1865; wounds.
Chitty, J. H..........	....	Aug. 15,1862	Aug. 15,1862	Disch. Feb. 21,'65, disabil.
Chitty, O. W..........	....	" "	" "	Mustered out July 9, 1865.
Chadoin. T. B	....			M. O. June 2,1865; disabil.
Carter, W. B..........	....	Aug. 1,1862	Nov. 4,1862	Mustered out July 9, 1865.
Crane, S. S	....	Aug. 15,1862		" "
Dorris, W. R	....	Aug. 1,1862	Aug. 1,1862	" "
Dorris, W. W..........	....			" "
Dungy, T. H..........	....	Aug. 15,1862	Nov. 4,1862	Deserted July 28, 1864......
Duncan, J. W.........	....	" "	Aug. 15,1862	Mustered out July 9, 1865.
Dry. George H	Montgomery co.	Mar. 31,1862	Mar. 31,1862	" "
Daugherty, W. G.....	....	Aug. 15,1862	Nov. 5,1862	" "
Erek, William........	....	Aug. 31,1861	Aug. 31,1861	Died at Andersonville prison June 18,'64. Gr. 2211
Fry, Simeon	....	Aug. 15,1862	Aug. 15,1862	Died Aug. 15, 1864.........
Fletcher, Calvin......	....	" "	" "	Mustered out July 9, 1865.
Gower. Jefferson......	....	Aug. 1,1862	" "	" "
Glass, Thomas	....	" "	" "	" "
Gregory, William	....	" "	" "	" "
Greiger. George	Lebanon.......	" "	Oct. 1,1862	Trans. to V. R. C. Nov.25,'64
Hicks, Samuel	....	" "	Aug. 15,1862	Absent, in confinement, at M. O. of organization....
Hoober Frank	Bond co	July 28,1861	July 28,1861	Mustered out Apr. 12, 1865.

Name and Rank.	Residence.	Date of rank or enlistment.	Date of muster.	Remarks.
Herron, Ephraim	....	Aug. 10, 1862	Sept. 5, 1862	Mustered out July 9, 1865 ..
Hill, W. J.	....	Aug. 1, 1862	Nov. 4, 1862	Mustered out June 16, 1865.
Jackson, Harvey J	....	" "	Aug. 15, 1862	Mustered out May 30, 1865 ..
Keys, John	....	" "	Nov. 4, 1862	Mustered out July 9, 1865 ..
Moynihan, Phillip.....	Montgomery co	Nov. 17, 1862	Nov. 17, 1862	Captured Oct. 27, 1864, near Rome, Ga.................
McLean, Alvin A......	" "	Sept. 24, 1861	Sept. 24, 1861	Mustered out Sept. 24, 1864.
Moake, Abraham......	Bridge's Corn's	Aug. 15, 1862	Nov. 5, 1862	M. O. June 23, 1865, G.O.No. 77, A. G. O.............
Mifflin, John.........	....	Aug. 1, 1862	Nov. 4, 1862	Killed Nov. 23, 1864, near Milledgeville, Ga ......
Nicodemus, M. H......	Montgomery co	Aug. 23, 1862	Aug. 23, 1862	Disch. May 9, 1865; disabil.
Phelts, Benjamin	....	Aug. 15, 1862	Aug. 15, 1862	Trans. to V.R.C.,Mar. 25,'65
Powel, John	....	Aug. 14, 1862	" "	Mustered out May 30, 1865 .
Poteete, G. W	....	Aug. 1, 1862	Nov. 4, 1862	Mustered out July 9, 1865 ..
Pitcock, Newton	....	Aug. 15, 1862	" "	" "
Richardson, Samuel ..	....	Aug. 14, 1862	Aug. 15, 1862	" " " "
Robertson, Samuel....	....	Aug. 1, 1862	Nov. 4, 1862	" " " "
Stephens, C. J........	....	Aug. 14, 1862	Aug. 16, 1862	" " " "
Stephens, David	....	Aug. 15, 1862	Aug. 15, 1862	" " " "
Stephens, F. M	....	" "	Nov. 4, 1862	Died Sept. 5, 1864 ....
Stroud, J. C	....	Aug. 14, 1862	Aug. 20, 1862	Mustered out June 13, 1865.
Stroud, J. P.........	....	" "	" "	Died at Andersonville prison, Oct.6,1864. Gr. 10,440
Spillers, Perrine	....	Aug. 15, 1862	Nov. 4, 1862	M. O. July 11, 1865, G. O. 27. Departm'nt of Kentucky
Stickel, F. M	Montgomery co	July 28, 1861	July 28, 1861	Taken prisoner Oct. 9, 1863, Salem, Miss. No. discharge furnished ....
Sharrock, D. L	Tower Hill	Sept. 3, 1861	Sept. 3, 1861	Mustered out Sept. 2, 1864..
Sweet, Thomas........	....	Aug. 15, 1862	Nov. 5, 1862	Mustered out June 2, 1865..
Turnage, Henry......	....	" "	Aug. 15, 1862	Deserted July 28, 1864......
Turnage, Phillip......	....	" "	" "	Mustered out July 9, 1865..
Talbert, William	....	Aug. 1, 1862	Nov. 4, 1862	" "
Winters, William H...	....	Aug. 15, 1862	Aug. 15, 1862	Died May 19, 1864 ....
Recruits.				
Duncan, Hiram M.....	....	Aug. 15, 1862	Nov. 4, 1862	Mustered ont July 9, 1865 ..
Folkner, Benjamin F.	....	Aug. 1, 1862	" "	" " " "
Folkner, Joseph J.....	....	" "	" "	" " " "
Folkner, James M.....	....	" "	" "	" " " "
Under Cooks.				
Bailey, Charles........	....	Dec. 18, 1863	Jan. 24, 1864	Mustered out July 9, 1865 ..
Dixon, Berry	....	" "	" "	Deserted................
Drake, Jack	....	" "	" "	Mustered out July 9, 1865 ..
Houston, Frank	....	" "	" "	Deserted................
Kimball, Jasper......	....	" "	" "	
White, Thomas........	....	" "	" "	Mustered out July 9, 1865 ..

COMPANY D.

Name and Rank.	Residence.	Date of rank or enlistment.	Date of muster.	Remarks.
Captain. Frank X. Wagner.....	....	Aug. 20, 1864	Oct. 11, 1864	Mustered out July 9, 1865 ..
First Lieutenant. Jacob Nicholas........	Chicago	Aug. 20, 1864	Oct. 11, 1864	Mustered out July 9, 1865 ..
Second Lieutenants. William Jones.........	....	Aug. 20, 1864	Not must'd.	Canceled ....
Isaac Smith..........	....	" "	Dec. 18, 1864	Mustered out July 9, 1865 ..
First Sergeant. Lewis L, Troy.........	Belleville.......	Mar. 31, 1864	Mar. 31, 1864	Promoted Adjutant........
Sergeants. Jacob Nicholas........	Chicago	Mar. 28, 1864	Mar. 30, 1864	Promoted 1st Lieut........
Isaac Smith..........	....	Aug. 15, 1862	Nov. 4, 1862	Promoted 2d Lieut.........
First Sergeant. William H. Slater.....	....	Aug. 15, 1862	Nov. 4, 1862	Mustered out July 9, 1865 ..

Name and Rank.	Residence.	Date of rank or enlistment.	Date of muster.	Remarks.
Sergeants.				
Henry Kremer........	Lebanon	Aug. 31, 1862	Oct. 31, 1862	M. O. May 26, 1865, by order War Dept ....
Christian Rose........	Chicago	Mar. 27, 1864	Mar. 27, 1864	Mustered out July 9, 1865..
William Felts	....	Aug. 15, 1862	Nov. 5, 1862	" "
James Leamster	....	"	"	" "
Corporals.				
Rolley Smith..........	....	Aug. 15, 1862	Nov. 4, 1864	Mustered out July 9, 1865...
Henry Miller	Chicago	Mar. 27, 1864	Mar. 27, 1864	M. O. July 9, '65, as Serg't..
James Smith..........	....	Aug. 15, 1862	Nov. 4, 1862	Mustered out July 9, 1865...
Louis Val-ntine.......	Mascoutah	Jan. 4, 1864	Mar. 26, 1864	M. O. July 9, '65, as Private
Frederick Koch	Chicago	Mar. 26, 1864	"	" "
William Morgenstern.	Belleville.......	Jan. 17, 1864	Apr. 16, 1864	Absent without leave at M. O. of organization...
Charles Wright	"	Aug. 26, 1862	Oct. 31, 1862	M. O. May 26, 1865, by order War department.........
Veterans.				
Brenner, Henry.......	Chicago	Mar. 26, 1864	Mar. 26, 1864	Mustered out July 9, 1865..
Balderman, William..	Hillsboro	Mar. 23, 1864	Mar. 23, 1864	" "
Deasch, George	Belleville.......	Mar. 26, 1864	Mar. 26, 1864	" "
Seibert, Charles.......	Chicago	Mar. 27, 1864	Mar. 27, 1864	M. O. July 9, 1865, as Corp.
Salzman, John M......	Bloomington ...	Mar. 23, 1864	Mar. 23, 1864	Trans. to Non-Com. Staff, as Chief Bugler..........
Vogel, Bernhard......	Belleville.......	Mar. 26, 1864	Mar. 26, 1864	Mustered out July 9, 1865..
Recruits.				
Adam, Christopher...	Summerfield ...	Jan. 14, 1864	Mar. 26, 1864	Mustered out July 9, 1865...
Bauer, George........	Belleville.......	Jan. 15, 1864	Feb. 8, 1864	" "
Brakebusch, Henry...	Alton	Feb. 6, 1864	Mar. 26, 1864	" "
Becker, Ferdinand....	Belleville.......	Apr. 8, 1864	Apr. 22, 1864	" "
Bullion, John..........	Fosterburg.....	Feb. 3, 1864	Feb. 3, 1864	" "
Hess, John	Alton	Feb. 14, 1864	Mar. 26, 1864	" "
Jargner, August	Fosterburg.....	Feb. 3, 1864	"	" "
Keller, Mathias	Centreville.....	Feb. 8, 1864	Feb. 18, 1864	" "
Mitz, Henry	Shipman	Jan. 22, 1864	Jan. 29, 1864	Absent, sick at muster-out of organization ....
Seiler, John	Belleville.......	Jan. 16, 1864	Feb. 8, 1864	Transferred to Co. F......
Sutter, Benedict	Summerfield ...	Jan. 14, 1864	"	Mustered out July 9, 1865..
Will, Michael..........	Belleville.......	"	"	" "
Webber, Benedict.....	Fosterburg.....	Feb. 3, 1864	Feb. 3, 1864	" "
Non-Veterans.				
Alexander, William B	....	Aug. 1, 1862	Nov. 5, 1862	Absent with leave at M. O.
Amand, William	Belleville.......	Dec. 16, 1862	Feb. 28, 1863	Mustered out July 9, 1865..
Crain, George W......	....	Aug. 15, 1862	Nov. 5, 1862	" "
Darrow, Joseph.......	....	Aug. 1, 1862	"	Transferred to Co. B......
Elliott, William D	....	Aug. 15, 1862	"	M. O. June 30, '65, G. O. No. 77, A G. O ....
Ekols, Thomas........	....	"	"	M. O. July 9, 1865, as Corp.
Ivans, James..........	....	"	"	Died Oct. 13, 1864 ....
Harris, Charles	Jerseyville	Sept. 6, 1861	Sept. 6, 1861	Mustered out Sept. 11, 1864
Hill, John A..........	....	Aug. 15, 1862	Nov. 5, 1862	Transferred to Co. F......
Hartwell, John L......	....	"	"	Mustered out July 9, 1865..
Hays, Henry	....	Aug. 1, 1862	"	" "
Howerton, William P.	....	"	"	
Hunter, Joseph	....	"	"	Transferred to Co. B......
Jackson, Nathan......	....	Aug. 15, 1862	"	Mustered out July 9, 1865..
Jackson, Josiah	....	"	"	Mustered out July 20, 1865.
Jones, William........	....	Aug. 1, 1862	"	Mustered out May 29, 1865.
Leamster, William C..	....	Aug. 16, 1862	"	Disch Mar. 21, '65; disabil.
Moore, James..........	....	Aug. 15, 1862	"	Mustered out July 9, 1865..
Moore, John S.........	....	"	"	" "
McAnnally, Mathias..	....	"	"	
McAnnally, Isaac.....	....	Aug. 11, 1862	"	Transferred to Co. F ......
Mennes, William T ...	....	"	"	Mustered out July 9, 1865..
Oemigen, F. W........	Belleville.......	Aug. 30, 1862	Oct. 31, 1862	M. O., order of War Dept. May 26, 1865.............
Recter, George W.....	....	Aug. 15, 1862	Nov. 5, 1862	Mustered out July 9, 1865..
Rusching, Hugh	....	"	"	" "
Rainey, Thomas A....	....	Aug. 1, 1862	"	" "
Rodgers, William.....	....	"	"	M. O. July 9, 1865, as Corp.
Stroutt, William	....	Aug. 15, 1862	"	Mustered out July 9, 1865..
Sanders, Isaac........	....	Aug. 1, 1862	"	" "
Schmid, James T......	....	"	"	" "
Smith, Thomas R.....	....	"	"	Mustered out July 10, 1865.
Spring, Moses........	....	"	"	Mustered out July 9, 1865..
Smith, George H......	....	"	"	
Schilly, Fridolin	Lebanon	Aug. 16, 1862	Oct. 31, 1862	M. O., order of War Dept. May 26, 1865.............

Name and Rank.	Residence.	Date of rank or enlistment.	Date of muster.	Remarks.
Sanders, George B....	....	Aug. 15, 1862	Nov. 5, 1862	Mustered out July 9, 1865..
Sanders, Jacob........	....	"	"	" "
Shadowing, David....	....	"	"	" "
Thalbert, Thomas.....	....	Aug. 1, 1862	"	" "
Thomas, Joseph......	....	"	"	" "
Thomas, Joshua	....	"	"	" "
Vantreese, Grierson ..	....	"	"	" "
Walker, George	....	"	"	" "
Walker, Silas........	....	"	"	" "
William, Alexander...	....	"	"	" "
Riley, Gulley..........	....	Aug. 15, 1862	"	Transferred to Co. B ......
Recruits subsequent to Re-organization.				
Hartly, Martin F.....	....	Jan. 1, 1864	Jan. 1, 1864	Mustered out July 9, 1865..
Hunter, Benjamin	....	Aug. 15, 1862	Nov. 5, 1862	Transferred to Co. F ......
Nugent, John.........	Chicago	Mar. 7, 1865	Mar. 7, 1865	Mustered out May 31, 1865.
Stilley, James A	....	Aug. 15, 1862	Nov. 5, 1862	Mustered out July 9, 1865..
Smith, James M......	....	Aug. 1, 1862	"	Captured at Salem, Miss., Oct. 8, 1863...............
Prisoners of War.				
Allison, William	....	Aug. 1, 1862	Nov. 5, 1862	Died Dec. 16, 1864 ....
Bunse, William	Alton	"	"	Mustered out Apr. 22, 1865.
Crain, Francis.........	....	"	"	Died, Annapolis, Jan 2, 1865....................
Luster, James........	....	"	"	Captured at Salem, Miss., Oct. 8, 1863 ....
O'Daniel, James H....	....	Aug. 15, 1862	"	Died, Anders'nville pris'n, June 1,'64; grave 1533....
Odom, Archi'd (Corp.)	....	Aug. 1, 1862	"	Mustered out May 30, 1865.
Reed, Nicholas........	....	Aug. 19, 1861	Aug. 19, 1861	Mustered out Feb. 2, 1865..
Smith, G. H	....	Aug. 1, 1862	Nov. 5, 1862	Captured at Snake Creek Gap, Ga.. May 18, 1864....
Sekinger, August.....	Belleville.......	Jan. 15, 1864	Feb. 8, 1864	Captured at Snake Creek Gap, Ga., May 18, 1864....;
Under Cooks.				
Carr, David..........	....	Dec. 18, 1863	Jan. 24, 1864	Deserted Nov. 12, 1864......
Drake, Jacob	....	"	"	Transferred to Co. C ......
Dixon, Berry	....	"	"	
Kimball, Pleasant.....	....	Dec. 10, 1863	"	Died June 21, 1864..........
Polk, James..........	....	"	Jan. 18, 1864	Mustered out July 9, 1865..
Sour, Alex...........	....	Dec. 18, 1863	"	" "
Smith, Aaron.........	....	Apr. 4, 1864	Apr. 4, 1864	" "
Townsend, Dick......	....	Dec. 18, 1863	Jan. 18, 1864	" "
Townsend, Simeon....	....	"	"	" "

COMPANY E.

Name and Rank.	Residence.	Date of rank or enlistment.	Date of muster.	Remarks.
Captain.				
Thomas C. Kidd	Springfield.....	Aug. 20, 1864	Oct. 11, 1864	Mustered out July 9, 1865..
First Lieutenant.				
Thomas F! McClintock	Aledo	Aug. 20, 1864	Oct. 11, 1864	Mustered out July 9, 1865..
Second Lieutenant.				
William P. Reese	....	Oct. 7, 1864	Oct. 10, 1864	Mustered out July 9, 1865..
First Sergeant.				
Thomas C. Kidd.......	Springfield	July 28, 1861	July 28, 1861	Promoted Captain ....
Sergeants.				
Thomas F. McClintock	Aledo	Mar. 25, 1864	Mar. 25, 1864	Promoted 1st Lieutenant..
William P. Reese......	....	Aug. 15, 1862	Nov. 4, 1862	Promoted 2d Lieutenant...
Joseph R. Cox.........	Aledo	Mar. 25, 1864	Mar. 25, 1864	Mustered out July 9, 1865..
George M. Gilmore ...	Boston..........	Mar. 31, 1864	Mar. 31, 1864	Trans. to non-com. staff...
Corporals.				
Frank M. Tilitson.....	Chicago	Mar. 25, 1864	Mar. 25, 1864	Mustered out July 9, 1864..
Thomas A. Edmonson.	....	Aug. 20, 1862	Nov. 4, 1862	" "
Michael Fisher........	Jonesboro	Sept. 14, 1864	Sept. 14, 1861	Discharged Sept. 19, 1864 ..
William Dillard	....	Aug. 15, 1862	Nov. 4, 1862	Mustered out July 9, 1865..
William J. Stevens....	....	"	"	

Name and Rank.	Residence.	Date of rank or enlistment.	Date of muster.	Remarks.
William H. H. Riley ..	Aledo	Mar. 25, 1864	Mar. 25, 1864	Mustered out July 9, 1865..
John W. Hoy...........	"	Jan. 28, 1864	" "	" "
James Miller..........	Chicago	Mar. 25, 1864	" "	" "
Musician.				
George W. Rose.......	Chicago	Mar. 25, 1864	Mar. 25, 1865	Mustered out July 9, 1865..
Veterans.				
Boyer, William........	Aledo	Mar. 25, 1864	Mar. 25, 1864	Mustered out July 9, 1865..
Dodson, Abisha.......	Keithsburg.....	" "	" "	" "
Frothingham, D. C....	Chicago	" "	" "	" "
Fulmer, John	Belleville.......	Jan. 4, 1864	Jan. 4, 1864	Died February 6, 1865 ......
Gilmore, James B	Boston..........	Mar. 25, 1864	Mar. 31, 1864	Mustered out July 9, 1865..
Graham, Elisha P.....	Chicago	" "	Mar. 25, 1864	Trans. to non-com. staff...
Hughes, Edwin........	" "	Jan. 4, 1864	Jan. 4, 1864	Mustered out July 9, 1865..
Hicks, James L........	Carbondale.....	" "	" "	" "
Jackson, Martin W....	Belleville.......	Mar. 25, 1864	Mar. 25, 1864	Died March 24, 1865........
Lyons, John	Chicago	" "	" "	Mustered out July 9, 1865..
Miller, Joseph L.......	Paducah, Ky ...	Jan. 4, 1864	Jan. 4, 1864	Trans. to non-com. staff...
McGinnis, John........	Rock Island....	" "	" "	Mustered out July 9, 1865..
Primley, William F ..	Chicago	Mar. 25, 1864	Mar. 25, 1864	Trans. to non-com. staff...
Shroyer, James.......	" "	" "	" "	Mustered out July 9, 1865..
Smith, William H. H..	" "	" "	" "	" "
Stewart, James........	Belleville.......	" "	" "	" "
Taylor, Ira.............	" "	" "	" "	" "
Triplet, William G	" "	" "	" "	" "
Ward, James	" "	Jan. 4, 1864	Jan. 4, 1864	" "
White, Jacob...........	Aledo	Mar. 25, 1864	Mar. 25, 1864	" "
Veteran Recruits.				
Hickman, Hugh A.....	Fayetteville	Feb. 5, 1864	Mar. 25, 1864	Mustered out May 30, 1865.
Kilpatrick, George W.	Aledo	Jan. 28, 1864	" "	" "
Miller, Eugene	Belleville.......	May 1, 1864	May 1, 1864	Deserted Nov. 13, 1864......
Mock, Abraham	BridgesCorners		May 11, 1864	Mustered out July 9, 1865..
Woods, Thomas W....	Belleville.......	Feb. 18, 1864	Mar. 26, 1864	" "
Non-Veterans.				
Anderson, T. C	....	Aug. 15, 1862	Nov. 4, 1862	Died March 24, 1865.........
Anderson, William G.	....	" "	" "	Mustered out July 9, 1865...
Allabaugh, Robert R..	....	" "	" "	Died September 16, 1864....
Ayers, Joseph	....	" "	" "	Mustered out July 9, 1865...
Allen, Viren H........	....	Oct. 1, 1862	Dec. 18, 1862	" "
Bevel, William S......	Jonesboro	Sept. 22, 1861	Sept. 22, 1861	Discharged Sept. 22, 1864 ..
Bayles, David S	....	Aug. 15, 1862	Nov. 4, 1862	M. O. July 9, '65, as Corp...
Bynham, William Y...	....	" "	" "	Mustered out July 18, 1865.
Burns, Thomas G	....	" "	" "	Mustered out July 9, 1865..
Curtner, Daniel	....	" "	" "	Mustered out July 17, 1865.
Carmichael, G. W	....	" "	" "	Mustered out July 9, 1865..
Cox, Augustus B	Aledo	" "	Aug. 15, 1862	Died in prison, Charleston, S. C., Sept. 16, 1864 ....
Dunn, William D......	....	" "	Nov. 4, 1862	Mustered out July 9, 1865..
Dunn, John R	....	" "	" "	" "
Dixon, John..	....	" "	" "	" "
Fox, Calvin E..........	....	" "	" "	Died, Andersonville prison, May 31, 1864............
Frazier, William	....	" "	" "	Mustered out July 24, 1865.
Ferrel, Wyatt C.......	....	Aug. 20, 1862	" "	Deserted ....
Feater, Anthony......	....	Aug. 15, 1862	" "	Mustered out July 9, 1865...
Gmelin, Henry	Belleville.......	Aug. 15, 1861	Aug. 15, 1861	Died, Anders'nville prison
Goodman, Henry	....	Aug. 15, 1862	Nov. 4, 1862	Mustered out July 9, 1865..
Hewlett, Altenmont...	....	" "	" "	" "
Hewlett, Lemuel	....	" "	" "	" "
Hall, Willis	....	" "	" "	" "
Hall, Russell	....	" "	" "	" "
Howerton, John P.....	....	" "	" "	Mustered out July 20, 1865.
Johnson, Lemuel......	....	" "	" "	Captured 1865; not heard from since................
Jones, James F........	....	" "	" "	M. O. July 9, '65, as Corp...
Morehead, John	Aledo	Aug. 6, 1861	Aug. 9, 1861	Died, Andersonville prison. Grave 2646...........
Miller, William T......	Carbondale.....	Sept. 18, 1861	Sept. 18, 1861	Discharged Sept. 19, 1864 ..
Martin, Samuel J. B...	....	Aug. 15, 1862	Nov. 4, 1862	Mustered out July 9, 1865...
Pembleton, Joshua....	....			
Rank, John............	Fayetteville	Aug. 15, 1861	Aug. 15, 1861	Mustered out May 31, 1866..
Reed, Alfred...........	Lebanon	Oct. 20, 1862	Oct. 20, 1862	Mustered out July 9, 1865...
Smith, Milton.........	....	Aug. 20, 1862	Nov. 4, 1862	
Swires, Frank N.......	Belleville.......	Oct. 20, 1862	Oct. 20, 1862	Trans. to non-com. staff...
Spinks, James J	....	Aug. 15, 1862	Nov. 4, 1862	M. O. May 31, 1865, by order War Department ....
Struble, David M. C...	Carbondale.....	Sept. 18, 1861	Sept. 18, 1861	Discharged Sept. 19, 1864 ..

Name and Rank.	Residence,	Date of rank or enlistment.	Date of muster.	Remarks.
Talday, William......		Aug. 15,1862	Nov. 4,1862	Died,Andersonville prisbn
Vestal, Neal	Aledo	Dec. 18,1861	Dec. 18,1861	Discharged Dec. 18,1864 ...
Warren, George W....	Carbondale.....	Sept. 16,1861	Sept. 16,1861	Discharged Sept. 16,1864 ..
Wilhelm, Marshall....		Aug. 15,1862	Nov. 4,1862	Mustered out July 9,1865..
Wollard, John R				
Forby, William........		Aug. 25,1863	Aug. 25,1863	Died July 24,1864, Rome, Ga
Recruits.				
Anno, Joseph..........		Jan. 1,1864	Jan. 1,1864	Absent, sick, at muster-out of organization......
Burd,William W		"	"	Mustered out July 9, 1865..
Barknar, John S		"	"	Absent, sick. at muster-out of organization......
Boles, Henry		Aug. 15,1862	Nov. 4,1862	Mustered out July 9,1865..
Bradley, Marcus				"
Bond, John P..........		Aug. 29,1861	Aug- 29,1861	Discharged Aug. 29,1864...
Chamness, Marsh'll E.		Aug. 15,1862	Nov. 4,1862	Mustered out July 9, 1865..
Chambers, Henry.....				Absent at M.O.of organi'n
Chitty, Tayfact........		"	"	Mustered out July 9, 1865..
Childers, Robert		"	"	Trans. to 31st Ill.Mar.28,'65. by order of War Dept...
Childers, Joel		"	"	Trans.to 31st Ill. Mar.28.'65, by order of War Dept ...
Duncan, Hiram M.....		"	"	Transferred to Co. C ......
Etherton, Charles.....		Jan. 5,1864	Jan. 5,1864	Absent, sick, at muster-out of organization......
Fleming, Frederick...		Aug. 24,1862	Dec. 1,1862	Absent. sick, at muster-out of organization......
How, Erastus C		Jan. 1,1864	Jan. 1,1864	Mustered out July 9,1865..
Hill, Radford.........		Aug. 15,1862	Nov. 4,1862	"
Harlow, Bapet........		Aug. 22,1861	Aug. 22,1861	Discharged Aug. 29,1864...
Meridith, William B..		Aug. 15,1861	Nov. 4,1862	Mustered out July 9, 1865..
McCormick, Wesley ..				"
Prouty, John M.......		Jan. 5,1864	Jan. 5,1864	Absent, sick, at muster-out of organization......
Price, Henry G........		Aug. 15,1862	Nov. 4,1862	Mustered out July 9, 1865..
Perry, Rols...........				"
Reily, George W		Jan. 1,1864	Jan. 1,1864	Mustered out July 13,1865.
Reed, Sylvester......		Aug. 21,1862	Aug. 30,1862	"
Roberts, Edwin B.....		Aug. 15,1862	Nov. 4,1862	Discharged March 29,1865.
Rols, George V				Transferred to Co. B......
Smith, George W.....		"	"	Absent, sick, at muster-out of organization......
Talbot, Squire........		Jan. 1,1864	Jan. 1,1864	M.O.as of 27th Inf. Jun.7.'65
Turnage, Henry.......		Aug. 15,1862	Nov. 4,1862	Died in field hospital, Va.
Waldron, Tefford		Jan. 1,1864	Jan. 1,1864	Mustered out July 9,1865..
Under Cooks and Teamsters.				
Anderson, Loyal		Dec. 18,1863	Jan. 24,1864	Mustered out July 9,1865..
Hewley, Sam..........		Jan 23,1864	"	"
Mason, Israel.........		Dec. 18,1864	"	Deserted Nov. 18,1864......
Peters, Davis.........			"	"
Talday, Jack		"	"	Mustered out July 9,1865..
Talday, Hartwell.....		Jan. 24,1864	"	Deserted Nov. 11,1864......
Williams, Simons.....		"	"	"
Williams, George		"	"	Mustered out July 9,1865..

COMPANY F.

Name and Rank.	Residence·	Date of rank or enlistment.	Date of muster.	Remarks.
Captains.				
William M. Cooper....		Aug. 20,1864	....	Dropped from rolls July 1, 1865, under G. O. No. 83, A. G. O., Mar. 13,1865 ....
Charles T. Hunter		July 9,1865	Not must'r'd	M. O. as 2d Lieut. July 9,'65
First Lieutenants.				
William M. Cooper....	Chapin	Apr. 4,1864	....	Promoted..................
Charles Wehling.....	Red Bud........	Aug. 20,1864	Not must'r'd	Canceled ....
Charles T. Hunter ...			....	Promoted..................
William M. Dearson ..		July 9,1865	Not must'r'd	Mustered out as 1st Sergt. July 9,1865...............

Name and Rank.	Residence.	Date of rank or enlistment.	Date of muster.	Remarks.
Second Lieutenants.				
Charles T. Hunter	....	Aug. 20, 1864	Oct. 11, 1864	Promoted......................
William M. Dearson ..		" "	" "	Mustered out July 9, 1865..
William Moore		July 9, 1865	Not must'r'd	Mustered out (as Sergt) July 9, 1865................
First Sergeant.				
William M. Dearson ..	....	Aug. 1, 1862	Nov. 5, 1862	Mustered out July 9, 1865..
Sergeants.				
Charles Wehling	Red Bud........	Aug. 25, 1862	Aug. 31, 1862	Disch. May 27, 1865, order War Department ....
Charles T. Hunter	....	Aug. 20, 1862	Nov. 5, 1862	Promoted 2d Lieutenant...
Charles W. Miller.....	O'Fallon........	Sept. 8, 1861	Sept. 31, 1861	Mustered out Sept. 9, 1864.
William Moore	Belleville.......	Mar. 26, 1864	Mar. 26, 1864	Mustered out July 9, 1865..
Corporals.				
Reuben Turnage......	....	Aug. 15, 1862	Nov. 5, 1862	M. O. July 9, 1865, as Sergt.
James Glenn		Aug. 1, 1862	" "	
Hezekiah C. Gill		" "	" "	Mustered out July 9, 1865..
James Hefflin		" "	" "	
Frederick Kramp	....	Oct. 2, 1862	Feb. 28, 1863	" "
William Lovell	....	Aug. 1, 1862	Nov. 5, 1862	" "
John W. Oden			Nov. 4, 1862	" "
John Fruind	Belleville.......	Mar. 26, 1864	Mar. 26, 1864	" "
Veterans.				
Bertram, Henry	Belleville.......	Mar. 26, 1864	Mar. 26, 1864	Mustered out July 9, 1865..
Caspari, Henry........	" "	" "	" "	
Euler, Jacob	Chicago	" "	" "	" "
Gartheoffner, Anton ..	" "	" "	" "	" "
Guckes, Gottfred......	Belleville.......	" "	" "	" "
Hauser, John	" "	" "	" "	" "
Lambe, Christian	" "	" "	" "	" "
Louth, Frederick	" "	" "	" "	" "
Scheide, John	" "	" "	" "	" "
Weiss, John...........	" "	" "	" "	" "
Zweibarth, Henry	" "	" "	" "	" "
Recruits.				
Knight, Thomas A	Anna...	Feb. 7, 1864	Mar. 26, 1864	Mustered out July 9, 1865...
Newhouse, Augustus .	Fosterburg	Feb. 3, 1864	" "	" "
Non-Veterans.				
Abney, Francis M.....	....	Aug. 1, 1862	Nov. 4, 1862	M. O. July 9, 1865, as Corp.
Abney, Paul		" "	" "	Transferred to V. R. C ....
Baldre, Richard		" "	" "	Mustered out July 29, '65. Absent, sick, at muster-out of organization ....
Baumgartner, Fredr'k	Mascoutah......	Aug. 26, 1862	Aug. 31, 1862	Discharged May 27, 1865, orders War Department.
Birdwell, John H......		Aug. 20, 1862	Nov. 5, 1862	M. O. July 9, '65, as Corp'l.
Deason, James A......		Aug. 1, 1862	Nov. 4, 1862	Mustered out July 9, 1865...
Dunn, Henry		" "	" "	Killed, Sandersville, Ga., Nov. 25, 1864.............
Eason, William L		" "	" "	Mustered out July 9, 1865...
Enoch, Leonard		Aug. 15, 1862	" "	" "
Flanagan, Richard		" "	" "	" "
Forbes, David		Aug. 1, 1862	" "	" "
Grissum, Thomas		" "	" "	" "
Hall, William.........		Aug. 15, 1862	Nov. 5, 1862	" "
Hazlewood, John		Aug. 1, 1862	Nov. 4, 1862	" "
Henry, John		" "	" "	" "
Hewlett, Martin R.....		" "	" "	" "
Howell, Jasper		Aug. 15, 1862	" "	" "
Hunter, William B....		Aug. 1, 1862	" "	Died September 1, 1864 ....
Jordan, William H ...		" "	" "	Died January 8, 1865 ....
Kassing, William		Jan. 9, 1863	Feb. 28, 1863	Mustered out July 9, 1865..
Ludwig, Balthersar ...	Red Bud........	Aug. 25, 1862	Aug. 31, 1862	Discharged May 25, 1865, order War Department.
Manning, Henry......		Aug. 1, 1862	Nov. 5, 1862	Mustered out July 9, 1865..
McCabe, James........		Aug. 15, 1862	Nov. 4, 1862	" "
McCabe, John		" "	Nov. 4, 1862	" "
Morris, Robert........		Aug. 1, 1862	Nov. 4, 1862	" "
Morris, William		" "	" "	" "
Neighbors, John C		Aug. 15, 1862	" "	" "
Peterman, Benjamin..		Aug. 1, 1862	" "	" "
Peterman, George ...		" "	" "	
Peterman, William G .		" "	" "	Died August 22, 1864 ....
Potter, Isaiah.........		Aug. 15, 1862	" "	Mustered out July 9, 1865..
Potter, William.......		" "	" "	Absent, sick, at muster-out of organization ....

Name and Rank.	Residence.	Date of rank or enlistment.	Date of muster.	Remarks.
Rice, Jeremiah M		Aug. 1, 1862	Nov. 4, 1862	Mustered out July 9, 1865 ..
Rumsey, George H				Captured Nov. 26, 1864 .....
Schloter, Jacob		Jan. 14, 1863	Feb. 1, 1863	Mustered out July 9, 1865 ..
Stalboris, Henry		Aug. 23, 1862	Aug. 31, 1862	Discharged May 27, 1965,. Order War Department.
Stevens, Thomas		Aug. 1, 1862	Aug. 4, 1862	Mustered out July 9, 1865 ..
Stevens, William				''
Thurston, James M		''	''	Disch. Mar. 12, '65; disabil.
Wattson, Joseph		''	''	Mustered out July 9, 1865 ..
Williamson, Cornelius		''	''	M. O. July 9.'65, as corp'l..
Prisoners of War.				
Carter, Sylvester		Aug. 1, 1862	Nov. 4, 1862	Died in Andersonville prison Sept. 28, 1864 ......
Clayton, George		''	''	Absent, sick, at muster-out of organization ......
Enock, John		''	''	Mustered out July 9, 1865 ..
Erbe, Joseph	Belleville.	Aug. 1, 1861	Aug. 31, 1861	Died, Andersonville prison, Sept. 25,'64. Gr. 9717
Forbes, Madison M		Aug. 1, 1862	Nov. 4, 1862	M.O.June 14,'65, as Wm. M. Forbes. Order W. D....
Hall, Joseph		''	''	Captured April 17, 1864......
Hohrein, John	O'Fallon.	Aug. 18, 1861	Aug. 31, 1861	Mustered out May 30, 1865...
Reither, Charles	Belleville.	''	''	Mustered out May 27, 1865..
Schultse, Henry	Edwardsville ..	Aug. 10, 1861	''	Mustered out April 14, 1865,.
Recruits, subsequent to Re-organization.				
Hill, John A		Aug. 1, 1862	Nov. 4, 1862	Absent, sick, at. muster-out of organization......
Hunter, Aaron M		Aug. 20, 1862	Nov. 5, 1862	Mustered out July 9, 1865 ..
McAnnelly, Isaac		Aug. 1, 1862	Nov. 4, 1862	M.O. May 30,'65. Telegram from A. G. O., May 6,'65 .
Phillips, Levi V		Jan. 1.1864	Feb. 25, 1864	Captured Nov. 30. '64 No discharge furnished.....
Rawls, George W		Aug. 15, 1862	Nov. 4, 1862	Mustered out July 9, 1865 ..
Seilas, John		Jan. 16, 1864	Jan. 16, 1864	''
Tramwell, Milo		Aug. 1, 1862	Nov. 4, 1862	'' ''
Under Cooks.				
Drake, Sam		Dec, 18, 1863	Jan. 24, 1864	Deserted March 15, 1865....
Grixby, Burk		''	''	Mustered out July 9, 1865 ..
Murray, Martin		''	''	'' ''
Simpson, Jesse		''	''	'' ''
Teamsters.				
Scott, James		Dec. 18, 1863	Jan. 24, 1864	Mustered out July 9, 1865 ..
Taylor, Jim		''	''	Deserted March 15, 1865....
Townsend, Abraham		''	''	Absent, sick, at muster-out of organization......
Townsend, Joe		''	''	Mustered out July 9, 1865..

COMPANY G.

Name and Rank.	Residence.	Date of rank or enlistment.	Date of muster.	Remarks.
Captain.				
Isreal G Heaps		Jan. 1, 1864	Jan. 27, 1864	Prisoner of war...........
Henry J. Martin	Winchester	July 9, 1865	Not must'd.	M. O. as 1st Lieut. July 9,'65.
First Lieutenant.				
James McNulty	Annawan	July 9, 1865	Not must'd.	M. O. as Serg't July 9,'65 ..
Henry J. Martin	Winchester	Jan. 11, 1864	Jan. 1, 1864	Mustered out July 9, 1865 ..
Second Lieutenant.				
John D. Long	Alton	July 9, 1865	Not must'd.	M. O. as Serg't July 9,'65..
First Sergeant.				
John D. Long	Alton.	Jan. 1, 1864	Jan. 1, 1864	Mustered out July 9, 1865 ..
Sergeants.				
James McNulty	Annawan	Jan. 1, 1864	Jan. 1, 1864	Absent on furlough at M.O.
David D. Fronk	''	''	''	Mustered out July 9, 1865 ..
Benjamin F. Hickok	Exeter			

Name and Rank.	Residence.	Date of rank or enlistment.	Date of muster.	Remarks.
Corporals.				
John J. Brady.........	Tiskilwa........	Jan. 1, 1864	Jan. 1. 1864	Mustered out July 9, 1865.
John H. Burdett......	Jacksonville ...	" "	" "	" "
John F. Cue..........	Walker's Grove			
William B. Fleming ..	Keithsburg	Nov. 18, 1863	Nov. 18, 1863	Absent on furlough at M.O
Laban B. Noble	New Boston....			Mustered out July 9, 1865.
Henry Smith	Annawan......	Jan. 1, 1864	Jan. 1, 1864	" "
Julius Vandeventer...	Versailles	" "	" "	" "
Frank Mott............	Newbern			
Privates.				
Banzhoff, John........	Exeter..........	Jan. 1, 1864	Jan. 1, 1864	Absent, sick at M.O. of org.
Bennett, Christoph. C.	New Salem.....			Absent on furlough at M.O
Boyles, Lafayette.....	Jersey Landing	Jan. 2, 1864	Jan. 3, 1864	Mustered out July 9, 1865.
Boggs, Joseph A......	Havana.........	Jan. 1, 1864	Jan. 1, 1864	" "
Boggs, Charles T......	" "	Mar. 9, 1864	Mar. 19, 1864	" "
Bouscher, William F..	Murphysboro ..	Jan. 1, 1864	Jan. 1, 1864	" "
Benjamin, John W....	Arcadia.........			" "
Benjamin, George T..	Yatesville......	Mar. 18, 1864	Mar. 18, 1864	" "
Carroll, George........	Annawan.......	Jan. 1, 1864	Jan. 1, 1864	" "
Connett, William......	" "			" "
Cassady, Peter........	Galena..........	" "	" "	M. O. July 13,'65, as of 27 Ill.
Cox, John.............	Waterford......	" "	" "	Mustered out July 9, 1865.
Collins, Alfred M......	New Boston....	" "	" "	" "
Cheatham, John.......	Murphysboro ..	" "	" "	" "
Chew, Andrew B	" "	" "	" "	" "
Crain, Dessney........	" "	" "	" "	" "
Creath, Phineas.......	" "	" "	" "	M. O. July 24,'65, as of 27 Ill.
Durham, Walter	Annawan	Mar. 25, 1864	Mar. 25, 1864	Captured, Franklin, Tenn., Nov. 30, 1864 ....
Dwyre, Michael	Galesburg	Jan. 1, 1864	Jan. 1, 1864	Mustered out July 9, 1865.
Davis, John H........	Jersey Landing	Jan. 9, 1864	Jan. 9, 1864	" "
Dixon, Henry C	Walker's Grove	Jan. 1, 1864	Jan. 1, 1864	Mustered out Aug. 5, 1865..
Essley, John F........	Eliza............			Absent on furlough at M.O
Flynn, John	New Boston....	Jan. 5, 1864	Jan. 5, 1864	No discharge furnished at M. O. of organization....
Fitzgerald, Patrick ...	Murphysboro ..	Jan. 1, 1864	Jan. 1, 1864	M. O. July 24,'65, as of 27 Ill.
Gochenouer, Henry...	Annawan.......	" "	" "	Absent on furlough at M.O
Gochenouer, William.	" "	" "	" "	Mustered out July 9, 1865.
Graham, Alexander J.	" "	" "	" "	Deserted June 22, 1865.....
Hale, James..........	Exeter..........	" "	" "	Mustered out July 9, 1865.
Hammonds, Albert ...	Versailles	" "	" "	" "
Holton, George........	Brighton	Nov. 18, 1863	Nov. 18, 1863	" "
Holliday, Henry.......	Murphysboro ..	Aug. 13, 1862	Aug. 13, 1862	Disch. May 28, 1865, order War Department ....
Heitz, Sopha	Concord........	Jan. 1, 1864	Jan. 1, 1864	Mustered out July 9, 1865.
Hanback, Charles.....	Quincy	" "	" "	" "
Johnson, John W......	Neponset	" "	" "	" "
James, Hurlbert F	Versailles	" "	" "	Captured, Franklin, Tenn. Nov. 30, 1864 ....
Jackson, Wiley T......	Eliza............	" "	" "	Mustered out July 9, 1865.
Kelly, James	Mineral.........	" "	" "	" "
Kimbler, John.........	Exeter	" "	" "	" "
Kinslow, Thomas......	Macomb	" "	" "	" "
Knep, Joel.............	Versailles	Mar. 31, 1864	Mar. 31, 1864	Absent on furlough at M.O
Kirsch, George........	Springfield	Jan. 1, 1864	Jan. 1, 1864	M. O. June 9,'65, as of 27 Ill
Lynch, Patrick........	Greenville......	" "	" "	Mustered out July 9, 1865.
Long, Owen	Galena..........			" "
Louke, George	Buck Inn.......	Mar. 14, 1864	Mar. 14, 1864	" "
Larby, Venton........	Butler	Jan. 1, 1864	Jan. 1, 1864	" "
Lester, Shipley W	Bath	" "	" "	" "
Lakey, Lewis.........	Keithsburg....	" "	" "	" "
Murphy, John.........	Annawan.......	" "	" "	" "
Meise, August.........	Springfield	Aug. 26, 1862	Aug. 31, 1862	Disch. May 28, 1865, order of War Department......
Mitchell, Marion J	Exeter..........	Feb. 19, 1864	Feb. 19, 1864	Mustered out July 9, 1865.
Mayo, Hugh L........	Perry	Jan. 1, 1864	Jan. 1, 1864	Wounded, absent in hospital at M. O. of org ....
Mayo, William H......	" "	" "	" "	Mustered out July 9, 1865.
Moore, John H	Miles' Station..	" "	" "	" "
Noble, Van A	" "	Aug. 14, 1862	Dec. 1, 1862	" "
Needham, John W. L.	Murphysboro ..	Jan. 1, 1864	Jan. 1, 1864	" "
O'Riley, Thomas......	Whitehall	Feb. 9, 1864	Feb. 9, 1864	" "
Parkhurst, Josiah C ..	Galena..........	Jan. 1, 1864	Jan. 1, 1864	Absent on furlough at M.O
Paul, William	Zanesville.....	" "	" "	Mustered out July 9, 1865.
Pigus, Thomas........	Alton			" "
Prouty, William H	" "	Aug. 13, 1862	Dec. 1, 1862	Capt. Franklin, Tenn., Nov. 30,'64. No disch. furnish.
Rader, Hiram..........	Naples..........	Jan. 1, 1864	Jan. 1, 1864	Captured Nov. 30, 1864.....
Richards, David	....	Feb. 19, 1864	Feb. 19, 1864	Mustered out July 9, 1865.
Rochester, John L	Bath	Jan. 1, 1864	Jan. 1, 1864	" "
Stevens, Peter	Wheeling.......	" "	" "	" "

Name and Rank.	Residence.	Date of rank or enlistment.	Date of muster.	Remarks.
Stillwell, Charles J ...	Annawan	Jan. 13, 1864	Jan. 14, 1864	Absent on furlough at M.O
Stillwell, William.....	''	Mar. 25, 1864	Mar. 25, 1864	Mustered out July 9, 1865..
Stillwell, George......	''			
Shives, William H....	Alton	Jan. 1, 1864	Jan. 1, 1864	'' ''
Stratton, William.....				'' ''
Sabins, Charles O.....	Millersburg ...	''	''	'' ''
Sargent, James M	Jacksonville ...	''	''	'' ''
Tracy, William V	Exeter	''	''	'' ''
Tribbet, Thomas......	''	''	''	'' ''
Tucker, Lewis A......	Mt. Sterling....	''	''	'' ''
Tempest, Robert......	Havana.........	''	''	'' ''
Thornton, Thomas C .	Millersburg	Dec. 17, 1863	Dec. 17, 1863	'' ''
Vizard, Martin	Neponset	Jan. 1, 1864	Jan. 1, 1864	'' ''
Williams, Robert F...	Miles' Station..	''	''	'' ''
Wadsack, Frederick ..	Eliza............	''	''	'' ''
Welsh, William	''	''	''	'' ''
Woodward, Joel N	New Boston....	Jan. 5, 1864	Jan. 5, 1864	'' ''
Woolsey, Joshua......	Murphysboro ..	Jan. 1, 1864	Jan. 1, 1864	'' ''
Woolsey, Richard.....	''	Aug. 10, 1861	Aug. 10, 1862	Disch. May 25, 1865, order of War Dep't ....
Watt, William J.......	Jacksonville ...	Apr. 11, 1864	Apr. 11, 1864	Absent on furlough at M.O
Under Cooks.				
Armstead, Stark	....	Mar. 3, 1863	Oct. 29, 1863	Mustered out July 9, 1866..
Collins, John...........	....			'' ''

UNASSIGNED RECRUITS.

Name and Rank.	Residence.	Date of rank or enlistment.	Date of muster.	Remarks.
Abbott, Jesse..........	Crab Orchard..	Mar. 20, 1864	....	Died Apr.15, '64; C'mp B'tler
Branch, Frederick....	Lebanon........	Oct. 22, 1862	....	....
Clark, John C..........	Frankfort	Feb. 2, 1864	....	....
Eichler, Man	Mascoutah	Feb. 13, 1864	....	Deserted ....
Garbar, Nicholas......	Dark co., Ohio .	Feb. 5, 1864	Mar. 27, 1864	....
Griffin, Benjamin.....	DeSoto	Feb. 10, 1864	....	....
Harrison, David......	Troy	Mar. 24, 1864	Mar. 24, 1864	Discharged July 1, 1864....
Johnson, Thomas	Belleville.......	Jan. 9, 1864	Feb. 8, 1864	....
Miller, Edward T	Shelbyville....	Dec. 29, 1863	Dec. 29, 1863	....
May, Benjamin F	South Pass.....	Mar. 9, 1864	....	Died Apr. 14, 1864; at Camp Butler ....
Miller, Joseph.........	Anna	Mar. 18, 1864	....	Discharged Apr. 20, 1864...
Niedermuiler, George.	Mascoutah	Jan. 26, 1864	....	Deserted ....
Osborne, Henry	Anna	Mar. 15, 1861	....	Rejected.....................
O'Brien, Dennis.......	Minonk	Jan. 11, 1865	Jan. 11, 1865	....
Offner, Henry.........	Lebanon........	Dec. 10, 1862	....	....
Ryan, Daniel	Edwardsville ..	Feb. 3, 1864	Feb. 3, 1864	....
Stotler, Jackson P	DeSoto	Feb. 10, 1864	....	Discharged..................
Salcer, Ernst..........	Mascoutah	Feb. 15, 1864	....	Deserted ....
Stillwell, John G......	O'Fallon........	Feb. 29, 1864	....	''
Vancil, Welles	Anna	Jan. 26, 1864	....	Discharged..................

HEADQUARTERS DEPARTMENT AND ARMY OF THE TENNESSEE,

SPECIAL FIELD ORDERS, }   BEFORE ATLANTA, Ga., *July* 21, 1864.
No. 74.   }

1st. The enlisted men of the Ninth Illinois Infantry whose term of service expires during the present month, with such officers of same as by reason of expiration of term desire to be mustered out of the service, will forthwith proceed to Chattanooga, Tennessee, under charge of Colonel Mersey, for the purpose of muster-out.

2d. The remaining men of the regiment will be consolidated into one or more companies of the legal maximum standard, under the command of Lieutenant Colonel J. J. Phillips, and the requisite number of other commissioned officers will be appointed and assigned on the recommendation of Major General Dodge, commanding left wing Sixteenth Army Corps.

3. Major General G. M. Dodge will order an officer from the Battalion thus organized to Nashville, Tennessee, to procure a sufficient number of Spencer rifles to arm the command.

By order of Major General JAMES B. MCPHERSON.

(Signed)   WILLIAM T. CLARK, *Assistant Adjutant General.*

JOHN Y. SIMON, professor of history at Southern Illinois University at Carbondale, is the editor of *The Papers of Ulysses S. Grant* and a founder of the Association for Documentary Editing. He has published more than sixty articles in such journals as *Military Affairs, Journal of American History, Ohio History, Journal of the Abraham Lincoln Association,* and *Journal of the Illinois State Historical Society.* The editor of *The Personal Memoirs of Julia Dent Grant* and the coeditor of *Ulysses S. Grant: Essays and Documents* and *The Continuing Civil War: Essays in Honor of the Civil War Round Table of Chicago,* Simon has held office in national professional associations and has served as a consultant for federal and state agencies, university and commercial presses, and other editorial projects.